DIRTY WATERS

CHICAGO VISIONS AND REVISIONS

EDITED BY CARLO ROTELLA, BILL SAVAGE, CARL SMITH, AND ROBERT B. STEPTO

DIRTY WATERS

CONFESSIONS OF CHICAGO'S
LAST HARBOR BOSS

R. J. Nelson

THE UNIVERSITY OF CHICAGO PRESS • CHICAGO AND LONDON

The University of Chicago Press, Chicago 60637
The University of Chicago Press, Ltd., London
© 2016 by The University of Chicago
All rights reserved. Published 2016.
Printed in the United States of America

25 24 23 22 21 20 19 18 17 16   1 2 3 4 5

ISBN-13: 978-0-226-33449-3 (cloth)
ISBN-13: 978-0-226-33452-3 (e-book)

DOI: 10.7208/chicago/9780226334523.001.0001

Library of Congress Cataloging-in-Publication Data
Names: Nelson, R. J. (Robert J.), author.
Title: Dirty Waters : confessions of Chicago's last harbor boss / R. J. Nelson.
Other titles: Chicago visions+revisions.
Description: Chicago ; London : The University of Chicago Press, 2016. | Series: Chicago visions and revisions
Identifiers: LCCN 2016007482| ISBN 9780226334493 (cloth : alk. paper) | ISBN 9780226334523 (e-book)
Subjects: LCSH: Harbors—Political aspects—Illinois—Chicago. | Political corruption—Illinois—Chicago.
Classification: LCC HE554.C5 N45 2016 | DDC 387.1/5092—dc23 LC record available at http://lccn.loc.gov/2016007482

♾ This paper meets the requirements of ANSI/NISO Z39.48–1992 (Permanence of Paper).

For Kris. All the love songs in the world cannot express mine for you.

To pour forth benefits for the common good is divine.

BEN FRANKLIN

CONTENTS

ACKNOWLEDGMENTS

Chicago's first black mayor, Harold Washington, changed forever the old Daley-style machine politics, and his reforms were naturally resisted by the vast patronage system that had been in place for generations. Outsiders like me whom Harold brought into the government were suspect, and various attempts were made to undermine our attempts to change the system. I saw the need to document my actions and experiences to the extent possible. From the first month of my tenure and especially after Harold died unexpectedly eight months later, I made detailed notes on conversations and meetings—including specific statements from participants—and I saved various memos, newspaper clippings, and other documents. Those notes, documents, and recollections are the basis of the material in this book.

While the spokes in the wheels under this book are many, my wife and childhood sweetheart, Kris, is the center. Being married to an activist and religious seeker is stressful enough; being married to a would-be writer for years requires the patience of Mother Teresa. In addition to emotional support she suggested many important changes as she proofread all drafts. Without her this project never would have materialized. My daughter, a former editor at Brookfield Zoo and now a professor at the University of Illinois at Chicago, was also invaluable, as was my son, his wife, and our two grandchildren, whose constant curiosity pushed the manuscript along.

Old friends Ron and Ute Carson, who never ceased badgering me to stop procrastinating and keep writing, can now finally stop rolling their eyes. Close friends from the boat business, T. E. Leonard and Grant Crowley, also provided motivation.

I deeply thank Tim Mennel, senior editor at the University of Chicago Press, who shocked me by e-mailing his interest a day after reading a sample and then accepting the manuscript. Bill Savage, editor, professional bartender, and Chicago lover extraordinaire, was extremely helpful in the revision process. To all the other editors and staff who transform rambling stories into books, I offer my admiration. Writing coach Whitney Scott suggested I read selections at open-mike sessions around the city, which resulted in positive feedback. Additionally Lisa Wroble helped me navigate the book into the world of publishing.

I owe a great spiritual debt to my theology professor and lifelong friend Bill Hamilton, who escorted me ethically out the side door of the Church; and to Michael W. Flamm, history professor at Ohio Wesleyan, who three years ago invited me to share my activist stories to his class on the sixties. His students gave me the kick I needed to finish my manuscript.

Finally my deepest thanks to the old-timers, not only at the park district, but at the many Chicago places I worked: the ship captains and boat builders at Grebe Shipyard, the angel carvers at the University of Chicago, the steel pourers at U.S. Steel South Works, the asbestos mixers at Chicago Fire Brick, the dying breed of elevator operators in the Monadnock Building, and the mom-and-pop owners of Belmont Foods, to name a few whose wealth of wisdom inspired me all my life.

DAWN CITY

March 23, 1987.

People asked me how a former college chaplain landed the job of director of harbors and marine services for the Chicago Park District, a position so mired in corruption that the last four directors before me went to federal prison.[1] I jokingly said that in my interview when asked what denomination I served, I answered, "tens and twenties mostly," and was hired on the spot. In truth the only qualification essential for this job was a sense of humor, especially irony.

Only ten days on the job, I was besieged and exhausted: I faced angry boaters who demanded to see me about their boat slip applications, harbor contractors with unpaid bills, lawsuits over slip assignments, and nervous staff members begging to keep their jobs. The *Tribune*, *Sun-Times*, and Channel Seven News, armed with Freedom of Information Act requests, copied files all week, chasing various stories of harbor corruption. FBI agents showed up every other day, opened file cabinets, and asked questions. They scared the hell out of me. In the sixties at Cornell, they investigated me for my antiwar activities, followed me everywhere, demanded to see my draft card, tapped my phone, and assembled a thick file on me, some of which is still classified, all of which got me fired. But this time around a generation later, they zeroed in on my predecessor, Gerald Pfeiffer. They were polite and asked for my help with records. I helped them.

The marine director's office was huge, with a double-wide window overlooking Soldier Field Stadium. The walls and ceiling were dirty and stained from years of chain-smoking. The florescent light fixtures were yellowed, and the threadbare carpet smelled of ground-in dirt from years of foot traffic. The broken glass in the office door, where the FBI officers smashed their way in, was still covered with plywood. A large safe in one corner could not be opened, because only Gerald Pfeiffer knew the combination. His fifty-gallon aquarium still bubbled away on one long wall. Dozens of tropical fish stared down at me. A cheap armoire in another corner was filled with Cook County sheriff uniforms. Pfeiffer used his clout to get appointed a deputy sheriff, a common perk for pols that allowed him to carry a gun and make arrests. With a .357 magnum on his hip, he often made surprise visits to the harbors looking for harbor rule violators to intimidate and punish.

About nine thirty in the morning, my secretary knocked on my door. "Luke Cosme, one of the lakefront engineers, is here to see you." He entered tentatively, peering around, carrying two thick, rolled-up sets of blueprints against his chest like an archaeologist carrying the Dead Sea scrolls. Luke—old school, way past retirement, with thick silver hair, and almost British in manner—wore a dark-blue pinstriped suit with a white handkerchief, a perfectly knotted striped tie, a light-blue shirt that looked new, and polished wing-tip shoes that lifted and set down in measured, short steps as he approached my desk.

"Do you know I have not been allowed in this office for ten years?" he said, shaking his head. "Your predecessor never once asked for our engineering opinion on anything in the harbors. When he wanted something, like specifications for that star dock contract that got him into trouble, for instance, he would gather us together in a conference room and dictate the specs he wanted. That was it."

I realized Luke was one of those lifers my father told me to look for wherever I worked, an elder whose knowledge and expertise were critical. And here he came looking for me.

"Worst of all, Mr. Pfeiffer always carried a gun," Luke continued.

"I knew he carried a gun in the harbors . . . but to meetings here?"

"Yes, and he would take off his suit coat so we could see the chrome barrel and bone handles. So intimidating, no one dared question him." Luke paused to look over my newly decorated office. He walked over to two enlarged photos of icebergs I had taken while sailing off the coast of Labrador four years ago with Tom Leonard, my former boss at Grebe Shipyard.

"What size was the iceberg?" he asked, as an engineer naturally would.

"About twice the size of Soldier Field Stadium, maybe three times as high." Luke was especially fascinated when told the berg was floating close to where the *Titanic* went down.

"The locals thought we were crazy to sail so close. See how the cone-shaped top is starting to crack? Icebergs shaped like that tend to split in two and create forty- to fifty-foot tidal waves. If that had happened, our forty-foot sailboat wouldn't have stood a chance. When fishermen see those cracked bergs, they get the hell away.

"One day sailing along in such dense fog, we couldn't even see the bow of the boat. Captain Leonard was down in the cabin hunched over the radar screen while I steered. Suddenly the steady wind stopped and the sails went limp. I told him I thought we must be next to an iceberg, but he scoffed: 'there's no berg on the radar screen.' We didn't know then that small radars don't pick up ice very well if at all.

"We argued a little. I had carefully read the Canadian government's maritime guide book, *Navigation through Ice*, which Tom had placed on a shelf next to the ship-to-shore radio. One chapter described a phenomenon called 'ice blink,' a yellowish glow high in the fog caused by the sun's rays bouncing off the top of an iceberg. The book warns that when you see ice blink, the berg is right on top of you."

"Ice blink. I've never heard of such a thing, but I'm not a sailor," said Luke.

"Well, I recognized it and yelled down to Tom. He ignored me and stayed glued to the blank radar scope. Suddenly we were bombarded by falling chunks of ice like ice-cube trays opened upside down. Out of the fog no more than fifty feet away, the berg appeared, a white cliff of ice towering over our masts making tinkling sounds, like glass wind chimes, as shards of thousand-year-old ice showered the deck. 'Ice berg off the port beam,' I shouted, turning on the engine, pushing the throttle to full, and spinning the wheel to head the boat away from the berg. Captain Tom rushed up the companionway, saw the gigantic berg, and froze. We had no idea how big it was or whether it formed a horseshoe trap around us, in which case we would surely collide, so I eased back on the throttle. Tom took the helm and sent me to the bow. I grabbed a handheld air horn and wedged myself into the bow pulpit looking pointlessly into the thickest fog I had ever seen. I pressed the air-horn button once, then twice, then twice again, listening for an echo off the ice. An immediate echo meant imminent collision. My heart pounded as I pressed the horn again. No echo, thank God. We were angling away from the berg. Within minutes the fog shroud around the berg cleared; the sun brightened, and we could see the forbidding granite Labrador coast. Behind us the floating ghostlike mountain of ice slogged off to the south, as I snapped pictures."

Luke nodded in rapt attention. "That's quite a story. I read in the *Sun-Times* that you sailed across the Atlantic, too."

Landlubbers, especially Midwesterners like Luke, are always impressed by tales of sailing across the Atlantic. While I didn't tell him, my voyage was to navigate through a midlife crisis. I put out to sea to cross an ocean of the past and sort out my future.

"Yes, with a couple of guys. But enough sea stories, Mr. Cosme; what can I do for you?"

"First, everyone calls me Luke. I thought you might like to see the plans for the Shedd Aquarium expansion and its big new seawall. It sticks out quite a ways into Monroe Harbor."

Luke unrolled the blueprints on top of my new round conference table and thumbed through to the scale drawings of the seawall. It was massive, ten feet off the water and made of reinforced concrete facing northeast, the direction of the worst Lake Michigan storms. The wall was concave like a snowplow blade, designed to scoop up waves and throw them back on themselves. I asked Luke if the Shedd engineers expected a tsunami to hit Chicago. He chuckled and reminded me that the lake just recorded its highest level ever; storm waves flooded Lake Shore Drive. The Chicago Yacht Club stuffed table linens under its doors to stop water from surging in. Glass windows on apartment buildings on Sheridan Road were smashed in. When Mayor Washington appeared at a news conference on the second floor balcony of one of those buildings to announce the creation of a "Shoreline Protection Commission," he and all the other dignitaries present were doused by spray from huge waves, all caught on tape for the evening news. The lake had been rising for several years. All the boat slips built permanently on pilings had to be retrofitted with riser platforms in order for boaters to get to their boats without boots.

"This is serious. Our lakefront facilities were not designed for such high water levels," Luke said authoritatively. I told him not to worry, that the day after I was hired lake levels started to recede.

With a high-pitched chuckle, Luke returned to the plans. In addition to the concave design, the engineers decided to dump tons of armor stones in the water in front of it to break up the waves before they hit. Unfortunately, they would encroach on the already narrow south entrance to Monroe Harbor. Boats trying to get in during storms or with motor trouble in calm weather would drift onto these boulders.

"Luke, obviously no boaters were involved in this design. How much time do we have to suggest changes?"

"Without discussion your predecessor signed off on the plans last year," he said dolefully. "The bids have already been awarded."

"There are no places for boats to tie up, only piles of rocks. Didn't anyone think to have a nice place for visiting boats to tie up and take in the aquarium, and its sister museums, the planetarium, and the natural history museum—all on the edge of the largest harbor in the city?"

"Believe me," Luke answered apologetically, "I tried to get the aquarium's engineering firm to test their seawall design in our wave tank. If they had done so, we would have proved it didn't need to be so massive."

"We have a wave tank?" This seemed unlikely to me. Wave tanks are basically swimming pools with machines that simulate waves against scale models of structures. Some are huge and can be frozen to test the effects of ice on navigation buoys, or even scale-model oil rigs.

"Under Soldier Field, built during the Great Depression to test the new seawalls and permanent piers the federal government constructed along the lakefront. I was a young man then," he said wistfully, paraphrasing the famous quote from Daniel Burnham, "we made no small plans."

I asked Luke to show me the wave tank. He looked at his watch and suggested we go right away. His crew of surveyors were testing a model replacement of Casino Pier, the quarter-mile-long structure that protects the entrance to Jackson Park Harbor. The pier was originally built to mark the entrance to the canals of the Columbian Exposition of 1893. Back then thousands of people strolled out onto the pier, but after a hundred years, it had deteriorated badly and was closed to public access.

Luke led me down the escalator to the basement and then through glass doors into an underground cave with steel roll-up doors at either end. This is where the commissioners, the general superintendent, and other big shots parked their cars. There were thirteen numbered spaces.

"Did you know that your predecessor was assigned space number 3 right behind General Superintendent Kelly and the board president?" We walked down a flight of stairs. At the bottom was an underground parking lot with 102 parking spaces assigned to various executives. My space was number 100, as far away from the stairs as you can get. Luke told me that it might take years to get a closer space, depending on how much clout I brought along. He paused with raised eyebrows waiting for me to disclose my political connections.

"You may not believe this, Luke—no one else does—but I have no clout. Absolutely none."

"Me neither," he said. "After forty-five years, I still have to park outside. I guess they want me close to the lake."

We continued to walk underneath the grandstands past numerous doors, some with glass panels marked in faded black letters indicating various trades: electrical, rigging, welding, carpentry, and mechanical. Other doors without glass were not marked; some were steel, some wood resembling weathered barn doors. These rooms were used for many different things to serve the downtown parks, and Luke knew them all.

"Soldier Field was built after World War I as an Olympic stadium with track and field, a soccer field in the center, and pageantry areas in the north end. The colonnades on both sides were designed to make it 'fit in' with the Field Museum next door. The south end of the seating area was designed as an amphitheater to mount classic Greek dramas behind a series of curtains, but was never used. Not too many Chicagoans interested in ancient Greek drama."

I listened carefully.

"During World War II the army installed rifle ranges, training facilities, and all sorts of offices down here. Top secret," Luke said holding his finger to his lips.

He led me down a long corridor with jail cells on both sides, where prisoners of war were occasionally held. At one time these cells were used during Bears games to hold drunks until the police hauled them off.

Somewhere beneath the fifty-yard line, Luke led me through a propped-open wooden door and then down four more stairs to a dirt floor. My glasses fogged up from extremely humid air that smelled swampy. We entered a large room with cinder-block walls painted navy gray that surrounded a shallow concrete pool the size of those at cheap motels, about ten by twenty feet. Solid two-foot-square timbers supported the ceiling under the stadium seating areas. These looked new, and Luke once again put his finger to his lips.

"See those cracks in the ceiling? The timbers are the only thing keeping the whole stadium from falling down. Those nice seating areas you see on television? Just a thin layer of latex concrete over the old crumbling concrete. The old stadium has to be replaced in ten or fifteen years. Don't worry. It's safe under here," he said, knocking for good luck on one of the heavy shoring timbers. The wave tank, illuminated by a grid of single-bulb porcelain fixtures, was full of dirty water about two feet deep. Three workers in park district uniforms and hip boots stood in the tank. From wooden bins along one wall, they picked various sized stones from quarter inch to half inch diameters, representing the armor and core stones at Casino Pier. The model pier angled across the pool at forty-five degrees and then turned back, forming a ninety-degree angle. In the far corner of the wave tank loomed a large motorized contraption with paddles and levers connected by camshafts.

"This is going to be noisy," Luke said as he reached into a rusty fuse box and threw a switch.

The wave machine started up, its paddles slapping water, undulating back and forth, created frothy waves chaotically at first, then in regular wavelengths.

"Watch how the machine simulates different height waves and frequencies," Luke shouted. Using a remote control box on a long cable with rows of lighted switches, he played with the controls. The machine groaned, changed paddle angles, and rhythmically pushed perfect model waves across the tank. As the waves became larger and more frequent, the surveyors took notes from gauges showing water depths at various points. Luke gradually pushed the machine to its limit. "These are the equivalent of twenty-five-footers," he said as two-footers crashed into the model seawall. Stones began to dislodge and tumble off their miniature piles. A breech opened up in the model, exciting the surveyors. As they focused a video camera on the widening breach, my ears felt like they were exploding. I tried to get Luke's attention to tell him I had seen enough, but he was lost in concentration.

The wave machine slapped furiously at the water until it strained beyond its limits and lurched off corroded mounting bolts. Shaft bearings squealed as paddles flew off the camshafts and flayed the water like a drowning man. The waves became irregular and washed over the sides of the tank. Luke dropped the remote and rushed to the fuse box while the surveyors sloshed their way to the wave machine. I backed away quickly and tripped as miniature waves washed over my ankles. My head slammed against one of the timbers. With a painful thud, I fell. Light fixtures dimmed and went black. My ears roared as if jammed with fire hoses. Semiconscious I heard a voice from the disabled wave machine hissing scratchy and high-pitched nonsense.

"Zacchaeus here, recruiter of pneumacrats to repair the world."

My head throbbed. Like many spiritual people, I have heard voices. As a small child I wandered into the Lake Michigan surf and almost drowned in the undertow. Before my mother could snatch me up, I experienced an out-of-body experience, ascended a vertical tunnel on a beam of blue-green light. At the top angels were singing beautiful hymns of welcome. But as my mother pulled me to shore and frantically placed her mouth on mine and forced air into my lungs until I spat up sand and water and started breathing, the voices went silent. The angels turned sad and whispered, "Go back, go back," and I descended on the blue-green beam into the water and then on a hot sand beach gasping for breath. When revived I told the story to my mother, who repeated it for years. While I never forgot the experience, I now imagine it as a metaphor for my spiritual journey.

"I am that Zacchaeus you admired in your seminary studies, the short in stature—some said disabled dwarf—chief tax collector for the Romans, who climbed a sycamore tree to glimpse the Lord. When he called me down and stayed in my house, my life changed forever. I longed to follow him, but the disciples would have none of it."

"But why?" I said. "The scripture only says you told Jesus you were giving half your wealth to the poor and would restore fourfold anything you defrauded from anyone."[2]

"The disciples convinced themselves I was a Roman mole, and the Romans suspected me of being a Zealot terrorist. After the crucifixion, they fled without me. The Romans fired me for my association with the Jesus movement, and I was shunned until the day I died."

"The point of my paper on you was that you deserved sainthood."

"Not a chance. No church will ever be named Saint Zacchaeus. If you think bureaucracies are bad on earth, they are much worse here. You Americans joke about the Eternal Revenue Service. Well, it's true. Bureaucracies outlive everyone. Bureaucracies are eternal. After my death the heavenly bureaucrats didn't know what to do with me, so they made me a pneumacrat recruiter. Most believers think they will meet God right after they pass. Well, good luck. My face to face with the Lord keeps getting moved back. The last unconfirmed date is two centuries from now.

"You have no idea what eternal life is like until you try to get something done. But enough about me; your file shows pneumacrat potential. I think your passion for sailing caught the Lord's eye. You remember that other paper you wrote that Jesus was a sailor, always getting into boats, sailing in fair weather or foul. Oh, how he loved to get into a boat and sail the Sea of Galilee."

"That was a long time ago," I answered, suddenly feeling nostalgic for my three years at Colgate Rochester Divinity School in the fiery sixties. I was mesmerized by Dr. William Hamilton, the theologian who started the "Death of God" theology, who taught that God, the problem solver, had disappeared, that the secular world had come of age, and did not need God, and that religion had become static cling in everyday life. What was needed was what the German theologian Dietrich Bonhoeffer called "a non-religious interpretation" of Christianity in which Christians participated in the sufferings alongside their neighbor in a godless world. Who was our neighbor? Those protesting injustice, civil rights, and the war, those involved in movements to change the world. Bill Hamilton kindled that fire in my belly and became a lifelong friend. I named my son after him.

"Zacchaeus, what do you mean you're interested in my 'pneumacrat potential'?" I vaguely recalled that strain of Jewish mysticism, Tikkun Olam, which holds that the world was shattered into fragments by sin and must be repaired morally and politically into a perfected world before God will even consider returning. Zacchaeus then began a sort of rant.

"All this repair work could have been avoided. Why did God rest after spending only six days on creation? Couldn't he have worked a little overtime and got it right? There's no planning. Everything is crisis management. Fix this, fix that. It would be more cost effective to tow the whole world in for repairs and get it over with. Finding handyman pneumacrats like you to do the work will take an eternity, which is exactly why they do it."

"Why me?"

"Your name came up in a lottery for church dropouts who cause trouble trying to repair the world, like my last assignment, Dietrich Bonhoeffer."

"You consulted with Dietrich Bonhoeffer, the German theologian who believed his Christian duty was to join the conspiracy to kill Hitler and was hanged by the Nazis?"

"Well, not really. I just love dropping his name. I was assigned to Corporal Knobloch, who was unfit for combat and assigned guard duties at Tegel prison in Berlin. When Bonhoeffer was arrested, the nightly bombings of Berlin were horrific and flattened the city, including parts of the prison. As a sort of comic relief, Knobloch ordered the great theologian to bend over and hold his ankles tight. When he obediently assumed the position, Knobloch shouted, 'Now kiss your ass good-bye.'"

As my face frowned, he whispered, "Don't be offended. Dietrich had a great sense of humor and laughed along with the guards. During the bombings he was a fearless counselor and comforted prisoners hit by shrapnel and others who panicked in their locked cells. Moved by Bonhoeffer's faith and courage, Knobloch befriended him and risked his life to smuggle out those famous letters and papers you and half the world so admire. Without this prison misfit bureaucrat's help, they never would have seen the light of day. Corporal Knobloch was a true pneumacrat. Do you understand?"

"I'm trying to."

"A pneumacrat follows the spirit of the law, never the letter. I know that sounds like a cliché. In truth, however, the spirit behind every law benefitting mankind is the Holy Spirit. Unfortunately mankind bureaucratizes eternal laws, like the Ten Commandments or your Bill of Rights for instance. Following the spirit becomes difficult. It constantly gets lost in bureaucratic rules. Pneumacrats find or make exceptions to rules for the common good, and when that happens, discover the divine like Ben Franklin said. It's like a spiritual scavenger hunt. Believe me, you will have plenty of opportunities, and be assured my disembodied spirit will stick to you like gum on the bottom of a church pew."

Suddenly the voice of Zacchaeus deflated like air from a tire. The surveyors covered their heads thinking part of the ceiling under the old stands was about to fall. Luke turned away from the wave machine and saw me lying in the mud. The surveyors sloshed over quickly and helped me to my feet. I was a little woozy. Supported by the surveyors, we walked tentatively up the stairs, then through another door to the field of the stadium. The fresh air cleared my head. I assured Luke I was all right. We walked back to the main building. Luke talked more about Lake Michigan. He smiled, looked at me and crossed his fingers. "I hope you're right about the water level going down."

Back in my office I started to sweat. The balmy late March day required no indoor heating, yet the Chicago Park District's steam furnace, like the sprawling bureaucracy it served, made no temperature adjustments until some fixed date later in spring. Steam hissed and banged through radiators around the room, encircling me like the government I was now part of. I removed my blue blazer and laid down on the floor to ruminate on my encounter with the voice of Zacchaeus.

There were two dilapidated folding tables against one wall. Around Christmas season these were placed in the hall outside my predecessor's office where vendors, contractors, and boaters heaped them with gifts. A second door from the office into the hall he had sealed up to keep all "wise guys" bearing gifts from trying to deliver them personally. No one, except his inner circle, entered without an appointment. If you were lucky enough to get an appointment, he kept you waiting.

For my only appointment during his ten-year reign, I waited three hours. That was eight years ago when I was sales manager of Grebe Shipyard, and our customers could not get any information on their mooring applications. I telephoned, wrote letters, but was totally ignored until an intermediary, George Feiwell, a boater and lawyer for the shipyard, persuaded him to see me. When finally allowed into his inner sanctum, he took my head off for contributing to the harbor masters' Christmas party without his permission.

"You'll never get a slip or mooring in a Chicago harbor for your customers while I'm harbor director," he screamed, pounding his desk. I was shocked. No moorings would quickly put me and Grebe's out of the yacht-selling business. He expected me to grovel, to "cooperate" with gifts or cash or services. I refused to take the bait and tried to be conciliatory: "I'm sorry you feel that way," I offered. It was not what he wanted to hear.

"Get out and never come here or call again!" he had shouted so that his entire staff and other waiting boaters would get the message that I was poison. That night I told my wife, Kris, the story, complaining bitterly about his blatant dishonesty backed by an iron fist—either pay to play or pay the consequences. "If I only had his job, everything would change. I know what to do. It's like I was born for that job," I said. Kris worried I would get caught up in the bribery scandals if I stayed in the boat business in Chicago. We argued. It never occurred to either of us that eight years later I would be given his job.

Pfeiffer's folding tables were now piled with unconnected computer equipment that my staff knew nothing about. I would find out later it belonged in the offices of Ed Kelly, the former park general superintendent who had been ousted by new mayor Harold Washington. When he was replaced, Kelly's computers were hurriedly moved into Pfeiffer's office just before the feds arrived with their battering ram. There was nothing incriminating on the hard drives (e-mail had not yet been invented). Their attempted removal was for spite, to make it as difficult as possible for the new African American mayor's administration to operate.

Pfeiffer's large desk, badly scuffed and stained with one drawer missing (no one knew why) was original issue from 1934 when the three city park districts were centralized into one. Two side chairs did not match, and one had a steel plate holding a broken leg together. His cheap swivel chair with only four spoke legs toppled if pushed off to one side or the other. One rusting World War II vintage file cabinet stood in the remaining corner and squealed when opened. Inside were aerial photos of the Chicago harbors that Pfeiffer had taken for one of his shakedown schemes: suggesting to prospective slip holders that they might want to buy a picture of the harbor they would be assigned to (price negotiable). I planned to enlarge and frame these harbor pictures to put around the office as an invaluable show-and-tell device about the most complex municipal harbor system in the country, if not the world.

Shabbiness was the perfect decor for a grafter who, during his thirteen-year tenure, reaped hundreds of thousands of dollars in bribes, many exchanged in this office. New furniture and carpeting were ordered, but like reform in government the process took time while the stench of chain-smoked corruption lingered.

There was a green phone on the windowsill. My desk held a traditional black business phone with four lines and an intercom, but the green phone was not connected to the desk phone. You see such old phones, with rubber feet and a headset the size and shape of a clown's bow tie, languishing in garage sales. Oddly it was attached through the wall on a very short cord and when I picked up all I heard was scratchy old record-player noise. While my desk phone flashed and rang constantly, the green phone never rang.

"That was Mr. Pfeiffer's personal phone," my inherited secretary informed me, but she did not know the number or why it was green— maybe because it was the color of all the bribe money he took over the years, I thought to myself.

When I asked to get the phone fixed, she dutifully typed up a work order and sent it to the "Telephone Communications Office," located at the other end of the hall. Two weeks passed and when no telephone repairman showed up, I asked her to follow up on the repair order.

"It won't do any good. When it comes to that phone, you have to talk to Miss Brett," she said, obviously wanting nothing to do with it. I decided to meet Miss Brett.

For years Kay Brett was in charge of the telephone system, which was originally installed in the 1930s and modified several times since. The system connected not only all the phones in the administration building, but also hundreds of phones in park field houses, harbor stations, Soldier Field, Lincoln Park Zoo, and all the repair shops. Kay Brett was the only person with full knowledge and control over its use. Several people told me, "You don't want to upset her." Her office was modest with several switchboard operators who faithfully answered queries from the public seven days a week. They knew more about the parks, operations, and special events than anyone, and if they didn't know the answer, they connected you to someone who did.

I tried calling Miss Brett but was politely yet firmly told by one of her loyal operators—more like bodyguards—that she was busy and to please call again in a week, which I did with the same result. Kay Brett was not the sort of gregarious employee you ran into walking down the hall, even though our offices were on the same floor. She rarely left her inner office except for lunch. I only knew when she was in because of the smell from the cigarettes.

Then one day in the cafeteria I spotted this heavyset, middle-aged woman wearing a little too much lipstick and far too much costume jewelry sitting by herself behind a large support pillar. Trying to get to know as many members of the old guard as possible, I asked if I could join her. She barely looked at me and said in her smoke-graveled voice, "As long as you don't ask for any favors." Then, to make sure I understood, she added, "If it doesn't come from the general superintendent, I don't do it." After pausing awkwardly wondering if I would have to bother my boss with a telephone repair request, I introduced myself as the new marine director. She smiled and began talking about her love of boating—powerboating that is. When I enthusiastically recounted sailing across the Atlantic in a killer storm, she listened patiently for a minute, then with her face tilted toward the ceiling and rolling her eyes, said, "You must be nuts or something."

I thought for a second and answered, "You are absolutely right. Why else would I take this job?"

Kay Brett laughed, sounding like concrete pouring down a truck chute, so loud the cashiers from the treasurer's office sitting at the next table stopped talking. After swapping boat stories until our lunch plates were clean, she lit a cigarette, took a deep drag, and after a long, slow cough asked, "So is it true the new bunch is going to outlaw smoking in the building?"

I assured her it would not happen anytime soon. That secondhand smoke was dangerous was still considered a loony idea, and besides, many of the new Harold Washington appointees were smokers. I took the opportunity to ask about the green phone. That set her off.

"That prick Pfeiffer went around me," she said all but spitting his name. "I only found out about his precious phone when I was going over the phone bills and saw this 'line secured' charge. What the hell was that?" she asked rhetorically, clanking the bracelets on her arms. "It took me a week to find out that Pfeiffer was behind it. When I confronted him, he cursed me out—none of my goddamned business. Well, he was sure right about that," her loud laughter punctuated by another cough.

"I had nothing to do with his funny business which ain't going to be so funny when they put him in the slammer. Good riddance, if you ask me." With that she abruptly excused herself, but not before whispering a warning. "Watch your back around here."

The next morning a telephone repairman arrived. He unscrewed the cover on the green phone. "Well, well, what have we here?" I peered into the phone at a small capsule-like attachment clamped onto the internal wires. "That's a scrambler," he said. "It makes wiretapping pretty much impossible. This is real state-of-the-art stuff."

No wonder the green phone never rang. Pfeiffer used it only to make calls, not receive calls. A "line secured" phone is equivalent to something in the Pentagon or the White House. Pfeiffer knew the FBI was tapping his regular phones, so he used his clout to install the scrambler on an unlisted one. Everyone, including me, knew the FBI was investigating him; two agents interviewed me at Grebe Shipyard, with questions about cash payments for moorings, and about how certain boaters—none of whom I knew—had obtained their boat slips. They asked if I would take a lie-detector test. With nothing to hide, I agreed but never heard back from them.

"You want me to take the scrambler off?" asked the repairman.

"You can take the phone out too, for all I care."

"Can't do that. Only Miss Brett can order me to do that," he said, placing the scrambler in his pocket as he screwed the cover back on. "The order said to get it working, that's all."

When he left I walked down to Kay's office. The cigarette smoke signaled she was there, and this time her operator-bodyguard flashed a pleasant smile and directed me to go right in. I didn't want any more reminders of my corrupt predecessor, but instead Kay Brett convinced me to keep the green phone.

"It's a gift," she said, pointing up to the ceiling as if a divine power was involved. Kay lit another cigarette and then said softly, "You know you can call anywhere in the world anytime. Why give it up when nobody knows it even exists?" Then she handed me a memo from Jesse Madison, Ed Kelly's replacement. "Have you seen this?"

The memo was a new policy for reducing telephone abuse. "Effective immediately long-distance calling features will be removed from all departments except law, medical, and offices of the commissioners and the general superintendent. All other long-distance calls have to be requested and approved through the telephone office." Apparently, long-distance calling to "1-900 sex talk numbers" was rampant, especially from remote phones in the parks. At three to five dollars an erotic minute, they added up and inevitably became a scandal exposed in the press.

"What genius thought this up?" Kay asked, as if I had been consulted. She explained that while the new procedure might stop the sex calls, it would create absolute havoc with legitimate long-distance calls.

"I'm supposed to decide what calls can be made? Do you know how many long-distance calls are made every day out of this place? Hundreds! In all my years here this is the stupidest thing I ever heard of."

I told Kay not to worry, the policy would collapse under its own bureaucratic weight after a few months and be replaced by strict rules against sex calls. "By the way, your green phone is not affected," she chuckled.

That same day I began using the green phone, first occasionally, then for all my outgoing calls. I even bought a long headset cord, in order to stand and move around the office while talking. And there was a bonus. Until the ban on long-distance calls by department heads was lifted, I allowed a trusted few planners, architects, and other new appointees to make their calls on the green phone but only after swearing a solemn oath of silence. I made a lot of friends with the phone that never rang. More importantly, it was my first act as a pneumacrat: bypassing the letter of a law to follow its spirit for the common good, exchanging a burglar's tool for a builder's.

Looking back, it was the only exception that caused me pleasure instead of trouble—the simple pleasure to never have to wait for a phone line on the office system to open up, to never have concerns about someone listening in from the other phones in the office—and no incoming calls, for neither I nor anyone else knew the number. Well, Kay Brett knew. The old-timers knew everything.

On my first day when ushered into the office of Jesse Madison, Harold Washington's choice for chief executive of the park district and the man who hired me, several members of his staff huddled around the speakerphone, finalizing money matters with my predecessor and his lawyer. How odd that I would be allowed to overhear such a conversation. Pfeiffer had been escorted out of the building three days earlier but was technically still employed. Somehow he managed to have his job designated as part of the civil service, the only senior management position in the park district with such protection, which meant he could only be fired for cause. While there was plenty of cause, nothing had yet been proven as the FBI methodically made its case. After holding out for months, he finally resigned, but for a price: a payout and a guaranteed pension even if indicted. As the discussion between the lawyers on the speakerphone ended with promises of putting it all in writing, I gagged in silence.

Sighing with relief, Jesse welcomed me to the park district and introduced me to his top staff members, including Tom Elzey, a tall, handsome young black man wearing a dark-gray suit and a cold, stony look to match. When Jesse said, "Tom is your boss," I did a double take. I thought I would report directly to Jesse. Not so. After shaking hands, the lawyers and Tom Elzey were excused; Jesse sat behind his desk and asked me in his characteristic soft voice if I had any questions.

"What will my salary be?"

"Oh, I'm sorry," he said lifting a copy of the budget from his top desk drawer. He cleared his throat and said, "I need to tell you that you won't exactly be paid as an employee but as an independent contractor until the park board decides whether or not to hire you as a full-time employee."

I did not expect this at all. I gave up a good job with benefits and a future to be an independent contractor? That's worse than being a patronage "temporary employee," no different than a day laborer without benefits: no medical, no pension, nothing. While he looked for the marine director's salary, I wondered what kind of an organization would spend hours negotiating benefits for my predecessor and not even know what his replacement would be paid. Suddenly I felt like a fool.

It took seven months to get to this point. All my letters, calls, and networking during Pfeiffer's holdout to get an interview had dead-ended. Totally frustrated I finally called my alderman and friend, Larry Bloom, who arranged an interview in the summer of 1986 with Jesse, whom I never heard of until then.

The interview went well. Jesse was the former city commissioner of consumer affairs and knew precious little about boats but a lot about politics. When I said I personified the exact opposite, he laughed. He had agreed to interview me after Larry Bloom asked him, as a courtesy to Bloom, whom he barely knew except as an early supporter of Harold. (Larry and State Representative Barbara Flynn Currie were the only white elected officials who endorsed him, which meant a lot.) That led to a long talk about our civil rights involvements in the sixties and then to Mayor Washington's vision for fairness and equal access to government services. We impressed each other apparently, because after an hour, he said so quietly I could barely hear, "Bob, I want to hire you, but there are complications," by which he meant the position of harbor director was politically sensitive. He said he would be in touch.

In the fall of 1986, I was interviewed again, this time by Walter Netsch, the famous Chicago architect who had been appointed president of the park board by Mayor Washington. Netsch had appointed himself micro-manager of day-to-day park operations, which by statute was not the board president's job; it was Jesse's job. But before George Galland in the Law Department straightened Mr. Netsch out, he insisted on interviewing any candidate for harbor director. The interview was held in secret as Pfeiffer was still at the helm of the Marine Department. After reading off several pages of harbor questions (fortunately I knew a lot more than he did), he gruffly informed me that I would not be hired as director of harbors. What? I thought the interview had gone so well and that it was the final step.

"We are looking for someone with professional qualifications and will conduct a nationwide job search of professional schools of harbor management," he said. When I felt compelled to inform him and his two advisors, who also knew nothing about boats or harbor management, that there were no such schools, Netsch's legendary temper erupted. He accused me of being "unprofessional and rude" and abruptly ended the meeting. I was flabbergasted and confused. Jesse, who sat in the meeting without saying a word, told me afterward to hang in there, that he and Netsch had a major disagreement over managing the parks. Once again he said he would be in touch.

More months passed with more news articles on corruption in the Marine Department but no criminal indictments. Repeated calls to Jesse went unanswered. But then unexpectedly at five o'clock on a Friday afternoon in March 1987, I received a call from the acting general attorney, George Galland, whom I had never met. "Are you still interested in the harbor director job?" he asked.

"Yes," I answered. Of course I was. To be in charge of Chicago's eight harbors was a dream job.

"If the position is offered to you, when can you start?"

I explained that I had a very good winter selling boats, and with customer commitments, commissioning the boats and all, I could start the end of May. There was a short pause.

"No, I mean what time can you start Monday morning," he said rather emphatically. "Mr. Pfeiffer is being escorted out of the building as we speak."

I arrived at 8:30 on that Monday morning at one of the most politically run agencies in Chicago with the improbable background of college chaplain, university administrator, and—for the last dozen dropout years—sailboat peddler, to accept a position waterlogged in corruption. My friends said I was naive, that I wouldn't last a year. They were half right; I was naive. I trusted people beyond a reasonable doubt and sometimes beyond a shadow of a doubt. But in the realm I had entered, trust had always meant political loyalty. As the old hymn goes, "Trust and obey, for there's no other way."

Jesse put the budget book down and took off his reading glasses. "Your compensation will be the same as Mr. Pfeiffer's: $53,000 annually," Jesse said.

I wiped my sweaty palms on my pants and took a deep breath. "That's not acceptable. With all due respect, you expect me to leave a good job in the private sector, take a job on a temporary basis without benefits, and be at the mercy of a board president who shows a distinct dislike for me?"

Jesse smiled. "Well, when you put it like that . . . what do you want?"

"Sixty thousand," I responded.

He jerked back in his chair. "That's more than most department heads."

"I don't know about that, but I know I'm taking a big risk. Starting as an independent contractor sounds very tenuous."

He thought for a few seconds and then surprisingly agreed. "OK, $60,000 it is." He did not offer a written confirmation or even write it down. Instead he picked up the intercom and called in Tom Elzey, whose office was across the hall. "You will report to Tom. He will take you up to your office and introduce you to the marine staff. Afterward you are scheduled for a press conference."

When Tom came into the office, I could tell by his same stony look he was not happy. He had no knowledge of my "appointment" until the previous Friday, and clearly did not want me. Out in the hall, he made his disapproval clear by deliberately not introducing me to the marine staff, leaving that chore to an underling, who gathered the staff and announced simply, "This is the new harbor director, Mr. Nelson," and then led me into my office and closed the door. He explained that he was my contact with Tom Elzey. All communications, letters, memos, calls, and so on, were to be sent to him first. What he did not tell me was that a new staff member, a young female friend or relative of Tom's, would be assigned that same day to the Marine Department to copy all incoming telephone messages, letters, and memos, and every hour or so take the copies to Tom's office.

Watching her nonchalantly pick up my secretary's phone log to copy convinced me to keep a journal with notes on conversations and meetings. Additionally, I would copy memos, policies and telephone messages. To offset the political machinations, I would create a "pneumacratic" record of my time at the park district, however short that might be. I would take them home each night to my basement office.

And that was my first day orientation to the Chicago Park District. No pamphlets, codes of conduct, budgets, ID, or even a building tour—nothing but an office key and a spy at the copier. As I got ready for the press conference announcing my "temporary appointment," I felt like Jonah swallowed up in the belly of a whale.

Ten exhausting days later, lying motionless on the worn carpet, I recalled laying on the deck of *Chasseur*, Tom Leonard's forty-foot sailboat. Two buddies and I crossed the Atlantic aboard her in 1980. On
clear nights after horrendous storms, I watched the moon rise and set,
slowly falling into the sea like a giant tablet with imagined plop and
fizz—an Alka-Seltzer moon bringing relief. Lying on my back, sighting the stars between my toes, I would meditate my way to deepwater
calm, the serenity Christopher Cross sings about. Since leaving the
life of the church, sailing had replaced prayer as my spiritual exercise.
When sailing, the world took on an awesomeness in which I felt part.

I remember one August single-handedly crossing Lake Michigan
from the Michigan City boat show to Chicago, an eight-hour overnight sail. A few miles out from Chicago on black night water, the sun
blipped over the horizon behind me like a miner's lamp on a seam of
coal. Chicago's skyline at dawn displayed a different kind of aurora borealis: crisp Canadian air mixed lake foam with morning sun as if to
scrub the buildings clean, power-washing the skyscrapers from tops
to street-level bottoms, the tallest first, reaching down floor by floor,
down masonry, steel, and glass to the treetops in the parks, Lincoln,
Grant, Burnham, and Jackson, brightening tree canopies in luscious
green over early morning joggers, cyclists, and the homeless in the hol-
lows. Sailing into that rarefied dawn city and seeing those waterfalls of
sunlight resembled the experience of a medieval pilgrim's first glimpse
of a great cathedral, or an immigrant sighting the Statue of Liberty—as
my grandparents had sighted it a hundred years ago. Awesome.

But on that threadbare carpet with no stars to sight between my toes
or Alka-Seltzer moons to imagine, I knew my spiritual resources would
be tested in reforming the harbors. According to scriptures, Jesus stood
on a hilltop overlooking the city of Jerusalem and wept emotionally just
before entering the temple to drive out the corrupt money changers. A
bold reform to be sure. While there is no indication what happened to
the money changers, we know what happened to the reformer.

But of course I was not Jesus, at best a bureaucrat like the tax collector Zacchaeus, a "publican" whose job was to collect taxes from resentful Chicago boaters. With an ironic smile, I stood up, dusted myself off, and walked over to the huge office windows and tugged the pulls. Amazingly one opened easily, the old counterweights faithfully doing their job defying gravity. Cool air poured in and a pile of papers fluttered to the floor, including an editorial clipped from yesterday's *Chicago Tribune*:

Signs of Spring at the Park District
Gerald Pfeiffer's resignation as director of the Chicago Park District's marine division is new proof that the old order is passing. For 13 years, Mr. Pfeiffer was in charge of awarding boat mooring assignments. Recently he was accused of accepting bribes; he failed to appear at a hearing on the charges and refused to answer questions from park district officials. On Monday, just as they were about to suspend him pending a civil service hearing, he quit.

On the same day, Robert Nelson, an official of a Wisconsin-based sailing firm, arrived to take over the job. For Mr. Pfeiffer, an ally of former park district Supt. Edmund Kelly, it must be a disorienting experience to lose his job to a reformer and face a federal investigation on top of that. What he is accused of doing had long been accepted park district procedure.

But suddenly time-honored Chicago customs like these are being treated as crimes (as they should be), and formerly well-connected officials are losing their jobs and otherwise feeling the heat for carrying on the tradition. For them, it's heat. For the rest of us, it feels like springtime.[3]

So it was official. The *Chicago Tribune* editorial said Pfeiffer's resignation was "proof that the old order is passing" and called me "a reformer." When Pfeiffer took over in 1975, he too was welcomed as a reformer in contrast to his predecessor who was shuffled off to federal prison. What happened? What turned the crusader into a criminal? Could it happen to me? I felt like a prostrate priest taking final vows of poverty, chastity, and—scariest of all—political obedience.

HARBORS AS NEIGHBORHOODS

Chicago's ten harbors are neighborhoods much like motor-home parks with docks instead of streets and sidewalks. Boats are floating mobile homes that move easily from one harbor to another; but like homeowners on land, boaters tend to stay put in the first neighborhood they choose. In older harbors, like Chicago's, it is not uncommon for boat slips to be passed along from one generation to the next. Boats have kitchens (galleys), bathrooms (heads), and bedrooms (cabins). Owners consider them second homes, and the IRS recognizes them as such. Boats are mortgaged like homes, often up to thirty years, and all interest is tax deductible. Boaters are both successful and thrifty and would rather buy than rent. While boats are not a good investment per se, using them regularly is actually cheaper than traveling on vacations. Boaters choose their marinas carefully, considering amenities, ambience, and cost. If dissatisfied, they can move anywhere they wish.

Chicago's harbor neighborhoods are as diverse as the city itself, each one having a distinct identity. For instance, the three harbors in Jackson Park are part of the 1893 Columbia Exposition's Grand Canal system; Monroe, with over a thousand boats, has no docks, only buoy moorings; Diversey became a harbor for powerboats only when the Lake Shore Drive Bridge was built across its entrance to Lake Michigan. Each harbor, like the entire lakefront park system, was man-made, nestled on park land. Chicago's lakefront planning began in 1836 when three civic-minded US government surveyors

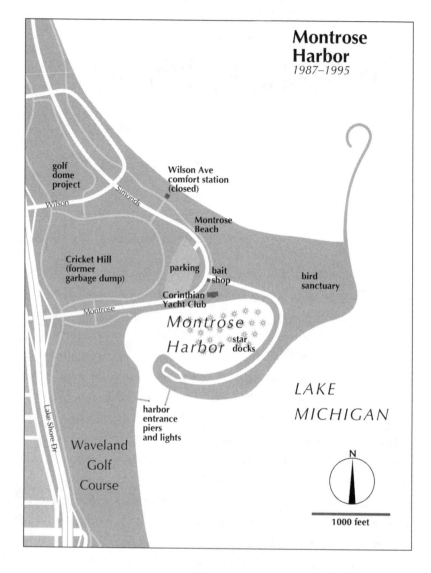

Montrose Harbor
1987–1995

golf dome project

Wilson Ave comfort station (closed)

Simonds

Wilson

Montrose Beach

Cricket Hill (former garbage dump)

parking

bait shop

bird sanctuary

Corinthian Yacht Club

Montrose star docks

Harbor

Montrose

harbor entrance piers and lights

LAKE MICHIGAN

Lake Shore Dr

Waveland Golf Course

N

1000 feet

refused to sell lakefront land to the state of Illinois for canal building, deciding instead to label much of it "Public Ground—A Common to Remain Forever Open, Clear and Free of any Buildings, or Other Obstruction whatever."[1] Ever since that momentous declaration, which became the legal basis for a hundred years of public trust court decisions, Chicago's lakefront and harbors have been the center of a classic American struggle between public and private use. For example,

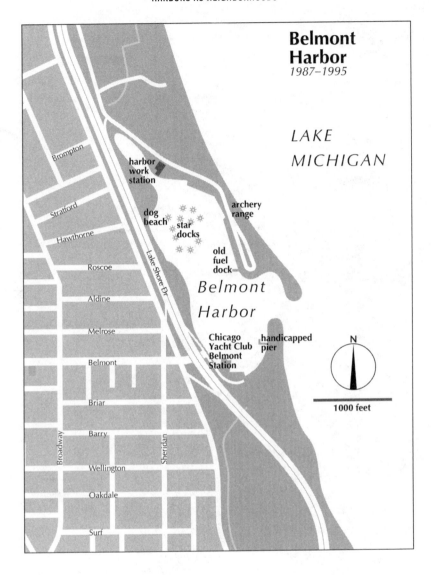

Belmont Harbor
1987–1995

LAKE MICHIGAN

harbor work station

dog beach

star docks

archery range

old fuel dock

Belmont Harbor

Chicago Yacht Club Belmont Station

handicapped pier

Brompton

Stratford

Hawthorne

Roscoe

Aldine

Melrose

Belmont

Briar

Barry

Wellington

Oakdale

Surf

Broadway

Sheridan

Lake Shore Dr

N

1000 feet

Chicago bans commercial advertising on the lakefront. There are no billboards on Lake Shore Drive or anywhere on the waterfront. Even the signage on the city's lakefront museums is highly restricted. One late Saturday night in the summer of 1991, I was called at home and told to do something about a "floating light ship" sailing in and out of the harbors with blinking ads on huge billboards on either side. The owner of the monstrosity insisted that because he was operating in the

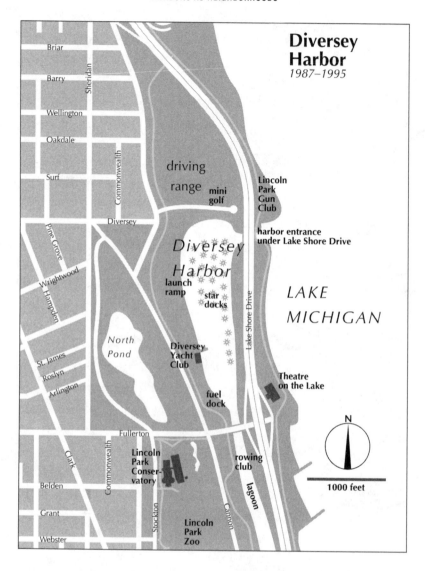

Briar

Barry

Sheridan

Wellington

Oakdale

Commonwealth

Surf

driving
range   mini
golf

Diversey

Pine Grove

Diversey

Harbor

launch
ramp   star
docks

Wrightwood

Hampden

North
Pond

Diversey
Yacht
Club

St. James

Roslyn

Arlington

fuel
dock

**Diversey
Harbor**
1987–1995

Lincoln
Park
Gun
Club

harbor entrance
under Lake Shore Drive

*LAKE
MICHIGAN*

Lake Shore Drive

Theatre
on the Lake

N

Fullerton

Clark

Commonwealth

Lincoln
Park
Conser-
vatory

rowing
club

Belden

lagoon

1000 feet

Grant

Stockton

Cannon

Lincoln
Park
Zoo

Webster

federal waters of the Great Lakes, he was not bound by Chicago's strict regulations, even though the city was granted jurisdiction right after World War I. He sued in federal court and lost. Judge James B. Zaegel upheld Chicago's police power over the harbors including commercial enterprises on its waters.

Chicago has ten harbors along fourteen miles of its thirty-one-mile lakefront, all made from swampy shoreline known to the Indians as

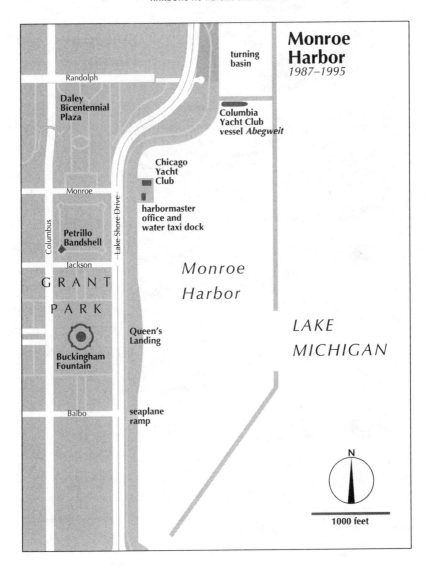

Monroe
Harbor
1987–1995

turning
basin

Randolph

Daley
Bicentennial
Plaza

Columbia
Yacht Club
vessel *Abegweit*

Chicago
Yacht
Club

Monroe

harbormaster
office and
water taxi dock

Lake Shore Drive

Columbus

Petrillo
Bandshell

Jackson

G R A N T

Monroe

Harbor

P A R K

Queen's
Landing

LAKE

MICHIGAN

Buckingham
Fountain

Balbo

seaplane
ramp

N

1000 feet

the "place of the stinking onions." The harbors were constructed with
various types of landfill: rubble from the Great Chicago Fire of 1871;
slag from the steel mills; and pure sand from Indiana's majestic dunes,
many leveled in the process. Montrose Harbor was built during the
Depression on landfill, much of it garbage dumped for years on top
of an abandoned water-pumping station on what is now Lake Shore
Drive. Much of the old mountain of garbage adjacent to the harbor

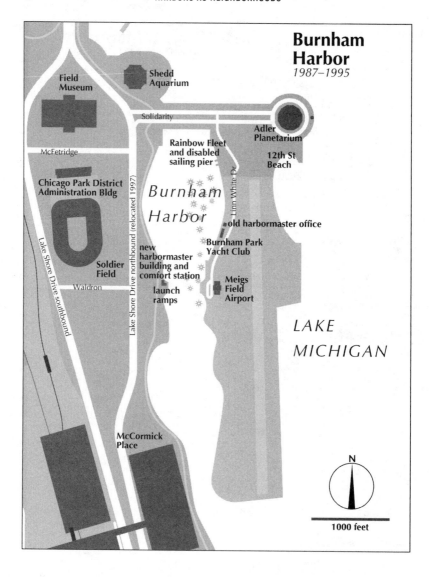

Burnham
Harbor
1987–1995

Field
Museum

Shedd
Aquarium

Solidarity

Adler
Planetarium

Rainbow Fleet
and disabled
sailing pier

12th St
Beach

McFetridge

Chicago Park District
Administration Bldg

Burnham

Harbor

Linn White Dr

old harbormaster office

Burnham Park
Yacht Club

new
harbormaster
building and
comfort station

launch
ramps

Meigs
Field
Airport

Lake Shore Drive northbound (relocated 1997)

Soldier
Field

Waldron

Lake Shore Drive southbound

LAKE

MICHIGAN

McCormick
Place

N

1000 feet

known as "Cricket Hill" was covered with soil and has been used for sledding by generations of children. The harbors were built according to a series of lakefront improvement plans spanning from the Civil War (Monroe Harbor was built by the War Department during the war) through the Great Depression of the 1930s. Only two, Monroe, at the entrance to the Chicago River downtown, and Calumet, at the entrance to the Calumet River ten miles south, were designed as anchor-

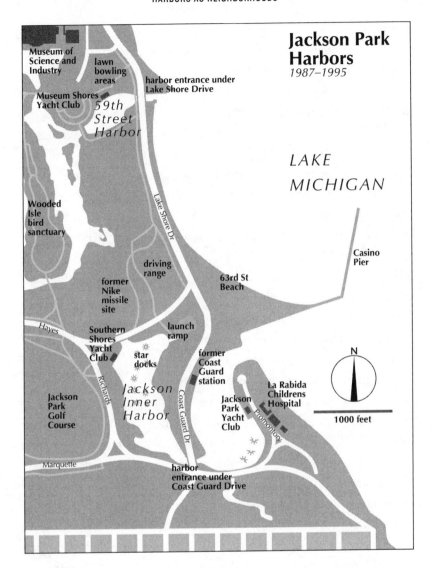

Jackson Park Harbors
1987–1995

Museum of Science and Industry

lawn bowling areas

harbor entrance under Lake Shore Drive

Museum Shores Yacht Club

59th Street Harbor

LAKE MICHIGAN

Lake Shore Dr

Wooded Isle bird sanctuary

Casino Pier

driving range

63rd St Beach

former Nike missile site

Hayes

Southern Shores Yacht Club

launch ramp

star docks

former Coast Guard station

La Rabida Childrens Hospital

N

Jackson Park Golf Course

Richards

Jackson Inner Harbor

Coast Guard Dr

Jackson Park Yacht Club

Promontory

1000 feet

Marquette

harbor entrance under Coast Guard Drive

ages inside stone breakwaters to protect large ships that are anchored, waiting to load and unload cargo at wharves up the river.

The other seven harbors were designed as lagoons in their respective parks for multiple recreational uses. If you stretched a string around the perimeters of the harbors, it would measure almost fifteen miles: fifteen miles of promenades, some twenty feet wide, extending for miles; grass embankments; walking and biking paths; fishing areas;

picnic areas; and other amenities. Perimeters of these "lagoons" are studded with major attractions: six major museums, four bird sanctuaries, five golf courses and driving ranges, an NFL stadium, a world-famous zoo, a former small airport, an international trade center, and a children's hospital, not to mention major annual events like the Air and Water Show, Taste of Chicago, and others that attract millions of people. This diverse public use of harbors and surrounding parks differentiates Chicago's harbor system from any other in the world.

It might seem odd that the harbors have not been named posthumously after famous Chicagoans except for Burnham Harbor, named after the great lakefront planner, and DuSable, after Chicago's first black settler whose cabin sat there. Like cemeteries and prisons, the other harbors are not named after people but mundane neighborhood streets that dead end at the lake making identification and directions practical and efficient like the city's grid system.

All commercial enterprises are prohibited on Chicago's lakefront. There are no privately owned restaurants or bars. The few that operate are "permitted" as concessions inside park district buildings or on its beaches. Yacht clubs have restaurants and bars but only for members and guests. Nor are there any repair facilities for boats. Those with serious repair problems must be towed miles up the rivers to private boatyards. Simple repairs and cleaning are done by licensed mobile vendors who come to the harbors and pay fees to the park district for providing ordinary maintenance and cleaning services. If these vendors utilize vans or trucks, they cannot use Lake Shore Drive to get to the harbors, as commercial vehicles are prohibited on that road. Such vehicles must use city streets that cross Lake Shore Drive and dead end into the harbors. Burnham, Fifty-Ninth Street, and Jackson Park Harbors have no cross-street access, so vendors and even boaters pulling trailers to the launch ramps in those harbors must use Lake Shore Drive anyway. Chicago police ticket them.

Chicago's park lagoons became "yacht harbors" toward the end of the nineteenth century. The Great Chicago Fire of 1871 created a building boom. Economic expansion of the city's manufacturing and transportation base brought prosperity and undreamed-of wealth. The city grew in all directions, annexing towns up and down the lakefront. In 1885 Congress announced plans for a world's fair to commemorate Columbus's discovery of America. Chicago decided to bid and passed a tax to pay for the costs, a tax overwhelmingly approved by the citizens bursting with civic pride. Chicago won over fierce competition from New York, and something unique to Chicago was born: citizen consciousness of the importance of the lake for everyday people. After furious infighting between the North and South Side park commissioners (the city had three separate park districts, south, north, and west), the South Side was chosen as the site, but only after the great landscape architect of Central Park, Fredrick Law Olmstead, weighed in. The unfinished Jackson Park and swamp land from Fifty-Sixth Street to Sixty-Seventh Street was chosen for the Columbian Exposition of 1893. The incredible success of the exposition, with its canals and tour boats, accelerated interest in recreational boating. While handfuls of boats had appeared in Chicago harbors in the 1870s, only after the exposition did boating begin to flourish and become organized around a series of yacht clubs. Because boating necessities like fuel docks, washrooms, and restaurants were forbidden on the lakefront, yacht clubs were formed, one in each harbor, sometimes two. Chicago Yacht Club, the most prestigious, was formally organized in 1875, and another ten followed as each harbor became populated with boaters who required basic amenities.

The birth of private yacht clubs, and their members' desire to build clubhouses, immediately clashed with Chicago's "forever open, clear, and free" advocates who feared that not only yacht clubs, but tennis, golf, and lawn bowling clubs, very popular at the time, would build private clubhouses. To this day, one active lawn bowling club with a stout brick clubhouse still exists on the perimeter of Fifty-Ninth Street Harbor.

There has always been tension between advocates for "green space use" and those for "blue space use," even though over a million people, boaters and their guests, visiting boaters, tour boat pa-

trons, fishermen, sailing school students, rowers, windsurfers, jet ski-
ers, and others use the blue space each year. While a bowling green,
golf course, or tennis court can be placed anywhere on land in "green
space," harbors and yacht clubs obviously have to be near water in
"blue space." It is no fault of the yacht clubs that the city owns all the
harbors and waterfront property. When yacht clubs prior to World
War I were denied building permits, the boaters built their clubhouses
on barges and floated them with federal waterways jurisdiction leases
for "anchorages," thus avoiding the city's direct control. To this day,
two of those early clubhouses still float: Columbia in Monroe and Chicago at Belmont (formerly the Lincoln Park Yacht Club), and others
have appeared in Belmont and, most recently, Thirty-First Street Harbor shortly after it opened.

Because of the "forever open, clear and free" doctrine, the Lincoln Park Boat Club in Diversey Harbor, like the Goodman Theater
in Grant Park, was required to construct its building entirely underground and out of view from the public using the park side of the lagoon. This was accomplished by landscaping a large mound over the
clubhouse complete with trees, shrubs, and walking trails. The one-
story concrete structure is buried several feet down with offices, classrooms, and storage for a hundred rowing shells. Except for a couple of
windows on the lagoon side, its only ventilation is through roof stacks
made to look like tree stumps. The entrance and docks on the lagoon
side are so low to the water that in periods of high water, like 1987,
the boat club floods.

One club, Calumet Yacht Club on the far south edge of the lakefront, never paid much attention to permits. Organized in a tavern in
1951 by about thirty working-class boaters tired of launching their
outboard fishing boats on a makeshift ramp, the club leased seven
hundred feet of beachfront property from the Falstaff Brewery. The
brewery's silos and distilling equipment, rising ten stories, sat about
two hundred feet back from the shoreline, while in the harbor was a
series of water intakes for making beer. As the club evolved, members
built a brick clubhouse with a full bar and restaurant and meeting

areas. In effect yacht clubs are no different than classic neighborhood taverns, bringing people together with shared values, supporting community groups and charities.

Numerous unsuccessful battles for permits and easements took place over the years. Calumet Yacht Club was undaunted. When the park district refused to supply water from its Calumet Park field house next door, the plucky club somehow obtained a Cook County permit to dig the only well on Chicago's lakefront. When easements for electricity were blocked, the club bought World War II army surplus generators. Slag from the mills was clandestinely dumped to build a wave-protecting peninsula out into the water as well as a parking lot and winter storage area for boats. The steelworkers in the club "borrowed" steel sheeting and long sections of fifty-four-inch-diameter smoke-stack liners they converted into caissons, sunk them into the beach sand, capped them with concrete, then attached piers and docks. They also fabricated a monorail boat lift from World War II surplus steel mesh used for portable runways.

Because Calumet Harbor was exposed to savage storm winds from the northeast, the club quickly discovered it would need additional breakwaters to protect its growing boat population. Junk barges were illegally floated in at night, sunk, and then filled with piles of damaged limestone donated by nearby quarries. Later some members managed to acquire a large crane and clam scoop from Commonwealth Edison's State Line power plant next to the club, and along with steel sheet piling and other structures "borrowed" from the mills, the break wall was completed—all without permits. If such a project were attempted downtown or on the North Side of the city, it would have been stopped; but Calumet is on the far southeast side of the city, an area rarely monitored. To this day, most boaters in Chicago, especially those in the downtown and North Side harbors, are unaware there is a marina and yacht club in Calumet Harbor.

The tensions between the yacht clubs and lakefront purists come and go like Lake Michigan squalls. In order to save money in 1934 at the height of the Depression, the three park districts of Chicago were consolidated into one with an independent board of commissioners. Along with all kinds of publicly owned facilities, the legal status of yacht clubs required clarification. The "forever open, clear, and free" forces squared off against "privileged yacht owners." In 1938 a blue ribbon citizens' committee was formed by Mayor Edward J. Kelly to "investigate the operations and expenditures of the Chicago Park District." A special section on "private clubs" reads:

> Private use of public property is undesirable. The only possible excuse for allowing such special privileges is where a particular recreational activity, by that means, is promoted, organized and directed for the people in general. It is difficult to advance any argument to support the policy of permitting private clubs, such as yacht clubs, boat clubs, gun clubs, lawn bowling clubs, or fly casting organizations, to continue the proprietary rights to some of the areas which they have acquired, to the exclusion of the general public. Carried to its logical conclusion this policy would turn the park tennis courts over to tennis clubs, golf courses to golf clubs, etc.[2]

This report, along with a 1944 court case questioning the rights of private clubs to be on the lakefront, became the impetus for strictly regulating the yacht clubs. On the day after Christmas in 1944, the park district passed "standards for operation of yacht clubs located on park lands or waters."[3] Eight standards basically gave the clubs year-to-year leases, with provisions that mandated membership open to any "resident of Illinois with a boat longer than 16 feet, or a 25% interest in such a boat, or a regular crew member of such boat located and with a permit in a Chicago Park District harbor." The Chicago Park District invoked its right to terminate a lease in 1991 when the Lincoln Park Gun Club, on the lake adjacent to Diversey Harbor's entrance, was disbanded. Under tremendous pressure from environmental groups, the park district refused to renew its eighty-year lease due to pollution issues from skeet shooting over the water. It took immediate possession of the building without any compensation and, after several attempts to use it for recreational purposes, tore it down.

Chicago Yacht Club, worried about these standards controlling its activities, dispatched politically influential members to Springfield to lobby for a bill giving it title to a small parcel of "bottom land of Lake Michigan" where they built their clubhouse. Chicago Yacht Club is the only club that owns its own land on the lakefront. However, the park district owns the land surrounding the clubhouse, including its member parking lot (which is leased). At various times of tension between the club and the district (especially when a new park administration takes over), this access is threatened. Compromises are forged, such as the club's late 1990s agreement to pay for a public washroom facility adjacent to the clubhouse.

In a wave of protest against yacht clubs in the summer of 1990, a Chicago alderman, Juan Soliz, challenged the closed membership policy of the Chicago Yacht Club by demanding to be served in its private dining room. When politely refused he immediately held a news conference on the club's front steps demanding that the rich man's club be closed and turned into a shelter for the homeless. This bizarre action prompted Mike Royko, the legendary Chicago newspaper columnist, to write one of his best satirical pieces on those who condemn yacht clubs.[4] For all the bad raps the yacht clubs have received, and certainly they are not perfect institutions on the lakefront, they are perhaps the best example of the highly touted "public private partnerships." The rich and powerful have as much right of access to the water as those less fortunate. But boating is hardly just a rich man's pursuit. This is why a second club, Columbia, was founded in the same harbor to cater more to middle-class boaters, the vast majority in Chicago harbors.

In the 1950s, a revolutionary change in boat manufacturing occurred that made boating affordable to the middle class. Experiments with fiberglass boats in World War II made it the chosen material for boat building; it could be molded into any hull shape desired and could be mass produced cheaply. It was also stronger and more durable than wood and required virtually no maintenance. Fiberglass boats last indefinitely, which is why damaged ones are banned from most landfills. The famed naval architect William Shaw when asked,

"How long will fiberglass boats last?" answered in a dry New England accent, "As near as we can tell, one day longer than rock."[5]

This new, less expensive way of building boats caused an explosion in middle-class boat ownership. By 1970 Chicago's harbors filled to capacity with long waiting lists. The supply of boat slips and moorings fell far short of demand, creating a perfect scenario for corruption: a government monopoly managed by government officials. By the time I assumed the position of director of harbors, the going rate for "consideration" of a boat slip was between $5,000 and $10,000. Mooring fees were kept low; cash payments, high.

The nature of boating allows for exemptions from certain strict park regulations. Because boats are floating domiciles, their owners are not bound by the park's 11:00 p.m. curfew and bans on camping. Boaters can sleep in their waterborne campers and party all night long. While the general public is prohibited from drinking in the parks, boaters can consume all the alcohol they wish. These privileges infuriate ordinary citizens, especially on hot summer nights when the police kick them out of the parks at curfew while boaters load cases of beer and liquor onto their boats. Such boater privileges cause a great deal of tension, especially with fishermen who argue for the right to fish twenty-four hours a day but are not allowed to do so except during smelt season. Perhaps the fact that harbors seem similar to gated communities, with docks accessible only to boaters and their guests, makes them unpopular. Yet, while gated off from public access by land, all harbors are open and accessible by sea. There are no gates across harbor entrances. Anyone in a boat, no matter its size, can come and go as they please.

There are no churches in the harbors or anywhere else on Chicago's lakefront. There are lots of statues, but no saints; lots of museums, but no cathedrals. I would posit that churches are not needed there, that Chicago's lakefront is the secular equivalent of sacred ground, that at the intersection of green space and blue space a reverence wells up in every individual soul.

Harbor management cannot be separated from other jurisdictions. I once made a list of all the governmental agencies, elected offices, not-for-profit organizations, and other entities that the director of harbors deals with on a regular basis. The total number was over 120, fewer than twenty-five of which had anything to do with boating.

My goal was to manage the harbors like neighborhood mom-and-pop stores, like the grocery store I worked in all through high school. Belmont Foods, at 107th and the Rock Island train tracks was a beloved institution in the Beverly neighborhood and the two generations of Schuenemans who owned it were highly respected for fairness and integrity. Employees from butchers to delivery order takers oozed with pride and could easily have written the manual for total quality management. There I learned that customer service was not something outlined in a book or seminar; it was a secret passed along by dedicated employees, a secret goodness to be discovered by customers. It was my goal to run the park district harbors honestly and fairly with equal access for all.

HARBOR RATS

March 25, 1987.

I decided to make a surprise visit to Belmont Harbor, the work headquarters for the harbors, three miles north of my downtown park district office. Gathered there are the men who run the harbors in the summer and maintain them in the winter. For decades they were masters of their respective harbors with the ability to make any boater's experience a pleasure or a living hell. Rather than call a big meeting of the maintenance staff downtown, I decided to meet them on their turf.

For fifteen years, most of them made my life as a boat peddler a living hell, because I did not "cooperate." When their hands were out, I never palmed off any cash. In terms of boat sales, it cost me dearly. The first question a boat buyer always asked was, "Where am I going to put the boat?" Outside of buoy moorings in the worst section of Monroe or remote sections of other harbors, a walk-on slip assignment required "consideration."

It was just after seven in the morning when I parked my car in the Belmont lot and sat for a few minutes wondering how the men would react to a surprise visit by their new boss. I entered the workstation building, a large, beautifully designed yellowish brick structure with a generous harbor master office overlooking the harbor. All other harbors had makeshift harbor master offices: wooden shacks at Jackson and Burnham, a trailer at Monroe, a tiny space in a toolshed at Fifty-

Figure I. Cluster of star docks in Burnham, originally invented by the park district in the I960s for the common good and never patented. (Photo by R. J. Nelson.)

Ninth Street, and small, uninviting rooms inside the yacht clubs at Diversey and Montrose. Not one displayed a sign or any harbor information. No wonder the harbor masters were referred to as "harbor rats." As the central maintenance facility for the entire harbor system, this split-level building includes cranes, workshops, and a marine railway system that pulls the large workboats and barges up to sixty feet long into the building. The harbors contained over five thousand boats, far more than they were designed for, often straining the maintenance system far beyond its capacity.

To make room for more boats, park engineers invented "star docks," floating dock wheels with spokes that held twelve small boats and only took up the swing space of four mooring buoys. They were installed in all harbors except Monroe, where wave action in storms made them unsuitable. There were several in Belmont.

A mysterious storage barn and work areas in the back were off limits to boaters or anyone else unless invited. This backroom was where payoffs were made and divided between my predecessor and his un-

derboss, the Belmont harbor master, Red Swanberg, who quickly retired at the end of 1986, and was later indicted when the FBI heated
up its investigation of harbor corruption.

I took a deep breath and walked down the stairs and hallway and
heard the employees talking over classical music, of all things, playing
in the background. When I entered the work area, they were eating
sweet rolls and drinking coffee. A rock-hard silence greeted me except
for a Mozart piano concerto, coming from an ancient Zenith radio on
a shelf high above a work bench, put there to prevent unappreciative
workers from changing the station. There were six men present when
there should have been ten. Two arrived a half hour late; the others
didn't show at all.

I could not help but savor the "what goes around, comes around"
moment. I saw the terror in the faces of my past tormentors; indif-
ference in others who were no doubt confident their political clout
would protect their jobs no matter what, and curiosity in the two
old-timers, Joe Kordecki and Mike Oltean—the classical music lover.
These two had accumulated many more years at the park district than
they needed to retire with good pensions. In their early sixties, both
sat together at the head of a large, heavy worktable.

Kordecki was a gruff character with thick white hair. He was a big
man with huge arms, a barrel chest, and hands that looked like leather
work gloves. My first encounter with him occurred in late spring thirteen years earlier in Burnham Harbor, when I brought my brand-new,
Canadian-built sailboat in to have the mast stepped at the Burnham
Yacht Club, which provided a small crane for the purpose. The previous fall, I had applied for a mooring in Burnham, paid my money,
and, as was often the case for those who did not cooperate, heard
nothing all winter and spring. A dozen phone calls elicited the same
curt response: "Your application is in process."

At Grebe Shipyard my boat was launched and had to be moved off
the busy shipyard dock. I took a chance and brought it down the Chicago River and into Burnham Harbor without a permit, figuring its
arrival would trigger an assignment. After stepping the mast, I found

Figure 2. Harbor master office at Burnham, 1987, formerly a toilet building from the 1934 Century of Progress. (Photo by R. J. Nelson.)

harbor master Kordecki busy filling soda-vending machines next to his office. Before I became director, all soda, ice, candy, and cigarette concessions were operated by the harbor masters below the radar of the park district accounting offices. It was my predecessor's way of spreading the wealth, you might say. Kordecki's nickname, "Six Bits Joe," related to his private vending operation. His machines only took quarters for cans of soda that cost fifty cents. Naturally, legions of boaters and park users needed change for a dollar. When they asked for change, he would reach into one of four pockets, each containing three quarters and say, "Sorry I only have six bits." The thirsty customers gladly exchanged their dollars for three quarters instead of four. Six Bits Joe made a 25 percent profit on change, not to mention on each can of soda.

I introduced myself to Six Bits Joe and asked if he had an assigned mooring for me on his list. He didn't even look at me. He continued to fill the machines until full, then locked them. Without saying a word, he walked into his office, a small dilapidated wooden building that leaned precariously toward the harbor and smelled of serious wood rot. He yanked hard on the top side drawer of a World War II vintage desk to get it open and pulled out three stacks of harbor permits, alphabetized in heavy black binders known in all harbors as the "Boater Bibles." Those recorded inside signed for their permit and were given a decal for the boat and a parking sticker. Boaters whose names and permits not recorded were damned to the Hell of consideration.

Joe pulled up his ancient swivel chair, looked through the permits tracing the lines with chubby fingers, and then slammed the binders hard on the old steel desk. "No Nelson," he said curtly, leaning back and finally looking me in the eyes.

"Well, can you at least call downtown? I applied last fall."

"I don't care what you did last fall." He sneered. "If you don't have a permit in here, you can't have your boat out there. Where's the boat now?"

"It's at the yacht club. I just finished using their crane to step the mast."

"Good. Now sail your fucking boat out of my harbor." He shoved the permits back in the desk and slammed the drawer. He looked at his watch. "It's three thirty. I'm off the clock. If your boat is here tomorrow morning, it will be impounded."

A harbor master could legally impound any vessel for the slightest rule violation. Impounded boats were towed and chained up in remote areas of harbors. No attempt was made to notify the owners. They had to come crawling to the harbor masters looking for their boats. Like cars towed to auto pounds, boats could rack up hundreds of dollars in fines and daily storage fees. Worse, impoundment could quickly lead to expulsion from the entire harbor system.

It was a Friday afternoon when Six Bits gave me his ultimatum. The marine office downtown was closed for the weekend. Desperate to avoid impoundment, I asked for help from the Burnham Yacht Club manager who said I could leave the boat overnight at its courtesy dock, which was leased legally and supposedly off limits to the

Figure 3. Harbor master office at Monroe, 1987, a condemned trailer with Porta-Potties in lieu of restrooms. (Photo by R. J. Nelson.)

harbor masters. The next morning I arrived at 7:30 just as Six Bits Joe pulled up to my boat in his beat-up red workboat, with towline, and lengths of rusty chains.

"I told you I would impound the boat," he shouted, his hand on the outboard motor steering his boat in a slow circle next to mine.

"I'm moving it now," I answered meekly, jumped aboard, and started the auxiliary engine. Circling until I was underway, he followed me for more than a quarter mile to the entrance of the harbor before turning back to his office. The yacht club manager had told me to forget about trying to deal with Kordecki. Instead he suggested I sail to Monroe Harbor and see the harbor master there, who would let me tie up temporarily and charge me daily fees designed for boaters visiting the city.

So I sailed my brand-new twenty-five-foot sailboat with canary-yellow hull—the "in" color in 1974—to Monroe Harbor and tied up outside the harbor master's office, a small construction trailer on cement blocks surrounded by chain-link fence and barbed wire and two huge dumpsters. A summer helper told me the harbor master was in the Chicago Yacht Club having breakfast and would be back in an hour. I waited. After two hours, he sauntered back to the trailer office with attitude. "I ain't helping you. You're illegal, but I'll do the Burnham Yacht Club a favor." He made it very clear that I could only stay one week at a time, cash in advance, and if I was one day late, my boat would be impounded. I obediently sat down on a worn-out couch while he filled out a temporary permit that looked anything but official.

The office trailer was small and dirty like those lined up in scrap yards on the Calumet River waiting for the crusher. Coils of line and boxes of swivel shackles lay all over the floor. Rusted, small boat anchors occupied one corner, and gas cans for outboard motors another. One dirty window overlooked the harbor, and under it was a makeshift counter with a coffeepot, a small black-and-white television turned on to some game show, and a marine radio turned off. By contrast the harbor master was neatly dressed in khaki shirt and shorts. As he hunched over the papers, I could see his balding head was covered with that black spray meant to look like hair. He reeked of cheap cologne that, mixed with the fetid odor of the trailer, almost made me gag. He assigned me a "temporary" buoy mooring straight out from Queen's Landing at the harbor's entrance, as far from shore as you could get.

When I asked for help to attach my mooring line to the buoy, he gave me a cold stare. "Where did you get that piece of junk?" When I told him it came from a yachting supply store, he scoffed and said he had no time—even though that was his job, a job that had to be done from a small dinghy or workboat, not from the deck of a sailboat five feet off the water. Harbor masters, particularly those assigned to Monroe with over a thousand boats on moorings, made up mooring lines as a side business, at hefty prices. Tips were encouraged.

"I can't leave the office unless it's important," he said, adding after a pause, "real important." He half-smiled out the side of his mouth and nodded to his summer helper, who got up and walked outside. Obviously some money would make attaching my mooring line real important. I was incensed. I thanked him for his favor to the yacht club manager, picked up my permit, and left. I borrowed a dinghy from a sailor returning from his boat and hooked up the mooring line myself.

After two weeks of paying daily fees, my brand-new sailboat was purposely moved from its temporary assignment to another in the worst section of Monroe Harbor where wave action during storms was severe. It shouldn't have mattered; my mooring line was stout with double leads. But it broke loose during a minor squall. When the harbor master moved it, he had to remove the proper stainless steel cotter pin that secures the clevis pin into the swivel shackle connecting the heavy line from the buoy to the boat. Instead of replacing the stainless steel cotter pin, he substituted a piece of coat hanger, an old trick guaranteed to make the shackle fail. Coat hanger wire is very soft and wears through quickly in a storm. My treasured new boat broke loose, drifted all the way to the Shedd Aquarium, and banged repeatedly into the concrete-and-steel harbor wall. The wall gouged the entire starboard side all the way through the fiberglass in some places, tearing off the deck rub rail and bending several lifeline stanchions. It would have sunk, had not the Marine Police Unit pulled it off the wall and tied it up at the Chicago Yacht Club until the storm blew over.

When I confronted the harbor master the next morning, he insisted that it was my fault, that there was no stainless steel cotter pin, and that he did me a favor by "temporarily" using a piece of coat hanger. But the brand-new mooring line and shackle did have a stainless steel cotter pin before it was moved. I had installed it myself! He meant it was my fault that I didn't buy the mooring line and shackle from him at almost double the cost of local marine suppliers. It was a boat protection racket. The system was feudal, and complaining was futile.

A month passed after my boat had broken loose before I was legitimately assigned a permanent mooring in Monroe. The daily fees had totaled up to half the cost of the mooring for the whole season. After my own initiation into the system, I carefully warned my customers to buy their mooring lines from the harbor masters. One customer refused. His brand-new, bright-red, thirty-five-foot sailboat mysteriously broke loose within a week and, battered by the harbor wall all night, sank at the south end of Monroe Harbor. On average, thirty to forty boats broke loose in Monroe Harbor each year. Those that sank were salvaged by the harbor masters and their scuba-diving friends who made very good money off the insurance companies, not only by raising the boats with inflatable air bags but also by selling items they purloined: winches, outboard motors, instruments, and personal effects of the owners.

About the time I interviewed for the director's job with Jesse Madison, one of the harbor masters was caught in scuba gear and tools salvaging a sunken boat. After an exposé in the press, he was fired, only to be later hired by the Chicago Fire Department—as a rescue diver.

Mike Oltean, Kordecki's friend, smiled when he saw me come through the doorway. We had known each other for many years. At Grebe Shipyard, Mike was a frequent visitor picking up parts for Marine Department workboats or bringing them up the river for service. Shirt open, cigarette dangling out the side of his mouth, he looked like Humphrey Bogart in *The African Queen*. Though never educated beyond high school, he listened to classical music all the time and could easily identify the symphonies from Bach to Brahms, Mozart to Mahler. Mike knew everything about boats but was not the best manager in the world. He was one of those people who complain about everyone else's mistakes and always have multiple excuses when things don't get done. He was old school, a tireless worker, and proud of his Eastern European Gypsy heritage. Mike had a dark side—"my Gypsy side," he once explained—he drank far too much, though never during working hours. But almost any late afternoon, you could find Mike at one of the yacht clubs, where every drink was paid for by boaters looking for favors.

But this time he smiled at me for another reason: his unmitigated hatred for my predecessor. Pfeiffer did not trust Mike, afraid he would

reveal too many secrets at yacht club bars. When he should have promoted Mike to harbor master, the highest pay level, he held him back
at "captain," which in the arcane park district system was a middle
rank. He despised Mike Oltean so much that he assigned him for two
years to the abandoned coast guard station in Jackson Park Harbor,
without heat or electricity or plumbing or telephone or even a desk.
When he could have transferred to another park department, Mike
stubbornly persevered. He rigged up a discarded boat generator from
Grebe's and a space heater from the Salvation Army. He would not give
in to Pfeiffer's machinations.

"Good morning," I said warmly. Only four of the men responded in
kind. The morning paper with the story about my appointment was
folded on the worktable, flat as their worried faces. Why the hell was
I there so early in the morning if not to fire them? I walked over and
helped myself to a cup of coffee and told the men to sit down around
the worktable.

"I am here for two reasons. The first is to introduce myself. Some
of you know me, some of you don't. For those who don't, you will
discover that I am honest and fair. My office door is always open, and
that means any of you can come in and talk directly and confidentially
at any time," I said, deliberately pausing and looking at each man in
the room.

"I know you are worried about your jobs. How you got your jobs
or who your clout is does not concern me. As long as you do your
jobs, you will have no problems." Only two of the men looked back
at me. Except for Mike and Six Bits Joe, they weren't buying my brief
inaugural address.

"Are there any questions so far?" A long silence ensued. These
men had been conditioned to do what they're told without questions.
When the top dog barked, they pulled the load.

"The second reason I'm here is to get your input on the condition of
the harbors. I know what the boaters need, but you know the harbors
and what equipment you need to do your jobs. My goal is to upgrade
the harbors so that the only thing you need to run them is pride."

I paused again and helped myself to another cup of their coffee. Mike Oltean opened a drawer under one of the workstations and pulled out a five-foot length of the chain used to connect all two thousand buoys throughout the system to huge blocks of concrete at the bottoms of the harbors. He threw the rusty chain in the middle of the table. The links were almost worn through.

"All the anchor chains have to be replaced, or we could lose two thousand boats this summer," said Mike lighting a cigarette. I hoped he was exaggerating. Replacing two thousand chains fifty to one hundred feet long would take all year at a cost well over $100,000, which I was sure was not budgeted. Mike then let out years of frustration.

"That motherfucker, Pfeiffer, substituted soft chain for the case-hardened chain the specs called for. Then he made the company bill us for case hardened, and got a kickback for the difference, the cocksucker."

With his nemesis gone, Mike was not afraid to say whatever he wanted. I picked up the worn length of chain and asked for three or four lengths to take back to the office. Joe Kordecki picked up a bolt cutter.

"Mike, don't scare Mr. Nelson on his first visit here," Joe interjected while snapping off three links like he was cutting thread with a scissors. He reminded me of the portly fireman at a demonstration in Rochester, New York, who easily cut through the case-hardened chains with the super-sized bolt cutters.

"Sure, there's a lot of soft chain out there, but it wears differently in different harbors. We don't have to replace it all at once." Joe picked up the links and handed them to me with a forced smile. "Some sections of Monroe are really bad. Burnham can wait a couple of years."

This was not the Joe Kordecki who threw me out of Burnham. Why was he suddenly so helpful? Already past retirement age and eligible for a generous pension, his family grown and prosperous, he didn't care about his job. Then it came to me. As gruff as he was, he never asked me for "consideration" to keep my boat in Burnham. The same was true of Mike. One of the FBI agents checking files in my office told me confidentially that they found no evidence of wrongdoing by Joe or Mike. The private vending machines were not illegal. Like Mike, Joe could not stand my predecessor.

From the far end of the table, a smooth yet assertive voice piped up. "We need new buoys. These old steel ones are relics. Some are so full of rust holes they sink, and the boaters hate them because they tear up the gel coat finish on their boats. Replace the buoys and boaters will love the park district." The speaker was an entry-level laborer, a Bahamas-born African American named Rich Tinker. I had never met him but liked what I heard.

"The boaters attach tires, wheels with rubber guards, plastic buckets, laundry baskets, even mattresses to the buoys. The harbors look like junk yards, and every fall during put-away, we fill up whole dumpsters with the junk."

I started taking notes. The subject of ice damage came up. Last winter was severe, especially in Belmont, where the harbor entrance is wide open to the lake. The ice layered up on itself and pushed like a glacier into the harbor, crushing several star docks. Mike was worried that the ironworker crews wouldn't be able to fix them all in time for the season. The district organized its craftsmen by geographic divisions: north, central, and south, including all 550 parks throughout the city. The harbors were not separate and were apportioned craftsmen according to need and season. But sometimes there was too much work. To keep up, the ironworkers designed and built self-propelled work barges with small cranes and diesel-powered saws and welding machines. But there were only two barges, and their ironworker crews were allocated a limited time in each harbor. To lift the star docks out each year required total disassembly and reassembly by ironworkers who couldn't spare the time.

Jimmy Halper, another young voice, piped up and said that Montrose Harbor, less than a mile away, had as many star docks as Belmont and never had ice damage because of its protected harbor entrance. "Forget the ironworkers. Our harbor crew can tow the Belmont star docks to Montrose each fall and back in the spring."

When I asked if they would fit, he answered, "Yeah, I pulled a favor from the park surveyors and had them measured. They'll fit fine, and we won't always be waiting for the ironworkers." This young man was another to watch, I noted.

I let the discussion go on for another half hour, listening to men who never before had been asked how they would improve the harbors. Then I took a quick tour of the facility. In one corner of the large room with the marine railway, I noticed a twenty-foot powerboat on a trailer. "Does that belong to the Marine Department?" I asked Mike. He admitted it belonged to the Monroe harbor master, one of the two no shows that morning.

"Why are we storing an employee's boat?"

"Nobody never said nothing before."

"Where does he keep it in the summer?"

Mike cleared his throat and answered, "Fifty-Ninth Street Harbor."

"Does he pay a slip fee?"

"That I wouldn't know. All that's done downtown."

"Well, you tell him to get his boat out of here by tomorrow night—and make sure he does it on his own time."

"Yes, sir," Mike responded—the first time he addressed me as "sir."

"And tell him if it's not out of here by tomorrow night, it will be impounded!"

The men got the message that I meant business, and not business as usual. I announced that until further notice, Mike would be in charge, and that when Mike was off, Joe would be in charge. It was late March. The boating season was on top of us. It would be virtually impossible to find, hire, and train new harbor masters. No one I knew called me for a harbor job. And besides the FBI said they were clean. Based on their hatred of Pfeiffer, I could trust them. I needed them both to do my job. I told them there would be weekly meetings in my office starting next Monday morning and to bring their lists of suggestions and needs.

I walked outside, and as I slipped into my car, I added one more thing. Pointing to the thirty-foot rusted flagpole in front of the building, which flew no flag for years, I said, "I expect to see that pole painted and a flag flying by Monday morning." This time there were two "yes, sirs," and whether offered out of respect or fear, it did not matter. For the first time in my life, I had been entrusted with power, real power, honest-to-goodness power, power wielded honestly for common goodness, the definition of pneumacratic purpose.

Like the maintenance staff at Belmont, my inherited office staff was on pins and needles. On my third day, Tom Elzey, the most feared hatchet man in the new administration, announced in front of them and me that all returning summer harbor attendants were summarily fired. He announced and walked away. How could he fire some twenty summer employees, many of whom had worked several seasons? Firing everyone was not only unfair but impossible, given various civil service protections. Worse, it was inefficient. The summer attendants handled all the launch ramps and manned the harbor offices when the harbor masters were out on the water. For my first boating season, I needed experienced summer workers who knew their way around and could run the launch ramps smoothly, not to mention addressing boater inquiries.

Joe O'Malley, the assistant marine director, was horrified at Elzey's announcement. Another lifer, Joe got his start in the Recreation Department and for years was a park supervisor. He claimed it was not his choice to be transferred to Marine, but thought it was a step toward a higher position in Recreation. Even though he had been working in Marine for several years, he knew virtually nothing about boats or marina management. He insisted Pfeiffer hated him, which is why he had no office, just a desk across the hall underneath a staircase. "Pfeiffer wanted me to sign purchase orders and contracts. I refused, so he moved me over there." Almost daily he felt he must assure me his hands were clean. The FBI agent confirmed his innocence.

Two years earlier, when I organized a charter fleet of sailboats in Monroe for Sailboats Inc., the Wisconsin company I worked for after leaving Grebe Shipyard, Joe was in charge of permits and inspections for all charter boats. Obtaining the permits was a nightmare. When I recalled my frustration, the veiled impoundment threats, the last-minute jumping through hoops just before the charterers arrived to go sailing, Joe nervously passed the blame onto Pfeiffer. "My hands were tied," he said earnestly.

I believed him and tried to convince him he would not be fired, but Joe remained unconvinced and terrified of Tom Elzey, Jesse Madison, and everyone else in the new administration. His assistant director title was exempt from the Shakman Decrees, a series of federal court rulings prohibiting hiring or firing for political reasons, with exemptions for top executive positions. My job and the fifty other top executive positions in the park district were exempt. This was proper, for any administration can't function without control over its own executive team. But for Joe, being designated "Shakman exempt" was like a sentence on death row. When I assigned him simple tasks, like answering a boater's letter of complaint or reconciling an inventory of maintenance supplies, he checked with me repeatedly to make sure he wasn't doing it wrong. If I gave him work that was not urgent, he apologized that he couldn't get it done by the end of the day. He was a "clean desker." By four o'clock in the afternoon, he sat with his hands folded like a Catholic schoolboy waiting for the dismissal bell. But the flip side of Joe O'Malley's fastidiousness was a dedication to public service and handling the public with fairness and honesty.

With great care I combed through my inherited staff's files to see which employees needed to be terminated. Other than time sheets required to justify payroll (Joe's indicated near perfect attendance), employee files kept by my predecessor were a joke. Favored workers' files burst with contrived letters of commendation from boaters. Over the years I sold boats, harbor masters asked me to write such letters, which I confess to having done. Files of disliked workers like Mike Oltean and Six Bits contained no such fluff letters; instead I discovered reprimands. Heavily clouted employees had nothing in their files.

It was difficult "weeding the garden." The first to go was Pfeiffer's right hand for assigning slips and moorings. It was not that she did anything wrong, but her close association with my predecessor, particularly on boat slip assignments, convinced me she had to go. Asking for her resignation was unpleasant. There were no blemishes on her record. Legally, it would be almost impossible to fire her for cause, and a long investigation might not prove anything. Her husband was a good friend of mine who managed a boat supply company I had dealt with for years

I called her in, and we sat down across Pfeiffer's old desk. After a few pleasantries, I apologized and said that I needed her resignation. She became predictably angry and insisted she had done nothing wrong. I understood but explained that there was no place for her on my team. She blustered and sighed but finally said she would decide by the end of the week. Thankfully, she delivered her signed resignation in a most professional way.

The second person I called in was the "marine sanitation inspector"—Pfeiffer's other right hand. Time sheets indicated she had been absent for months. I was told by Joe that she was on "I" time, a category of time off for medical disability with 75 percent of salary. The district had its own Medical Department, which authorized such things. According to Joe, she claimed to suffer from a neurological disorder that caused her cheeks to twitch in public situations, and that this "twitch" gave her such embarrassment and mental anguish that she could not function in her job until the condition subsided. When I asked where she was, Joe shrugged. "Her whereabouts are unknown."

I was not surprised. Last year when I pleaded with Joe for my charter boat sanitation inspections, he told me I had to contact the marine inspector directly. She had a private telephone number, an answering machine, and her own office at Burnham Harbor in a tiny building used by the charter boat fishermen. Several times I drove to her office, which was always locked, and she never answered my messages.

A marine sanitation inspection is an onboard check to certify that all marine heads have holding tanks with no through-hull valves allowing sewage discharge into the water. It was a simple inspection.

If there were no "Y" valves in the lines from head to holding tank allowing the switching of sewage either into the tank or into the lake, then the boat passed and a permit was issued. If there were multiple valves and lines, the marine inspector poured a little green dye—the same bright-green dye used to color the Chicago River green on Saint Patrick's Day—into the toilet and flushed. If any green showed up outside the boat, a fine was imposed and the boat was impounded until fixed.

In spite of numerous calls, daily visits, and notes taped to her office door, she was nowhere to be found. Desperate, I sent off a certified letter to Pfeiffer, insisting on an inspection or waiver so that my charterers could go sailing. I could not afford having twelve charter boats, all owned by prominent Chicago investors, impounded. The letter, with a veiled threat to contact the press, worked. The day before several charters were scheduled, I received a call from the marine inspector who made an appointment. I waited for two hours on the first boat in Monroe to be inspected, but she didn't show. I called her answering machine several times. Finally, she called back claiming that she was at Monroe Harbor at the appointed time, but that the water taxi was not operating, and so she left. We rescheduled the next day—opening day for chartering. She was an hour late when I picked her up in my motorized dinghy. The first thing she did was cite me for operating a motorized vessel in Monroe Harbor without a permit.

"But my dinghy is kept at Columbia Yacht Club on its private dock," I responded.

"I don't care. You're using it in park district waters," she said in true bureaucratic monotone.

"Inspector, there are a couple of hundred other dinghies at Columbia and Chicago Yacht Clubs without any such permits."

"Really. I had no idea. You should have reported this to me sooner," she said with a straight face. I took her out to the first charter boat, where my twenty-year-old son, Bill, who worked for me in the summers getting boats ready, was waiting. He helped her climb onto a brand-new, thirty-six-foot sailboat, owned by a prominent neurologist.

She asked me to show her the boat's sanitary system and, after verifying it had a holding tank and no "Y" valve for overboard discharge, sat down in the cockpit and filled out the inspection form without saying a word. As she was over an hour late, I couldn't spare more time to chauffeur her around to the other five boats, and explained that Bill would do that and anything else she required. She nodded and I left.

That night at dinner I asked Bill how the inspections went. "Oh, fine," he said. "I took her to one of the other boats, and then she quit."

"What do you mean she quit?" All I could think of was my other charter boats without permits would be impounded.

"She asked if the other five boats were like the first two, and when I said yes, she filled out their inspection forms and gave me the charter permits."

"She never inspected the other boats?"

"No, she was in a hurry to get back to shore." My lanky son reached into his back pocket, pulled out the folded inspection forms, and put them on the table. "Chill out, Dad. I already put the permit decals on the boats."

That was the previous year. Now she was outside my office. She had just finished a physical examination ordered by the new medical director appointed by Mayor Washington, who found nothing wrong and immediately took her off "I" time. Now it was my turn to examine this phantom marine inspector. Dressed in her brown Marine Department uniform and boat shoes, pen and clipboard in hand and with an unusual tan for March in Chicago, she came into my office and sat down. She did not appear nervous and displayed a nontwitching smile as if there was nothing wrong, as if she was about to get a new assignment from me.

I had done my homework. Among other things, I discovered she and her husband operated a charter fishing boat out of Montrose—from a choice slip, naturally, and that she was an officer in the one of the large fishing charter associations. I had directed Joe to search the office for all her inspection records. There should have been thousands; he found less than a hundred. Her personnel file contained numerous fluff letters and her original job description, written and signed by Gerry Pfeiffer. The document was specific, requiring annual inspections of *all* boats in *all* harbors. Because her job was doubly protected by both civil service and union contracts, I had to be very careful not to mention our encounter from last year. Lawyers love to use "retribution" as a basis for personnel cases.

"I have reviewed all inspection records but can only find about a hundred relating to sanitation."

She acted—and I emphasize "acted"—surprised, insisting that all the records were carefully filed in her desk. When I told her the desk was all but empty, she insisted with a straight poker face the records must have been stolen. When I asked why anyone would want to steal toilet inspection records, she responded immediately that someone in the department wanted to make her look bad, but she wouldn't say who. I asked her to go look through her desk and her Burnham office if necessary, search for the records, and return in an hour. She returned with no records or paperwork except a handwritten note from Pfeiffer telling her to attend a series of charter fishing meetings on his behalf.

"What is this?"

In a more desperate tone, she explained that Pfeiffer sent her to numerous meetings and functions related to charter fishing, which was the major part of her job, and that was why there were so few marine sanitation inspections.

"Really? I also have a note from Mr. Pfeiffer." I pulled out her job description, read it to her, and showed her Pfeiffer's signature. "There's nothing here about charter fishing responsibilities." At that point she started to cry. I handed her a tissue and said softly that it would be best if she resigned, that if she refused I would initiate a full investigation of her work.

I let her cry for a few moments and then placed a sheet of Marine stationery in front of her with a pen. "Just write 'I hereby resign,' then sign and date it." To my surprise she signed, although not before insisting she was being betrayed.

A month or so later, I was summoned to a fair labor practices appeal hearing where predictably she insisted I had forced her to resign for political reasons. She brought her husband as a character witness who told the hearing officer what an asset to the park district, especially the charter fishing business, she had been. The hearing officer appeared to believe her and raked me over the coals for pressuring her to resign. He said I had crossed the line between firing for cause and demanding resignation, and that because her personnel file was clean and filled with letters of commendation, the firing was—in his opinion—politically motivated. The district's disciplinary process of reprimands and suspensions was not followed in her case.

His formal decision arrived in two weeks: she was not entitled to her job back but was entitled to full unemployment benefits. The Law Department did not contest the decision; instead the general attorney, like the hearing officer, politely reprimanded me for not following disciplinary procedures. It was the first of many such reprimands for following the spirit of the law instead of the letter.

A BOAT SLIP AND FALL

April 4, 1987.

I waited almost half an hour for the first of my newly scheduled weekly meetings with Tom Elzey. A memo from his assistant, Kirk Lawson, stated: "Marine Department issues and concerns, including every aspect of the yacht clubs, their leases, membership, guest privileges, etc.," will be discussed. I noticed his title had changed from "special consultant" to "assistant budget director," a classic example of the political back door—from independent contractor to full-time position, the same pathway Jesse had indicated I would follow.

I carried a folder full of documents regarding the clubs, their leases, and so on. Kirk ushered me inside Tom's office, then left, shutting the door. Tom was standing with a stern look on his handsome face. I wondered if he was still recovering from the Hyde Park Lawn Bowling Club fiasco that was plastered all over the front pages of the newspapers.

The lawn bowlers, all elderly and of European extraction, numbered less than a hundred. They could be seen every Sunday afternoon from Lake Shore Drive in their dress whites bowling on the greens— two large rectangular lawns meticulously watered and cut like any champion golf course and rolled perfectly flat every Friday afternoon by the Golf Division. Years ago the greens were enclosed by five-foot chain-link fences with signs every twenty feet or so that read "Keep

Out," to keep picnickers from spreading out on the manicured playing surfaces. These rusty signs and fences were anonymously brought to the attention of Elzey as examples of white racism and segregation on Chicago's lakefront. Immediately adjacent to the Lawn Bowling Club was the Museum Shores Yacht Club, an all-black club at Fifty-Ninth Street Harbor, and it had no fences. Why else would the white lawn bowlers have fences?

Had Tom investigated he would have discovered that the bowling club had no fences around its clubhouse either—only around the bowling greens. Jackson Park Golf Course (less than a block away), where most golfers were black, was also fenced—except for the clubhouse—to keep people off the course during play. Had he checked with boaters at Fifty-Ninth Street Harbor, he would have discovered that the lawn bowlers for years tried recruiting black boaters into their sport—without success. Without investigating, without telling Jesse Madison, Mayor Washington, or anyone else, Tom, who prided himself on acting decisively, ordered park district workers to take down the fences late on a Friday afternoon. The weekend bowlers were horrified, and by Monday morning all hell broke loose. The newspapers had a field day with the story trying to trace Elzey's decision back to the mayor, who knew nothing about it and was politically embarrassed. Board president Walter Netsch apologized to the lawn bowlers, and by the following weekend, shiny new chain-link fences were installed around the bowling greens.[1]

Tom gestured for me to sit down. My lower back tightened up as he began pacing.

"I am informed you are talking to park district commissioners and other city officials about boat slips. Is that true?"

My face reddened. What was he asking? Handling boat slip inquiries was my job. Commissioner requests were the least of my problems. They knew the FBI investigations were ongoing and were always polite when I refused their requests. It was the city alderman, ward committeemen, county commissioners (including the county board president, George Dunne), state of Illinois legislators, judges, and

even US congressmen that made my integrity shiver. Not a day went
by without one of them calling on behalf of some influential constituent who needed a slip.

"Yes, that's true," I replied without elaborating. Tom walked to his
desk and sat down hard on a high-backed leather chair.

"Well, that all ends as of this moment. From now on, all requests,
inquiries, discussions of any kind regarding boat slips in the harbors
by public officials are to be referred to me. Is that clear?" What arrogance. Just like the lawn bowling incident. Maybe I should have given
him that gag plaque, found in countless boats, that reads:

> Our Captain
> is always right, misinformed perhaps,
> sloppy, crude, bullheaded, fickle, even
> stupid, but Never Wrong.

I wondered which public official I had offended who then complained to Tom. And why that would matter. I was brought in by Jesse
to clean up the system, not perpetuate it. Besides, Tom had no idea
how complicated every inquiry could be. So I appealed to his practical side.

"I don't think that's workable, Tom. With eight different harbors
and slips of all different sizes built over fifty years, you wouldn't know
what boat will fit into—"

He cut me off, standing again so abruptly his chair slammed into
the wall.

"When I need information about a damn boat slip, Kirk will contact you, but under no circumstances do you deal with public officials
unless I tell you to. Do you understand?"

We locked eyes. I understood all right; I was a subordinate independent contractor with zero protection. I answered yes.

"Good," he said and sat back down, folding his hands on the desk,
and wasted no time getting down to business. "I need a fifty-foot slip
for a very important person in the mayor's office. It has to be in Burnham Harbor."

I was speechless and had difficulty maintaining eye contact as he tapped his fingers impatiently. Assigning a slip without following the rules? He knew that was wrong, but apparently did not care. I had to fight back.

"Tom, you can't assign a boat slip like that. No one in the mayor's office, of all places, can get special treatment. Who is this person, anyway?"

"That is none of your business. Give Kirk the information by to-morrow," he said indicating an end to the discussion.

I was about to argue that it damn well was my business, when he leaned back, hands behind his head and almost yawning said, "By the way, I understand that you and Jesse and the mayor receive complimentary memberships in the Chicago Yacht Club. I expect to have one as well, by this afternoon. I want to eat dinner there this evening. Take care of it."

So this is what the yacht club memo was really about. The issue of free memberships in yacht clubs was under conflict-of-interest review by the general attorney, for God's sake, and he demands a membership. What balls! The yacht clubs had their protocols. Except for the traditional membership for the harbor director, I honestly didn't know how they decided which public officials received memberships. Tom put his elbows back on the desk and was about to say more when he received a confidential phone call. With his thumb he gestured me toward the door and swiveled his chair around facing the wall to answer it. I couldn't get out of there fast enough.

God I hated clout, maybe because I had none.

Who could I call? I had never even met Mayor Washington, let alone pressed doorbells for him. I knew none of his inner circle except Jesse and barely knew him. Larry Bloom, my alderman and close supporter of Harold? I hadn't talked to him since I asked for the interview with Jesse and didn't know his inner circle of political advisors either. I walked slowly back to my office upstairs, my knees so weak I held onto the railing. Joe O'Malley stopped me outside my office.   •

"Are you all right? You look like you've seen a ghost."

"Something like that," I replied and burrowed into my office to write down a summary of the meeting to take home for my basement files. This was crazy. I felt like an informant wearing a wire. I decided I had to talk to Jesse and the sooner the better. I called his office, but he was out until Monday. Fine, that would give me time to cool off. The worst thing would be to march into Jesse's office right then with some ultimatum like, "Either he goes or I go." That would be a no-brainer decision for Jesse: Tom was backed by city hall. I was only a temporary contract employee.

I decided to find out who the VIP was that needed a big slip in Burnham Harbor. I assumed the mystery boater was black, which narrowed it down. There were a couple hundred black boaters, most of whom moored in the far south harbors in small boats up to thirty-five feet or so. There were very few black boaters in Burnham. One was the commodore of Burnham Yacht Club. I could have called him, but decided not to. Discussing a slip assignment with him would be awkward. If not a close friend of the mystery boater, he certainly would know him.

That night as I pulled into my driveway, I saw Jim Montgomery, one of my black neighbors, getting out of his car across the street. As we exchanged waves, it occurred to me that Jim moored a small power-boat in Burnham. He was also the corporate counsel for the city of Chicago and one of Harold Washington's most trusted advisors. Big-time political meetings were frequently held at Jim's house with the mayor, aldermen, and other politicos. Was he the mystery boater? I walked over and exchanged pleasantries. A tall, distinguished-looking man with gray hair, Jim appeared as tired as I was from a long, tough day. But when I asked him about his boat he became animated.

"I sold it and bought a bigger one. The problem is it won't fit into my slip, and I can't get any information about a larger slip."

"Why didn't you call me?"

"I was told to call Tom Elzey."

"Yes, I know. He mentioned it to me this morning," I replied casually, as if Tom had given me Jim's name. I didn't mention the confrontation. For all I knew, he and Elzey were close friends.

"Your situation is not a problem, Jim, not like the old days when even if you had a slip for twenty years, then bought a larger boat you'd have to apply all over again. Under my reformed system, slip holders who buy bigger boats are assigned before new applicants on the list. That's only fair."

Jim's face lit up with relief. Boating was his escape from the tensions of the mayor's office. I asked for the information on his new boat and told him it would be taken care of first thing Monday morning and that I would drop off his new slip assignment at his house.

"You mean I don't have to go to the park district and stand in line with a certified check and all that?"

"Not any more. Everything can be done by mail now. I'll include your new bill. Just send a check and let me know when you want to move your new boat into Burnham."

He gave me a pat on the shoulder and walked up to his front door as his lovely wife, Pauline, opened it, smiled, and waved. I walked back home where Kris had dinner on the table. When I recounted the Elzey story, she shook her head in disgust, pointing out I had only been marine director for a month and managed to start an ethics war with my boss. I told her the real confrontation would occur Monday in Jesse's office, which could be my last day at the park district.

My meeting with Jesse was awkward. No big boss thinks well of a subordinate leapfrogging over his immediate superior and whining, but I had no choice. If I turned slip assignments over to Elzey, God knows what favors would be handed out. Jesse would be tainted and lose all credibility as one of Washington's reformers. If the special treatments were leaked to the press and became a scandal, Tom would fire me in a heartbeat and claim he was shocked by my ethical failure, how it never would have happened if he had been consulted when I was hired.

Pat Day, Jesse's executive secretary, welcomed me to Jesse's outer office and said, "Go right in." Jesse was sitting in one of the leather side chairs in an area used for small conferences, reading through a stack of papers, but put them down when he saw me.

First, I apologized for bothering him. He had a lot on his plate, and the last thing he needed was friction among his execs. Then I got to the point: who assigned slips? I recounted my meeting with Tom. Jesse listened squeezing his brow with his right hand without saying a word. As soon as I finished, he reached for the telephone and instructed Pat to call Tom in. I did not expect this instantaneous response, and my palms began sweating. When Tom walked in and saw me sitting there, he knew something was up. He had fire in his eyes as Jesse told him to sit down and demanded to know if what I alleged was true. At first he denied it, but then launched into a diatribe about there being nothing wrong or illegal with "helping our friends." Jesse remained calm and firmly stated that I would make all slip assignments without interference, that all inquiries, whether from politicians, public officials, or boaters, would be handled by me and me alone. He punctuated his directive to Tom with, "Do you want that in writing?" Tom answered no, looked at his watch, and rudely stormed out of Jesse's office while I sat stunned.

Then Jesse asked me if I wanted his directive in writing, but like Tom, I declined. I was gratified by Jesse's confidence, but at the same time wondered what price I would pay for ratting out my volatile boss. Jesse paid no attention to Tom's walkout. Presumably it had happened before on other issues. Jesse sensed my discomfort and gave me his take: "Tom has lapses of judgments from time to time. He'll get over it," he said. I was not so sure.

"How do I relate to Tom after this?"

Jesse assured me not to worry, that I would be protected as long as he was in charge. And how long would that be? I thought. Pat Day appeared in the doorway and announced that Jesse's next appointment, board president Walter Netsch, was waiting in the outer office. Jesse exhaled deeply and said with a smile, "You think you have problems with your boss?"

A few weeks later at a Monday morning executive staff meeting, Tom took his pound of flesh. These weekly meetings were the power center, where all policy decisions were formulated, run past the mayor for his blessing, sent to the park district board for approval, and then implemented. I had waited all my life to be included in such a magic circle.

Rarely were we given written agendas. Jesse started each meeting casually with comments about the week's news stories pertaining to the parks, an anecdote or two, and then turned the meeting over to the general attorney, Nancy Kaszak, or Al Nieman, his special assistant and troubleshooter in the parks. That day there was big trouble in the parks. Two children had drowned over the weekend after climbing through holes cut in inadequate pool fences. Pool drownings had occurred regularly and had to be stopped. Heavy wrought iron fences were being designed and installed, but they took time and there were dozens of unsecured pools. A new employee, Bob Wulkowicz, an inventor hired by Walter Netsch, had looked into the pool problem and invented a "pool spider," a floating mat-like structure with rope webbing that covered the entire surface of a pool, but tests revealed technical problems and it wasn't a ready solution. As a stopgap, security guards had been hired to watch over some of the more vulnerable inner-city pools 24/7.

Also over the weekend the newly formed Investigations and Inspections Department uncovered a dog-fighting operation built and run by park employees. The employees were fired on the spot. Fortunately for Jesse and staff, this scandal somehow did not find its way into the press.

Next up, the playing surface of Soldier Field had flooded again. The director of engineering explained how all rainwater falling onto the stands drains to the edges of the playing field and then into a large pipe that extends underground eastbound about a city block into Burnham Harbor. The all-time-high lake level was well above the pipe outflow, forcing the storm water to back up into the stadium on the playing field. He proposed an emergency no-bid contract to build a two-foot concrete retaining wall around the entire playing surface before the Bears played their first home exhibition game in August. There was much discussion about using sandbags versus the cost of concrete and the legality of a no-bid contract. Tom Elzey chimed in that as long as he was in charge of the stadium, no ugly sandbags were going to be stacked up for sports reporters to make jokes about. There was not enough time to prepare and advertise bid documents, a process that at minimum took three to four months. Jesse told Engineering to go ahead with a no-bid contract. The meeting dragged on.

I was asked by one of the black directors why the Marine Department still used the term "harbor master." She insisted "master" was racist. Like "plantation foreman" (a job title for nursery supervisor recently eliminated for that reason), "harbor master" had to go. I explained that "harbor master" was a term universally used by boaters and, like "concert master" or "toast master," it had nothing to do with race. We argued without resolution. Jesse said nothing.

The meeting rolled on for nearly two hours before we arrived at "roundtable" where department heads reported on problems in their areas; some were concise, some were verbose, others were not prepared and said nothing. I announced the purchase of six eighteen-foot Boston Whaler patrol boats (to replace old beat-up skiffs) as a way of professionalizing the staff and showing boaters that real change was coming. There was some bickering over the $125,000 special allocation to the Marine Department when other departments needed money for more important things, but Jesse quieted the jealousy and instructed me to buy the boats.

"Also I have completed removal of all barbed wire from harbor perimeters and dock entrances and have convinced the yacht clubs, including Chicago, to do the same."

I ended my two minutes with a plea for more bathrooms. In all eight harbors, there were only four public washrooms, and Monroe (with 1,100 boats) provided only Porta-Potties. My fellow department heads were less than sympathetic, pointing out that many of the neighborhood parks had no washrooms and used Porta-Potties also; boaters at least could join yacht clubs that had washrooms and showers. Looking at his watch Jesse asked if there was anything else. Tom Elzey said there was and stood up.

"These meetings are too long. Much of this department reporting is unnecessary. There is no reason, for instance, for the director of harbors to be here. The directors of the other Special Services, Parking, Golf, Concessions, Soldier Field Stadium, the Grant Park Symphony are not invited here. As their supervisor I address their concerns. From now on any issues involving Special Services, of which Harbors is a part, will be brought to these executive meetings by me." Then, looking directly at me he announced, "This will be the last meeting attended by the harbor director." He picked up his briefcase and walked out. To my astonishment Jesse also left without saying a word. What was going on? Did Jesse know ahead of time what Tom was going to do? Was this the payback for Tom's reprimand? I was confused. My face turned blood-red from embarrassment. I shrank into my chair as my fellow execs avoided eye contact as they left the conference room. I had been rudely pushed out of the circle like an overpowered wrestler, marginalized—the worst thing that could happen to a pneumacrat trying to make a difference.

What would Zacchaeus, who was pushed out himself, do? Perhaps he went sailing in spite of storms on Galilee, as I once sailed across Lake Michigan in a gale on my canary-yellow C&C 25. Even with sails down, the howling wind on the rigging alone drove the boat at hull speed. Thrashing around in twelve- to fifteen-foot waves, I glued my eyes to the compass, held course, and ducked the waves crashing over the bow and cabin roof. Without a radio I could not call the coast guard, but I didn't panic. I harnessed in and sailed the best I could with full faith, not in a higher power, but in the boat, which was designed and built for heavy weather. I arrived in Milwaukee safe and sound and exhilarated.

"You have a phone call," Linda, slouching in my office doorway, announced. I took the call at 11:30 a.m. I know the exact time, because as soon as the conversation was over I typed up notes. The caller was Barry Cronin, the *Sun-Times* reporter, who a month earlier crafted a nice half-page piece on me as new marine director complete with a flattering color photo. While the article intimated that I got my job only because of my association with Alderman Larry Bloom, it was balanced: "He may find his ministerial training will come in handy in resisting the temptations offered by well-heeled boat owners." When he interviewed me, we immediately hit it off. Both of us had University of Chicago ties; his as a student, mine as an administrator. We talked freely, and I answered all his questions honestly. The article ended with his observation that I had a realistic view of my new job with my comment, "I hope I don't get chewed up."[2] The purpose of his call was not journalistic, however. He apologized, saying the publisher of the *Sun-Times*, Robert Page, all but ordered him to make it. I got suspicious. Maybe this was a journalistic set up of some kind; I wrote down his words verbatim.

"Mr. Page has asked me to call you on behalf of Neil Ramo, CEO of Carson Pirie Scott, who needs a boat slip," he said softly. I could tell he was embarrassed as he explained the close relationship between Page and Ramo—as if I cared. When he danced around the question of a boat slip, I interrupted.

"Why are you calling me?"

"I don't really know," he replied sheepishly.

"Well, I know why. Yours is the fourth or fifth call for harbor favors this morning, and from you, of all people. I want you to tell Mr. Page—and please get this quote straight—that I am deeply insulted, not only because he would use his position to intercede for his friend over a boat slip, but because he put his own reporter, whose beat is the park district, in the position of running the errand. Will you tell him that?"

After a pause Barry promised he would relay my message to the publisher of the *Sun-Times*, and we hung up. While he would continue to pound away on park district matters, especially the growing rift between Tom and Jesse, he never called me again.

I typed up my notes, a copy of Lawson's memo, and sealed them in an envelope to take home to join the growing files in my basement.

FEET WET

July 1987.

Tom and I avoided each other as much as possible. He followed Jesse's order to forward all slip requests to me without interference; on other issues we interacted mostly through memos, his requesting all sorts of reports, mine asking for basic improvements, like replacing the old rotary phones in harbor offices, which he approved. He also approved my recommendation to promote Rich Tinker to marine inspector, the first African American to be elevated to a supervisory position in Marine, but denied my request to increase the number of summer ramp attendants, even though the expansion would increase revenue and efficiency. Seasonal employees were a sensitive political issue. Summer plumbers, electricians, ironworkers, and carpenters as well as ramp attendants were counted in regular employee totals. At the end of summer, when these hourly workers were laid off, press releases were issued to show how many positions had supposedly been cut. To convince the public they are cutting labor costs, all new administrations pull such tricks; similarly to increase employees, new administrations use independent contractor positions and establish "pilot programs," which are conveniently not included in worker totals.

My first summer on the job I learned so much. I became a freshwater sponge, soaking up park district history and institutional culture. I scoured every nook and cranny of the old Central Office building. At lunch I alternated between eating with the young architects Walter Netsch hired and the old-timers in the cafeteria. The basement cafeteria was a huge carpeted dining room the size of a hotel ballroom with decorative pillars, ornately plastered walls and ceiling, and a platform with a grand piano in one corner. It was not uncommon for art and music instructors in park programs to play everything from classical to jazz and pop music after finishing their lunches. The entire east wall of the room consisted of French doors that opened up into a walled garden, beautifully designed fifteen feet below grade with lime stone walkways, stone benches, and patio furniture. At lunch time this amazing hidden garden, flooded with noon hour sun, filled with workers, guests, visitors, and employees from neighboring museums, the Field, Shedd Aquarium, and Adler Planetarium.

The cafeteria seated two to three hundred people at round and square tables. There was no head table. Top executives rarely ate there, preferring working lunches in their offices, or in downtown restaurants. The cafeteria was for the working stiffs and middle managers, the people who got things done. Sitting with cliques of secretaries and assistant managers, I listened to their stories and insights into management. For instance, when I asked the manager of the central security desk in the lobby (manned 24/7) what his biggest problem was with the harbors, especially at night, he said, "Getting in touch with boat owners for emergencies: fuel leaks, sinkings, thefts, and those kinds of things." I couldn't believe that security did not have a list of boaters' names and phone numbers. Later my staff would confirm that Pfeiffer insisted the list was private and not to be trusted to Security. What a control freak. After lunch that day, I personally delivered a list to the director of security with my home phone number at the top.

Because I was hired in March, three months after the budget for 1987 was approved, I had no input. Unfortunately, my predecessor requested no money for harbor improvements: his priority was saving his own skin, not public funds. Except for the special appropriation for the Boston Whalers, I could only implement small, inexpensive improvements. For instance, I worked on better communications with boaters. Except for an annual short letter with their invoices, and of course notices of fines and impoundments, no communications existed between the marine director's office and the five thousand boaters in the harbors. I created a simple information sheet on the harbors and a quarterly newsletter to inform boaters of harbor advisory council meetings, events, and future capital improvements plans. I also changed the hours of harbor workers. Instead of the traditional industrial labor model of 7:00 a.m. to 3:00 p.m., I changed the hours to coincide with when boaters actually used their boats—late morning to sunset. Surprisingly, the union contract allowed management to change hours with only forty-eight hours' notice. My hand-me-down staff was not happy, being used to goofing off between seven and nine in the morning when no boaters or supervisors were around.

Satisfying legitimate boater complaints often required very little expense. For instance, in Monroe Harbor a decade before I started as harbor director parkland was extended into the water at Randolph Street. The park district installed a curvy sheet-piling wall three to four feet off the water between Chicago and Columbia Yacht Clubs, a distance of a quarter mile with an adjacent promenade and bike bath. On any given weekend, a hundred or so boaters attempted to tie up along this wall to visit the various activities in Grant Park like Blues Fest, Taste of Chicago, and numerous free concerts. Unfortunately, the wall was built—like the Shedd Aquarium seawall—with no provision for docking boats. Not to be deterred, boaters stretched their dock lines across the promenade to various trees, lampposts, and park benches. Not only did the lines damage the young trees, they created tripping hazards resulting in lawsuits. My predecessor responded with a crime-and-punishment scheme: he made mooring of boats along this wall illegal and regularly fined and impounded those that did. Then he justified the action as "revenue producing."

At the first angry Monroe Harbor Advisory Council meeting, the lack of temporary docking was brought up. Why, I thought, would the marine director infuriate boaters trying to enjoy the city? The

solution was so simple: weld mooring rings or cleats to the steel seawall. Let boaters tie up for free during the day and charge only those
who wished to stay overnight. I asked Luke to design a combination
pad-eye and mooring ring, which he delighted in doing. Luke accomplished it all in six weeks—a record in the park bureaucracy. By the
Fourth of July, the mooring rings were welded in place. Boaters were
pleased, and the increased overnight revenues paid for the rings with
a surplus of tens of thousands of dollars the first summer. This was
pneumacracy in action: changing the letter of an unjust and counter-
productive law to the spirit of the common good benefitting boaters,
bikers, and joggers, while increasing revenues.

I spent most of my first summer rotating among harbor offices. On
weekends I conducted harbor council meetings packed with boaters
venting their frustrations over the facilities and poor service, insti-
tuted council "walk arounds" in each harbor, and took photos and
copious notes on everything from thick seaweed that stopped powerboat propellers to lack of "No Wake" signs to sewer water bubbling
up from broken pipes. I explored every building, every locked room,
and every toilet facility. I discovered two "marine service" buildings
I was unaware of: one at Seventh-Sixth and South Shore Drive built
years ago to store and service the old wooden patrol boats used by
lifeguards, and the other at Nineteenth and Damen, nowhere near the
water. This facility contained a complete woodworking shop used for
storing and working on the personal boats of well-connected pols,
former general superintendent of the parks Ed Kelly being one. There
I discovered a sleek twenty-three-foot Boston Whaler runabout, all
tricked out in teak trim, built-in fishing rod holders and coolers, a
two-hundred-horsepower motor, and custom trailer. It had no name
or registration, but it did have park district ID numbers. Mike Oltean revealed that the park district owned it but only Pfeiffer used it,
mostly for fishing.

I had an idea and ordered Mike to move it down to Jackson Park
Harbor. My plan, or experiment, was to commute by sea to my downtown office, a distance of just over five miles from Jackson Park Har-

bor, which is four blocks from my house. With two hundred horse-power, it would take about ten minutes. More importantly, I could duck in and out of four harbors on the way and see what went on early in the morning. One morning about seven, I walked over to the harbor and started up the boat. The engine kicked over reluctantly and sputtered. After warming up the motor, I cruised out the entrance of Jackson Park Harbor into the rising sun. At Casino Pier I turned north and throttled up. The Whaler surged and started to plane when suddenly it stalled and slumped lifelessly into its own wake. Not worried—being very accustomed to boats acting up—I checked the gas tank, which was full, then the fuel lines and hit the start button. The starter whined and turned over, but the motor would not start. I tried fifteen or twenty times. Nothing. I turned on the ship-to-shore radio to call Mike, who was always at Belmont early. But sparks shot out and blew a fuse. Before cell phones ship-to-shore radios were the only way to communicate. I was adrift.

With a sigh of disgust, I looked around for help, but there were no other boats. The lake was like glass, but a gentle wind stirred from the west pushing me ever so slowly farther out. I moved forward to the anchor locker. At least I could anchor until a boat came by. But the anchor locker was empty except for a couple of dirty orange life jackets. I rummaged through various lockers and found four empty fuse boxes, a dim flashlight, a flare gun without flares, a flagstaff without a flag (flying Old Glory upside down signals distress), and no paddle. I fiddled with the choke and tried the starter several more times until the battery died.

Murphy's Law was surely discovered on a boat.

The Whaler slowly drifted toward the state of Michigan some forty miles due east. At least this was not the Atlantic. In the worst scenario, I would drift onto sandy Michigan beaches by the next day. If I didn't come home that night, Kris would call the coast guard. I shuddered at being rescued. What an embarrassing story for the gossip columns!

I could swim the quarter mile to Casino Pier, perhaps even towing the boat. But then I spotted an old green skiff coming out of Fifty-

Ninth Street Harbor with two men and a whole lot of gear of some
sort between them. They headed toward Casino Pier. I tied one of
the life jackets to a mooring line and threw it high in the air several
times. They saw my signal for help and headed toward me. They were
the same two surveyors I had met in the wave tank under Soldier
Field. They pulled alongside, fastened a towline and asked humorously, "What did you hit your head on this time?" They explained
they were taking depth soundings around the pier for engineering
design purposes. I looked at their unsteady skiff that appeared to be
World War II surplus and wondered how they could work without
capsizing.

"Oh, we've been dunked a few times," one said without giving details. "For ten years we have put in requisitions for a new boat. All we
get is promises and more work."

Luke Cosme was halfway out on the pier waiting for the surveyors
when we passed by. He shook his head and walked over to the old
Jackson Park coast guard station to meet us.

"Pfeiffer's revenge," I said climbing carefully out of the Whaler onto
the old and disintegrating steel coast guard dock. We shared a good
laugh. As the surveyors eyed the Boston Whaler's flat stable deck,
center console, and wide beam with envy, it occurred to me that the
boat would be better utilized by the surveyors, especially with Mayor
Washington's plan to reengineer the shoreline revetments. The Whaler
would double their efficiency not to mention their safety. Besides, my
commuting experiment was only a whim and not very practical. If I
wanted to visit the harbors by sea, I had six brand-new Whalers to
use anytime. Most importantly, I didn't want anything reminding me
or the boaters of a very expensive boat used by my predecessor for
personal use.

"Take the boat. It's yours," I announced. They thought I was kidding. But I was serious and said I would have the engine fixed and a
new radio installed before officially turning it over to Luke and the
Engineering Department. Furthermore they could moor it anytime in
any harbor without prior permission, which my predecessor required.

Pfeiffer loathed Luke and the engineers and went out of his way to make their work difficult. Luke shook his head in delight.

"Are you trying to bribe us with a new boat?" he asked playfully.

"Absolutely. Moral bribery is what pneumacrats do." They didn't ask for an explanation.

HAROLD

Thanksgiving 1987.

In less than three months, not the six I had expected, the board converted my independent contractor status to full-time employee. By fall I had accrued enough vacation time for a trip to London to visit our son, Bill, and his future wife, Kelley, in their junior-year exchange program. On Thanksgiving Day as Kris and I were trying to find a turkey dinner served somewhere, our daughter, Karin, a senior at the University of Chicago, called to say that Mayor Harold Washington, Chicago's first black mayor, had died the day before at his city hall desk of a massive heart attack. Kris and I looked at each other without speaking. How could this be? Harold was just reelected to a second term by a large majority, giving him the power to end the city council wars, pass his reform agenda, and appoint progressives. Harold Washington brought such promise and hope to a city so divided over race and class for so long. Some pundits had predicted the brilliant coalition that he put together would make him mayor for life, but no one predicted such a short life.

I did not know the mayor politically or personally. I met him only once, just over a month before at a fund-raiser on a party charter boat in Burnham Harbor. I was not invited and only put in an appearance to make sure there were no harbor problems that might spoil the event. I was walking around the docks when the boat's owner

Figure 4. Mayor Harold Washington and the author on a boat in Burnham Harbor, summer 1987. (Photo by A. Paul Knott Jr., MD.)

and captain, Dr. Paul Knott, a black cardiologist who loved chartering parties for money as much as doctoring, recognized me and invited me onboard his vintage sixty-five-foot Chris Craft. He then took me below where a line had formed to meet and be photographed with the mayor. Paul insisted I get my picture taken, so I stood in line and met the mayor. He had no clue who I was. When I told him I worked for Jesse as director of harbors, he looked at me with that trademark smile and said, "So you're the one in charge of this mess." That was the extent of our conversation. The photo-op line was long, the time for photos short; no time to discuss eliminating the city's crippling 50 percent mooring tax, which the city council enacted in Harold's first term and which had boaters up in arms and fleeing Chicago's harbors. We shook hands for the camera, and after a happy slap on my shoulder, I was escorted back on deck by one of his aides. Paul Knott told me that once it was autographed by the mayor, he would drop off the photo to my office. A month or two after Harold's death, Paul delivered it, unsigned, one of a stack still on his desk when he died.

Harold endured Jim Crow northern racism all his life in Chicago. My mother, father, and all their church friends were part of that racism. When housing covenants were declared illegal and blacks started moving into white neighborhoods, my parents fled from Eighty-Sixth and Elizabeth in Brainerd to the furthermost section of Beverly/Morgan Park west of Western Avenue. All my aunts and uncles fled to the suburbs. Dad enthusiastically joined the "Morgan Park Improvement Association," fictionally portrayed in Lorraine Hansberry's play *A Raisin in the Sun*, to buy houses for sale before blacks could or to persuade them not to move into Morgan Park.

When church friends gathered for "progressive dinners," all the rage in the fifties, Dad would retell his boyhood prank of calling blacks on the phone (in those days telephone number prefixes were letters and indicated which neighborhoods they serviced) late at night saying he was from the water department warning that the water would be shut off possibly for several days and suggesting they fill their bathtubs until the water main was fixed. An hour or two later, with his friends listening he would call back and ask if they had filled their bathtubs. If they said yes, he would shout into the phone, "Good, now take a bath you dirty nigger." The story always brought laughs at those dinners, while I cringed.

If we were driving on Garfield Boulevard and were passed by a black person driving a Cadillac, he would say, "How did that nigger get a Cadillac?" That puzzled me until years later I learned that until the 1960s dealerships refused to sell luxury cars to black customers. A black man would have to find a sympathetic white liberal to take his money, buy the car, and quietly transfer the title. Dad loved boxing and regularly watched the Friday night fights on our new Zenith television. If the fighters were both white, he would watch; if one was black and the other white, he would always cheer for the white fighter; if both fighters were black, he would turn off the television in disgust with the comment, "let the niggers beat each other's brains out."

I remember one gathering of the "Christian Forum" church group in our living room, where one of the deacons brought a record called "The Peasel Tree," a stereotypical satire on an illiterate black preacher who opens the Bible on Sundays confident that God will reveal the right scripture. He opens to the "Psaltre," and not knowing its meaning, makes up a sermon about a tree full of "peasels." The Christian Forum laughter was sickening. I could not fathom why my parents and their friends were so prejudiced. Our high school, Morgan Park, was integrated, and four of the ten brightest students were black. I had a serious crush on one of them.

Mother was scared of black people. When Com Ed started hiring black meter readers, she refused to let them into the house for fear they would steal or worse. When I brought home an African student from college for a one-night stay, she locked up her jewelry. The next morning as soon as he left, she stripped the bed sheets, mattress cover, spread, and towels—anything he might have touched—and washed them thoroughly with bleach.

But then an extraordinary change happened. Dad was promoted to the Telephone Detective Division of Illinois Bell, whose main purpose was to work with police solving thefts of pay phones, which at the time were located on practically every corner, park, restaurant, and building lobby in the city. One night (I was a senior in high school), he came home so agitated, mother thought he might have been fired. He waited until after dinner to tell us the cops had called him down to the precinct to identify a coin phone they had recovered so they could close a case. Because it was a mayoral election year, the cops were under great pressure to close cases. They escorted him down to a small windowless room in the basement where they were holding the alleged thief, a middle-aged black, homeless drug addict handcuffed to a chair. As soon as Dad entered, three officers started beating the man, with nightsticks on his fingers and knees and with thick Chicago telephone books on his head, which the officers gleefully pointed out didn't leave marks but hurt like hell.

They beat him for close to an hour until he confessed, not only to stealing the coin box the cops claimed they found under his bed, but to some fifty other phone boxes stolen all over the city, which was impossible. Dad almost gagged recounting the sergeant's words, "George, with this nigger's confession we just closed some fifty open cases, and we're going to put you down as being a valuable key witness." My father, discomforted, politely thanked him, and lent his signature to their report, knowing it would look good in his personnel file; but as he drove home, he felt ashamed at his complicity in convicting an innocent black man. Dad never used the "n-word" again.

My crush on the statuesque and smart black girl in high school turned into a lifelong crush on African Americans. My wife thinks I secretly want to be black. There is some truth in that. When Emmett Till's horrible murder in 1955 captured the liberal conscience of the nation, it captured mine as well. America as we know it without the role of the black experience is unimaginable. The racism and hypocrisy of my parents led my spirit into the moral black underground that in the sixties erupted like a volcano taking me with it.

In 1963, during my years at divinity school in Rochester, New York, Rev. Franklin Florence organized a sit-in at the city jail against police brutality. Three formerly convicted felons who had served their prison terms were arrested on suspicion of robbery, beaten badly with identical fractures around their knees, fingers, and noses, and then released without being charged. When the three found the courage to file brutality complaints, the police countered with charges of resisting arrest, conviction of which for past felons mandated long prison terms.

I was told about Reverend Florence's jail protest at an interdenominational clergy luncheon whose theme was brotherhood. Without eating I left and joined the sit-in. The police threatened to arrest us, but when the media showed up, they allowed us to sit down in a corner next to a bank of radiators while they worked around us. I remember the smell, a mixture of sweat, urine, and dried blood from generations of prisoners handcuffed to those radiators. The sit-in drew unwanted attention, and charges against the three men were quietly dropped.

In the spring of 1964, a black woman, Marie Fitzhugh, with a master's degree in social psychology, started her own clinic. When she attempted to rent in three apartment complexes in an all-white neighborhood, landlord after landlord refused. Outraged, she tried to enlist public officials to intercede, but only foot dragging resulted. She appealed to one of my classmates, Ken Dean, a white Mississippian, for help. First, Ken applied to the same three apartment complexes for an apartment and was immediately offered a room in each. He organized a small protest, but it fizzled. Ken then called an urgent all-school student meeting. Ken made the case that Rochester displayed more racial hatred and more de facto segregation than any town in his home state. The meeting was packed, and Ken, quoting from King's "Letter from a Birmingham Jail," called for civil disobedience, specifically blocking—during rush hour—a main artery of the city, Genesee Street, near where the apartment incident occurred. Out of a hundred seminarians, only sixteen volunteered. It was to be my first foray into the world as an anonymous Christian suffering with those treated unjustly.

Preparation was haphazard: a few hand-lettered signs, a bullhorn, and a much-debated decision to wear suits and ties instead of clerical collars. To me the event lacked drama, so I suggested chaining ourselves across the street (theology students can't resist symbolism.) Chains were approved—only if I paid for them. I visited the site and paced off the width of Genesee Street, then went to a local hardware store and selected lengths of the heaviest case-hardened chain I could afford along with seventeen padlocks. When the clerk asked if I wanted the locks keyed alike, I smiled and said without explaining that the keys would be thrown away.

The afternoon of the demonstration we waited for traffic to clear on Genesee Street between traffic lights and quickly chained ourselves across the street between two utility poles, wrists to ankles to poles and clicked the padlocks shut sans keys. We sat down with our placards held high as rush hour traffic came to a halt a few feet away. Ken, our spokesman (and not chained), turned on the bullhorn and quoted one of King's favorite scriptures from the book of Amos: "Let justice roll down like waters, and righteousness like an ever-flowing stream."

While we waited for justice to roll down Genesee Street, some Rochester commuters did not. A young man in a Ford Mustang pulled around his lane of trapped traffic and inched toward the center of our line, racing the engine and blowing the horn. Ken ran over to him, "They're chained. They can't get out of the way." But the young man ignored Ken. Either he didn't believe him or didn't care. He nosed the car's front bumper against the shoulders of Bobby Joe G. Mills and Ron Carson, who immediately stood up and displayed the chains and pointed at the padlocks. The motorist gave the finger to Bobby Joe, who was black, and kept inching the Mustang forward. Instinctively we all stood up and stretched our chained arms and legs until all the slack was gone. Bobby Joe and Ron lifted their legs as high as they could to get the chain lengths over the top of the car, its engine screaming. The rest of us stretched toward the center as chains clanked on the Mustang's windshield and stretched taut. Our bodies were about to be drawn and quartered. As the chain yanked, my ankle crunched and the skin tore. Ron and Bobby Joe jerked the chain barely over the top of the car when the enraged driver popped the clutch,

peeling rubber as it raced under the chains tearing off its radio an-
tenna.

My left ankle, right wrist, and shoulder throbbed with pain. Looks
of disbelief passed up and down the line. We believed civil disobedience would awake the sleepy will of the people to end violence, not
cause more. The rallying cry "Power to the people" had a dark side
that on that day almost ended in tragedy. And I was the idiot who insisted on chains and locks without any keys!

Ken Dean ran up and down the line asking if everyone was all right.
Aside from some minor cuts and bruises, we were fine. We decided
to remain standing, our chains and placards held as high as possible
for drivers to see while we waited for the police. As traffic backed
up, a hostile crowd quickly gathered and started a makeshift counter-
demonstration. After fifteen or twenty minutes, the police and the
media finally arrived. The cops maneuvered squad cars on both sides
of our line with lights flashing. With sighs of relief, we sat back down
in the street, and the demonstration continued in earnest. Ken read a
prepared text and handed out fliers.

The police demanded the padlock keys, and Ken referred them to
me, chained to one of the utility poles on the sidewalk. An older officer
walked over, gave me a painful kick in my thigh and demanded the
keys. When I informed him there were no keys, he roughly searched
my shirt and pants pockets. Finding nothing but sweat, he took off my
shoes and socks and searched them. Another cop with a pair of side
cutters attempted to cut the case-hardened chain. Not a chance. More
officers, with gold braid on their hats, arrived, looked at our suits and
ties, the chains and locks, and then conferred next to an unmarked car
bristling with antennas and flashing lights. A captain removed a much
more powerful bullhorn than ours from the trunk and informed us we
were blocking a public right-of-way.

"What about landlords blocking the right to rent?" we countered.

"Leave immediately or face arrest," he announced at full volume.
We couldn't leave if we wanted to, but nobody wanted to. We wanted
to sing "We Shall Not be Moved" and chant "right to rent, right to

rent." Then the fire department arrived in two pumper trucks. While one firefighter roughly slid my chained wrist up the pole level to his waist, another tried a slightly larger pair of bolt cutters, also useless. I was so proud of my work until one of the fireman called on his radio for a pair of "ball buster" bolt cutters.

The crowd became noisier and more hostile. Motorists caught behind the human barricade got out of their cars and screamed at the police to do something. A beer can was thrown and clanked on the street at Ken Dean's feet. When a bottle hit one of the police cars the officers put on helmets and formed lines to keep the crowd confined to the sidewalks.

A young mother in her twenties pushed toward me, screaming epithets in both English and Italian. She held a toddler on one hip with her left arm while she shook a clenched fist with the other. When she stood directly over me, I could see the veins bulging in her neck, her forehead contorted with hate. When I offered a peace sign, she lost control and kicked my chained hand hard. I noticed she wore a silver crucifix around her neck, and for a split second I swear I saw a smile on the tiny Jesus.

"Nigger lover," she screamed. And then, as people cheered and the police did nothing, she leaned over and spat in my face to the delight of the crowd. If we are created in the image of God, it must be a spitting image, I thought. She kicked me again as her little boy started to fuss and told her he had to pee. "Good," she said, and put him down, then pulled down his pants. She held him by the shoulders and positioned him on the curb next to my outstretched arm padlocked to the pole. I assumed she was going to make him pee in the gutter, but no, she held his shoulders firmly so that he peed on my hand and arm. I could see the stream and feel the warm urine running under my suit coat down my arm to the elbow, soaking my shirt. The crowd laughed at the unexpected entertainment. I looked into the chubby face of the little boy who smiled with relief like an enlightened Buddha.

"Nigger lover," his mother screamed again as she pulled the boy's pants up. As his urine cooled on my arm, I wondered what impression might stick in his young mind. The police ordered the woman to move back. The show was over. She moved away shouting "nigger lover" over and over. She was right. On that day I became a "nigger lover." If killed there in the street, they could have chiseled on my tombstone, "He Was a Nigger Lover," and I would have been proud.

Finally the "ball buster" bolt cutter arrived. With difficulty our steel umbilical cord to mother justice was cut, and we were arrested. In nonviolent tradition we refused to walk to the police wagon. Having never arrested divinity students before, the police showed cautious deference, not dragging us and almost polite as they carried us like children into the smelly wagons, the training wheels for moral protestors the world over. At the police station, we were fingerprinted and charged with disturbing the peace—exactly our mission. We refused to post bail and were locked up—their turn to hide the keys.

Later that night the divinity school president, Dr. Gene Bartlett, quietly bailed us out. Clearly nonsupportive, he said nothing and left as quickly as he had arrived. Kris drove me back to our student housing apartment where we watched the late-night news. The footage centered, not on Ken Dean and his oratory, but rather on Ron Carson and his full-length beard. Beards in those days were sure indicators of Communists plotting to take over America. After all, Karl Marx had a full beard, so did Fidel Castro; therefore, any protestor with a beard must be a Commie. If the little boy peeing on my arm was caught on film, it was never shown.

We were found guilty in court and fined fifty dollars each, which, again, President Bartlett paid on the condition we not talk to the press. Unintended consequences followed our "chain gang protest," as it came to be known. Alumni contributions came to a halt. The school gained an unwanted reputation for radicalism and was scolded in the media for months. There were editorials and sermons against us misguided divinity students taking to the streets instead of pulpits where we belonged. Telephone death threats and hate mail arrived. The faculty held meetings to consider our expulsion. Bill Hamilton, the only professor who stood with us from the beginning, passionately defended us, and fortunately we were not expelled.

But taking to the streets is only one way to bring about change.

Harold Washington did not take to the streets. Unlike Martin Luther King Jr. or Malcolm X, often called "outside agitators," he was an inside agitator, like that in a washing machine. Harold agitated inside the machine politics of the Chicago Democratic organization. His father was a precinct captain; so was Harold. He became a rising star in Harold Metcalfe's powerful South Side black organization. But when he started speaking out against police brutality and other abuses of the machine, he was shunted off to the Illinois State Legislature, a common tactic to sideline dissenters by moving them up and out. But Harold became more outspoken. To get him out of Chicago machine politics, he was slated for US congressman, where he also upset apple carts and railed against Ronald Reagan's conservative policies. Harold gathered a coterie of black activists around him, and when Richard M. Daley challenged Jane Byrne's reelection in the 1983 primary, they seized their long-awaited opportunity. Knowing that Daley and Byrne would split the white vote, Harold knew he could win if the historically low black turnout turned into a tsunami.

The main bearings of the machine, like the wave machine under Soldier Field, squealed as it began to come apart: old-line bosses either endorsed outright a hapless Republican candidate named Bernie Epton or encouraged their troops to do so privately. T-shirts proclaiming "Vote White, Vote Right" and buttons with a black slash through a watermelon were common. One of Epton's ads read "Before It's Too Late." Every time Harold campaigned in a white community he was jeered. At a Palm Sunday service on the northwest side, he was met by a mob that had painted "Nigger Die" on the church door and would not allow him to enter.[1] Bernie Epton, the Great White Hope, who didn't want to run in the first place, almost won, with Harold receiving a bare 51 percent of the vote but only 12 percent of the white vote. Harold was not a perfect candidate by any means, and the press repeatedly brought up his failure to file income tax returns.

Nonpayment of federal taxes is the one thing Harold and I had in common. Harold didn't pay income taxes for some years; I refused to pay LBJ's telephone tax to pay for the Vietnam War. As part of Nixon's revenge, both of us were tracked by the FBI and snared by the IRS in 1971. Harold, who owed $508.00, was sentenced to forty days in the Cook County Jail, an unusual penalty for a misdemeanor. In my case, after being harassed for three years, I was threatened with wage garnishment and agreed reluctantly to pay my back war taxes and penalties of $2.92.

There is no question that Harold was an inside agitator, which according to Zacchaeus was a synonym for pneumacrat.

Our London Thanksgiving dinner turned into a solemn affair as we contemplated a loss so distant yet so close. The privilege of working for his movement, however tangentially, had been taken away. I tried not to worry about who would become mayor and my future at the park district. My family consoled me.

When Paul Knott delivered the unsigned photo of Harold and me, I reflected on our only meeting. We were not actually shaking hands. His right arm was coiled around my shoulder, his left hand raised and closed. My hands were crossed at the beltline. We were both smiling for the photographer who took too much time, causing Harold's eyes to blink the split second the camera flashed while mine remained wide open. You can tell he is speaking, and I will always remember his words, "So you're the one in charge of this mess."

Since then, every Thanksgiving I drive to Oak Woods Cemetery to visit Harold Washington's tomb. Less than a mile from my house in South Shore, Oak Woods is one of Chicago's oldest cemeteries, not large, only a half-mile square with a high concrete and brick wall that separates it from the surrounding Woodlawn neighborhood, one of the poorest black neighborhoods in the city. No one in my family is buried there; perhaps I will be the first.

The cemetery is historically famous for an unusual and spectacular monument to Confederate soldiers. In 1867 the US government acquired one and a half acres of land in the cemetery for the burial of Confederate prisoners who had died of epidemics in a notorious

Union prison in Chicago between 1862 and 1865. Known as Camp Douglas, the prison was located on the edge of Stephen Douglas's farm three miles north on Cottage Grove Avenue, one of the streets that now borders the cemetery. Over six thousand Confederate soldiers who died of disease are buried in unmarked graves in circles around a forty-foot-tall column. On top is a life-sized statue of a Confederate infantryman, slumped over in sorrow, facing north toward the prison. On the four sides of the pillar are large bronze panels with bas-reliefs. The first shows General George Washington (admired by the Confederacy for being a slaveholder); the second is titled "Call to Arms"; the third, "A Veteran's Return Home"; and the fourth, "A Soldier's Death Dream." Beneath the romantic panels is a massive trapezoid base of pale granite quarried from Constitution Hill in Georgia. It resembles the ironclad ship *Merrimac*, which famously battled the Union's *Monitor* and marked the end of the wooden tall-ship era. The sides of the monument are clad in bronze, with lists of over four thousand names of the prisoners that authorities were able to identify. A small plaque recognizes two thousand more that could not be identified. The pillar stands in the center of a large grassy mound where the soldiers are buried in unmarked concentric circles. Four Civil War cannons and piles of shot are located at the corners of the monument, and these have their own history, having been used by both Union and Confederate armies in various battles. On the north side of the monument is a tall flagpole that flies the US flag.

The monument was built with private funds and dedicated on Memorial Day, May 30, 1895. Newspapers noted the ceremony as profoundly moving and estimated the crowd at over one hundred thousand people, including large contingents of both Union and Confederate veterans who marched together. Memorial ceremonies are no longer held, but wreaths and small Confederate flags are still anonymously placed around the mound. I have counted as many as ten.

At the eastern edge of the mound, deliberately placed on the fringe outside the monument border, stands a cenotaph of pink granite, four feet wide, five feet tall, and nearly three feet thick, deliberately massive to deter vandalism. The shape is irregular with jagged edges, as if purposely cut to look flawed and discarded by stone masons. Erected anonymously, it reads:

> To those unknown heroic men,
> Once resident in the Southern states,
> Martyrs for human freedom,
> Who at the breaking out of the Civil War
> Refused to be traitors to the Union;
> Who, without moral or material support,
> Stood alone among ruthless enemies,
> And, after unspeakable suffering, either
> Died at their post of duty,
> Or, abandoning home and possessions,
> Sought refuge,
> And scant bread for their families,
> Among strangers at the North;
> To those pure patriots who,
> Without bounty, without pay,
> Without pension, without honor,
> Went to their graves
> Without recognition even by their country,
> This stone is raised and inscribed,
> After thirty years waiting,
> By one of themselves,
> An Exiled Abolitionist.

A small US flag is often stuck in the ground next to the cenotaph, unfortunately not the abolitionist flag, which was identical to the US flag except missing the stars and stripes of the slave states. The abolitionists were the earliest civil rights group to "desecrate" an American flag as a protest symbol against the hypocrisy of America's founding on equality and justice, which purposely did not include black people.

When Oak Woods opened in 1853, it was located on the outskirts of the village of Hyde Park. Later the city of Chicago annexed the village, as European immigrants looking for jobs in the new boomtown of Chicago after the Great Fire of 1871 poured into the area. One of those immigrants was my grandfather on my mother's side, an Englishman with a German wife. He was a bricklayer and built his own Chicago-style bungalow a mile directly west of the cemetery in Englewood, now one of the city's most blighted and dangerous neighborhoods. The house is still there. Unfortunately, he died when I was very young and could not show me which downtown buildings he was so proud to have helped build in the twenties and thirties.

As the surrounding neighborhoods changed color, so did the cemetery. Now, the burials throughout the cemetery are mostly African American; at one time, there was one segregated area reserved for "Negroes." One of the first African Americans to be interred at Oak Woods was Jesse Owens, the great Olympian track star who sprinted to victory in 1936 in Germany, shattering Hitler's super-race theories. Now, black businessmen, artists, and politicians are buried here.

Mayor Washington's mausoleum, like his life, is modest, designed with simple rectangular lines and built of Chicago gray granite with narrow bronze and glass doors and one small stained-glass window on the back wall facing the setting sun. Along with birth and death dates, and those of his public service as a state legislator, US congressional representative, and mayor, his epitaph is chiseled next to the entrance: "Remember me as one who tried to be fair."

The epitaph expresses the black tradition of political reform. Whereas white notions of government reform have to do with efficiency, eliminating corruption, and reducing the role of government, the black tradition is based on black church culture and the civil rights movement, viewing government as a central agent of change, distributing resources according to neighborhood needs, including city jobs—these were distributed politically, of course, but fairly. Harold was the first mayor to sign onto the Shakman decree prohibiting political hiring, firing, and promotion.

In a flower circle in front of the tomb, with gray granite benches on either side, is a small stone that reads, "He loved Chicago," a vow he kept until that last full measure of devotion, dying at his mayoral desk. The understated message rekindles my love affair with the black experience.

Each time I visit Oak Woods, I follow the same ritual, walking the hundred yards or so from the mayor's tomb to the Confederate Mound. There I count the anonymously placed Confederate flags, read a few names aloud as they do in New York at Ground Zero, then pause at the cenotaph to rub my hands along its rough edges and recite its bitter lament—and wonder: Had I lived then, would I have joined that noble abolitionist cause? Would I have taken its extreme risks, allowed my barn or fruit cellar to be used as a rest stop on the Underground Railroad? I would like to think so. At the very least, I would have joined one of those churches that split from their established denominations over slavery.

Three blocks due north of Oak Woods at Sixty-Fourth and Kimbark is one of those churches, First Presbyterian. In 1845, the church rocked the governing presbytery with a resolution denouncing slaveholding as a "heinous sin against God."[2] The tradition lived on through the twentieth century. In 1958, Martin Luther King Jr. preached in this church, as it committed itself anew to the civil rights movement. Alas, like so many other Protestant churches who adopted the "Social Gospel," a popular turn-of-the-century theology I had soaked up like a sponge in seminary, First Presbyterian has fallen victim to blight, abandoned space, and urban weariness. With only a handful of active and aging members—its gray stone edifice in desperate need of repair—the church is dying.

A lagoon separates the Confederate Mound from the area where Harold's tomb is located. There are plenty of available grave sites on the banks of this lagoon, the preferred sites being up on the gentle knolls. There is one large waist-high crypt here, newly installed on the bank under a huge oak tree. Etched into the polished black granite is the familiar inscription: "The song is ended, but the melody lingers on."

I end my walks here on the bank of the lagoon, the Confederate Mound off to the south and Mayor Washington's tomb to the north. From here the Confederate flags appear the size of dandelions as leaves take aim on the mayor's tomb. Ironies swirl around this place.

This could be a perfect spot for my father's ashes, still waiting over fifteen years for a proper burial. My mother wanted them discarded by the funeral director. A product of the Great Depression and always practical, she saw no reason to spend hard-earned money on a grave, and when one of the relatives inquired about the cremains, mother blurted out, "Throw them in the garbage. What's the difference?" A huge argument took place. The relatives offered to pay for a grave, but mother adamantly opposed the idea. When a solution seemed impossible, I volunteered a temporary interment at our summer cottage in Michigan, where his ashes remain.

Two years before his death, I had taken my father sailing at the cottage on White Lake, his only time on a sailboat. He and my mother were visiting when I jokingly suggested we go for a sail on our new Ghost 13 day-sailor. Dad's prostate cancer had spread to his bones making him weak and withdrawn. But when I suggested sailing, he perked up. Mother opposed the idea. She had watched me sail the Ghost with my ten-year-old and eight-year-old, deliberately tipping it over several times in order to teach them how to right a small sailboat. Mother was sure that my inexperienced father would fall overboard and drown. But when I saw his eyes light up, a rarity at his terminal stage, I had to take him out on the water.

I piled several life jackets on the dock and eased him down on the cushions, then pulled the life jackets to the edge of the dock and swung out his legs. I jumped in the water and held the boat while Dad pushed himself off the dock, my mother gripping him under the arms. I could see he was in pain as I moved his body as forward and extended his legs aft as close to the centerline of the boat as possible. In his condition there was no way he could shift from one side to the other when tacking or jibing; it would be up to me, hanging over the side if necessary, to compensate for his dead weight. I put on a life jacket and strapped one on him.

We pushed off in a breeze with puffs of ten to fifteen knots and wind shifts off the dunes that surround White Lake. I explained that because the small boat was only one foot off the water, waves would splash in, but that they would drain out the back of the cockpit, and then added, "Dad, it's unlikely but we could turtle in a puff. If that happens, hold onto the boat." He laughed at such a funny expression. He assured me he could hold on and extended his arm to prove his strength.

"Take my hand," he insisted, and he squeezed until the veins in his forehead stood out. There was barely enough strength in his grip to hold a cup of coffee, let alone the slippery side of an overturned boat.

"Not so hard," I said as convincingly as I could. He was so pleased.

In steady wind we sailed quickly across the lake, a distance of a mile and a half. I worked the mainsheet, letting it out when strong puffs heeled the boat forcing the rails under water. Dad got soaked from the waist down but didn't seem to mind. I tacked to the light-house marking the channel into Lake Michigan, where I wanted to tell him that from there we could sail out the Great Lakes through the Saint Lawrence to the Atlantic to anywhere in the world but Dad had fallen asleep.

Rather than sail out the channel, I jibed the boat downwind and headed back to the cottage. Sailing downwind, I didn't have to hang over the side for balance. I swung my legs inboard, my feet touching his. I looked intently at my father, wedged into the narrow cockpit of the day-sailer, his head slumped on his chest—like looking into the bed of a sleeping child. As the wind lifted the boat gently down the lake, tears filled my eyes. Our bodies faced each other; mine forward in full charge, his in reverse toward a helpless infantile state. I could feel heat transfer from his feet to mine—from his generation to mine.

Later, my mother no longer remembered that day. She was slipping away with Alzheimer's and obsessed for hours over calendars spread out on the washer and dryer trying to figure out what day it was. Last spring on one of my increasingly frequent visits, she refused for over an hour to let me in, convinced I was a burglar; and later that night she wandered naked into the neighbor's house to steal candy and candles. I will never forget trying to look the other way as I wrapped my naked mother in a blanket and brought her home. The dreaded moment of placing what was left of her in a facility would come soon enough, and she would spend the rest of her days, zombielike—a dead woman walking.

A breeze tiptoed across the lagoon and brushed my forehead with another idea. If I bought a family plot on the lagoon, perhaps the cemetery would allow me to sail. The lagoon, a far cry from sailing across oceans or Great Lakes, is large enough for sailing a dinghy. An absurd thought, but you never know. I would be the only cemetery sailor in Chicago. The press could do one of those fuzzy Chicago interest stories, and I could sail until too old or sick; then my fiberglass dinghy would be pulled up on shore and turned upside down.

RAINBOWS AND RIOTS

December 18, 1987.

Harold hadn't been officially pronounced dead when the city council machine politicians met and pulled their sneak attack to select a new mayor and put an end to Harold's reform movement. A tremendous round of "council wars" followed with both sides reluctantly compromising on Eugene Sawyer, a black South Side machine pol who was also the first black committeeman to support Harold in the primary. But Sawyer, who did not want the job, was a quiet, uncharismatic man who could be swayed easily, and so progressives became anxious.

The park district exuded a funereal somberness. Jesse, anything but a political ally of Sawyer, skated on thin ice. Obviously under great strain, he assured us at staff meetings that he would be staying on as chief executive. But he was given no new contract and would not receive one.

Because I used up my vacation time in London, I had to work between Christmas and New Year's, the week most employees traditionally take off. The park building was a ghost town. Phones were silent. Execs presumably had their beepers on. The security guard in the lobby was reading a magazine and ignored me. The escalator was turned off, so I had to walk the three flights to my office. I made a pot of coffee and while it brewed took a walk down the hall to Recreation.

Sitting behind one of the many desks was a short, slightly overweight man, who glared at me, adjusted his glasses, and returned to reading spread sheets. I introduced myself.

"I know who you are," he said sharply, adding, "Kulovitz is my name."

Ron Kulovitz was the acting director of recreation and another lifer, a workaholic obsessed with sports programming in neighborhood parks. When I mentioned I had no vacation time, he scoffed,

"I never take vacations. Is there something you need?"

"No, but I would like information about the Rainbow Fleet Sailing Program."

I knew a little about Rainbow Fleet. For generations it trained young people to sail. Starting in the wood shops in public high schools in the 1920s, students built wooden sailing dinghies and then sailed them in park lagoons and later Burnham Harbor. At one time there were twenty-four junior Rainbow Yacht Clubs around the city. During the Depression the schools cut the programs and transferred the boat building equipment to the park district. There they flourished and became so popular that a boathouse facility was built in Burnham to organize teaching and racing. But in the last ten years, due to lack of interest in wooden boat building, the wood shops moved to other activities, like allowing budding carpenters and handymen to use them until they could afford their own equipment and establish small businesses. Reluctant wood shop instructors still doubled as sailing instructors. Ron listened somewhat bemused as I explained my love of sailing, how I had set up the commercial sailing school program for Sailboats Inc., how one of my goals was to bring dinghy sailing back to the old boathouses in Garfield, Columbus, and Humboldt lagoons, historic parks that had become run down in inner-city neighborhoods. "I want to expose inner-city kids to sailing," I said earnestly.

"I love you liberals always trying to change the world," he answered, and then with authority added, "You want Rainbow? It's yours."

"Are you serious?" I asked, expecting studies, committees, and a long drawn out turf battle between Recreation and Marine. But Ron was dead serious and had the power to transfer the program. He was obviously delighted to get rid of sailing with one condition: there would be no sailing budget per se, not even for replacement sails and rigging parts. I had to take the program without transfer of funds or personnel. The only assistance would be from the Beaches and Pools Division, which provided lifeguards in boats to follow the teaching sessions and regattas on the water. When I asked how I was going to hire sailing instructors and staff, he said nonchalantly, "You rag boaters are always saying, 'the wind is free and everything else should be.' You figure it out." His sarcastic voice sounded a lot like Zacchaeus.

That was it. No discussion, no analysis, no committees. He handed me some thin files and a worn blue folder on the history of the program. What was I going to do with a program scheduled to teach six or seven hundred youngsters how to sail in six months? My staff would have a fit. Not one of them knew anything about sailing. Where would the money come from? All I knew was that after accepting Ron's offer, I was now in charge of one of the oldest and largest community sailing programs in the country, one in need of total rebuilding.

I did my own due diligence. First, I attended a national Community Sailing Conference in California to learn trends and strategies for revitalizing struggling programs. What impressed me was a lively discussion on disabled sailing by a group of activist sailors who either through accidents or disease had become disabled but refused to give up their passion for sailing. They had worked with a New England boat builder, Freedom Yachts, to design and build an accessible boat and attended the conference to persuade more sailing programs to include the disabled.

Their stories were so moving I experienced a pneumacratic moment. What better way to repair the world than to provide the disabled access to sailing on Lake Michigan? On the red-eye flight home, I worked out a plan.

For that first summer, Jesse allowed me to hire a sailing consultant—an independent contractor naturally—and set up a pilot program. Oh, how I came to love using that government sleight of hand.

I talked a political science professor, Dr. Richard Farkas, into both studying and operating Rainbow Fleet. Dick was something of a sailing legend in Chicagoland, having established a wildly successful "Off the Beach" sailing program in Wilmette. After that first summer and Dick's recommendations, Jesse found some money to buy all new sailing dinghies and, more importantly, hire a full-time sailing coordinator, Jeff Fetkenhauer, for the following year, 1989.

That was the year the US Congress passed the Americans with Disabilities Act, which required access to everything from buildings to buses to recreational programs. The park district scrambled to prioritize compliance projects. Unfortunately, in spite of my pleading, disabled sailing did not make the list. So in our restored Rainbow Fleet program, I decided to add "handicap accessible" to our meager advertising and to accommodate disabled sailors as best we could until a permanent program could be officially authorized. I was not reprimanded, most likely because nobody in the Law Department noticed the fine print invitation on our posters.

But the disabled in Chicago did. At the end of the sailing season, I scheduled a public evaluation meeting of the effort. Amazingly, over a dozen paraplegics showed up on a bitter-cold and rainy evening at Columbia Yacht Club to tell their stories: "I lived in a one bedroom apartment with a narrow view of the lake through several other buildings. For ten years I watched the sailboats glide through my brief glimpse and wanted so bad to go sailing. This year you made that possible," recounted a middle-aged double amputee.

A paralyzed man in his twenties who had been a sailor before his auto accident, related, "I was told sailing was too dangerous and out of the question, but this park district program proved otherwise." A Vietnam veteran whose wheelchair bogged down on the sand beach where we offered sailing on sixteen-foot Hobie catamarans refused to be deterred. "A couple of buddies placed boards on the sand while I wheeled myself along. When I reached the end of the boards, they would move them until we got to the boats." Because his war injury paralyzed him from the waist down, his instructor strapped him onto the catamaran canvass and off they sailed, up and down the lakefront.

When I asked if he knew what could happen if the catamaran capsized with him strapped on underneath the water, he paused for a moment and said, "Believe me, there are a lot worse ways to go."

As I listened to their life-changing stories, the ordinary evaluation session turned Quakeresque. What the Quakers call "the inner light," what I would call that glow from the eternal flame of the human spirit, everyone present experienced. I overheard that old publican, Zacchaeus, whispering that disabled sailing access was my pneumacratic struggle, staying true to the spirit of the ADA law by making an unauthorized exception to park bureaucracy that would be up to me to make a standard. Call it a moral imperative or a movement like the civil rights and antiwar movements where rules were transcended and unjust laws broken and replaced with just laws. All who were involved in those efforts experienced the same quaking and trembling inner light. Did Jesus, who was an avid sailor, who spent so much time healing the crippled, take them sailing on Galilee? Of course he did—in my moral imagination.

A simple makeshift exception to make sailing on Lake Michigan accessible had profoundly changed lives. As the attendees continued telling their stories, I thought of ways to expand the program. There was enough money to buy three Freedom 20 sailboats, with their special seats that automatically swiveled back and forth from port to starboard during tacking and with all control lines leading to two crew positions, one forward, and one aft.

But selling a program that allowed the paralyzed, the heart attack and stroke victims, the seizure prone, and the mentally ill to steer and control small boats in all kinds of weather to a governmental bureaucracy turned out to be a pneumacratic struggle indeed. Park lawyers raised all sorts of concerns over compliance with the act and liability. Assisting disabled sailors from a dock into the boats became a huge issue. Other programs across the country employed a "transfer box," a simple vinyl-covered box with a hinged plank that extended from dock to boat. Disabled sailors sat on the box and slid across where they were assisted into the cockpit by an instructor.

This tried-and-true procedure alarmed the lawyers. What about restraints to keep clients from falling into the water? What if a participant had a stroke or heart attack on the water? They searched for boarding alternatives such as a crane with safety belts, which the lifeguards had developed for getting the disabled into field-house pools. They never stopped pointing out that the Americans with Disabilities Act guaranteed public access to the edge of Lake Michigan, not onto boats sailing miles off shore. The most vexing question was, how will paraplegics and quadriplegics pass the swimming tests required for the Rainbow Fleet Sailing Program? My answer was counterintuitive: eliminate the swimming requirement. As all sailing school managers know, on the rare occasion a small boat sailor drowns, it's from getting caught in the rigging under a capsized boat, not from lack of swimming ability. All Rainbow Fleet participants would wear life jackets, which obviated any need for a swim test. I was determined to establish a first-rate disabled sailing program in spite of the obstacles. I learned quickly that bureaucracies are designed to keep bad things from happening; the problem is they also keep many good things from happening.

But good things did happen. Peter Goldman, a Chicago businessman, and his family donated three Freedom 20 sailboats in honor of his father, Judd, who had a spinal disability but refused to let it keep him from sailing. They established the Judd Goldman Adaptive Sailing Foundation by the end of the year. The lawyers went silent when the park board gladly accepted the gift and a pledge from the Goldmans to raise future funds for operations.

The program began the following summer. One day while planning a regatta for disabled sailors with my new sailing coordinator, Ted Sutherland, I watched Gerry Dahl, one of our disabled sailors, a diabetic since childhood, painfully make his way on crutches down the hall to my office. His knees had required more surgery after gangrene complications following amputation of his legs the previous year. He should have been in a wheelchair, but, except for one freight lift, there were no elevators in the park district building. Grimacing, he walked right by my secretary, set his crutches against a file cabinet, hobbled over to a chair, sat down, and said, in his own brand of humor, "You know the wheel was not invented to make work easier; it was invented by people tired of hauling cripples in and out of caves like this place." Gerry was a football lineman–sized guy in his mid-forties with Scandinavian features, a full beard down to his collar bone, which would have qualified him for a department store Santa Claus except for its reddish color. Due to strokes and deteriorating circulation, he was gradually losing not only his legs, but his hand-to-eye coordination, which all but eliminated his profession as a carpenter.

"I need a job," he announced. "I want to teach sailing."

Ted had already talked to me about Gerry, who had been teaching informally all summer. Gerry loved the program. He'd never sailed before in his life until a therapist at the Rehabilitation Institute recommended it. He was a fast learner and by the end of the summer won or placed in almost every regatta for disabled sailors. On top of that, he had a knack for teaching, especially breaking down psychological barriers, such as fear of falling overboard and drowning. Ted related how Gerry would get into a boat, take off his artificial legs, strap on a life jacket, then jump overboard and float for a few minutes in front of the startled students. "See, you won't drown except in self-pity. And besides, you just get a real bath instead of a sponging."

Ted and I were just talking about the need for instructors with disabilities when Gerry walked in. It turned out he had taught carpentry and gardening skills (Gerry was both a journeyman carpenter and a certified master gardener) to disabled folks for years. He was just what the program needed.

"You're hired," I announced shaking his hand.

Gerry showed no emotion and gave me a polite nod as if he expected the job, which I dutifully explained was part-time and unfortunately included no benefits. Already on Medicaid he didn't care. "I don't worry about that stuff anymore," he replied. Fatalistic about his diabetes, he knew there were few plateaus left on the downside of his life. "I want to die on a sailboat," he said emphatically. I was not shocked but moved.

I changed the subject to the upcoming boat show at Navy Pier where I wanted him to work the Goldman Foundation booth, which displayed a Freedom 20 sailboat. He smiled ear to ear. Then, out of the blue, he asked if he could take the tillers from the three Freedom 20s home and refinish them over the winter. The factory only sprayed two coats of varnish on the tillers, and they were peeling and looked like sticks with acne. For a half hour, we talked about one of my favorite pastimes, the art of varnishing, pros and cons of urethane versus traditional spar, number of required coats—I argued four were adequate while Gerry insisted on at least five—which grits of sandpaper to use between coats, and the absolute necessity of using beaver-tail brushes. We were both amazed at how much varnish trivia we shared. Unfortunately, I had to inform him that taking park district equipment home for any reason was a rule violation. He countered by asking who was going to refinish the tillers.

No one of course. Paying a boatyard to do it was out of the question. When I suggested that I might persuade Grebe Shipyard to donate the work, Gerry stared hard, testing my ability to make exceptions to rules, something I would discover he had done all his life. The park rule on taking equipment home was to prevent abuse not improvement, so I gladly relented.

"OK, but only because you know so much about varnish. Take the damn tillers home. Just keep it quiet." The hint of a twinkle sneaked out of his eyes. Then he stroked his painful knees; he had to go home. A friend was out front with a car. With a painful effort that made me wince, he stood, fit the crutches under his arms, and walked gingerly into the hall.

It was close to five o'clock in the afternoon when Rich Tinker tapped on my door. Excited, he showed me, of all things, a sample of the new mooring fee invoices about to be printed. "They need your approval by today if you want a message to the boaters printed on the bottom." Rich's suggestion was to remind boaters to obey all the new harbor rules. I had a different idea: a tax deductible donation request for the disabled sailing program that would reach all five thousand boaters in the system.

I wrote out a simple message: "If you wish to add a tax deductible amount to your fee payment for the Judd Goldman Adaptive Sailing Program, you will help provide much needed access to Lake Michigan for sailors with disabilities."

To my pneumacratic delight, hundreds of Chicago boaters added ten, twenty, fifty, and occasionally hundreds to their mooring fee payments. A tradition was born. Over twenty years later, that donation line still appears on Chicago boater statements raising over a quarter of a million dollars, a large amount in the world of community sailing, all for access to sailing by the disabled on public waters.

Marketing the disabled program at Chicago boat shows was a priority, and Gerry Dahl worked them all. But the February 1991 one was most memorable. Saturday, the longest day of the Strictly Sail Boat Show at Navy Pier, ended at 9:00 p.m. As I closed up the Chicago Harbors booth, I noticed Gerry in his wheelchair with a lost little boy look. Gerry had worked the Goldman Adaptive Sailing booth tirelessly all day, standing on his prostheses and crutches much of the time; he hated sitting in wheelchairs. He was supposed to be resting at home, but Gerry insisted, "There is no rest for the wicked," and he did have a wicked streak. For instance, I would find out later Gerry frequently impersonated me as harbor director, particularly during Bears games or other crowded lakefront events when police shut down access to the Rainbow Fleet sailing center in Burnham. He carried some of my park district business cards and flashed them to the cops, who read the card, took one look at his legs and crutches and let him through.

"I'll bet you need a ride home," I said, trying not to notice traces of blood soaking through his bandaged knee stumps. Cringing in pain he related that the volunteers at the disabled sailing booth left without him. He said he would take a taxi, but I knew he couldn't afford one. Gerry barely got by on social security. I insisted on driving him. On the way out of Navy Pier, we stopped for a beer, which led to history lessons regarding the disabled.

He told me about a monastery in England in the seventh century where a monk, who could not tolerate the vow of silence, began experimenting with sign language, which was not tolerated. But sign language persisted and became very popular in monasteries. Later the Venerable Bede saw this new language as a tool for preaching the gospel to deaf people and systematized it. Now, hundreds of years later, the language of signing is all but universal.

"That monk was a fellow pneumacrat," I said. But Gerry heard "doomacrat," and asked what the hell I was talking about. "Never mind," I answered.

Those beers made it a chore getting him out of the wheelchair into the front seat of my car. As I headed north to his house, he stopped me. "No, no, I have to go back to the nursing home tonight." He explained that Medicaid required nursing home care until he recovered from his surgical wounds.

The nursing home was on a busy corner in the River North district, not far from Navy Pier. It was almost midnight when I parked in the no loading zone and helped Gerry back into his wheelchair. Because he was dead tired, I wheeled him inside. Gerry pointed to the elevator, but we were stopped by a security guard, who checked his patient list for Gerry's name. Gerry was not on it.

"That's bullshit," Gerry shouted with alcoholic help. "My clothes and stuff are in room 804. Check for yourself, you idiot."

The glaring guard dutifully called up to the nurses' station on the eighth floor while I asked Gerry what was going on. He shrugged as the guard put his hand over the mouthpiece. "Mr. Dahl, you were admitted here under strict orders not to leave the facility until released by your doctor. When you left without authorization, you became a nonpatient."

"A nonpatient," Gerry smirked. "That's a new one. I could have sworn the nurses changed the 'nonbandages' on my stumps this morning." He glared up at the guard and fumed against Medicaid and all doctors. I attempted to calm him while the guard asked the head administrator to get hold of Gerry's doctor—at midnight on a Saturday.

After about twenty minutes of phone calls, the guard reluctantly waved us toward the elevator. Gerry was seething as we wheeled in and slowly ascended to the eighth floor. When the door slid open, we were greeted by two nurses, three orderlies, and the administrator who looked anything but friendly. She sternly laid into Gerry about the importance of Medicaid rules and the liability the nursing home incurred because he left without permission. When he sneaked out without telling anyone, he set off an emergency alert. Staff physically searched the ten-story building for him. The police were called to initiate a missing persons' case.

"Excuse me," I said jumping into the fray. "Gerry did not sneak out. He was scheduled to work the boat show at Navy Pier, recruiting disabled sailors for the Judd Goldman Adaptive Sailing Program. He is a paid employee of the Chicago Park District."

"That's admirable but where he went or what he did is not our concern," the administrator replied. And then Gerry butted in.

"Your only concern is this nursing dump not getting paid or getting called on the carpet by some federal bureaucrat for billing a patient who technically is not here." Gerry spit out his words. "I'm tired of this crap. I'm going to my room."

When he started to wheel himself to the room, the orderlies restrained him. There was a scuffle. I put my hand on his arm to calm him down, but he would have none of it.

"Take me back outside. I'll just sleep in the street. I've done it before. Just give me a blanket and a piece of cardboard, and I'm out of here." We all stared at Gerry. As curious patients came out of their rooms, the administrator took a phone call—Gerry's doctor. I prayed they worked things out. My feet were killing me, and I had to pee badly. The administrator hung up the phone hard.

"Mr. Dahl, this care facility cannot accept liability for your reckless behavior. I have talked with your doctor and he agrees. The only way you will be allowed to stay here is for an immediate relative to assume guardian status for your person."

Immediate relative? Gerry was divorced; he had no children. The only family I was aware of was a brother out of state whom I had never met. During the pause that followed her demand, I glanced at my watch. It was after one in the morning. Gerry leaned sidewise in his chair and gestured toward me with his thumb. "This is my brother. He'll do it."

As the administrator turned doubting eyes on me, I couldn't believe Gerry threw me a line like that. We did resemble each other, both from Scandinavian ancestry, blond with beards. The administrator was skeptical. "And what is your name?" she asked. After a pause I gave her my real name for fear she would demand an ID. Then I performed my own improvisation. "We are brothers by different fathers," I said tongue in cheek, holding back a beer belch.

For whatever reason, she bought it. She ordered us to stay put while she retrieved a form from the nurse's station, handed it to me, and demanded to see my driver's license, as I had expected. While I complied and filled out the form, Gerry was allowed to go to his room escorted by the orderlies. When I joined him a few minutes later, he was already sitting in bed swallowing pain pills while one of the nurses unwrapped his bloody bandages. I was stunned by the oozing purple and blue stumps. As one nurse gently cleaned and wrapped them with new dressings, another prepared a syringe of insulin and asked Gerry which arm. "I don't care," he said slurring the words. As she prepared his left arm, Gerry scrunched up his nose, then closed his eyes hard and gritted his teeth. Here was a guy with no legs, who sailed fearlessly in Lake Michigan squalls, yet so afraid of shots he held his breath. From countless daily injections since childhood, he was still terrified of needles, stinging reminders of his terminal disease. The nurse finished, and Gerry, with tears in his eyes, exhaled forcefully as if surfacing from Lake Michigan. Once he gained his composure, I indicated I was not thrilled to be his new imaginary brother. "I thought you believed in that being your brother's keeper stuff," he said with a muffled belch.

"OK, but I don't want to see you tomorrow at Navy Pier, do you understand?"

"Sure thing, *bro*," he said adding with a flourish, "but the show must go on." We started laughing like teenagers after a successful prank. "You know, I almost introduced you as my twin brother. Then what would you have done?" I hadn't the faintest idea and quickly made use of his private bathroom.

The next day at about three o'clock in the afternoon, Gerry showed up at the boat show, in his wheelchair, taking a different aisle to the Goldman Adaptive Sailing booth, as if I wouldn't notice. I was not surprised and wondered what story would have to be invented this time. No beers tonight, I reminded myself. Then the phone in the booth rang. It was Kris. "Someone from a nursing home is looking for you," she said perplexed, "something about your brother, Gerry."

As the disabled sailing program grew, it networked with other private programs, mostly on the east and west coasts, which hosted a series of regattas, like the national Freedom Sailing Regatta in San Diego. Gerry, I, and Stan Stanford, another double amputee, attended.

Little did I, or anyone else, know it would take place during the Rodney King riots of May 1992. Twenty-five people were killed in the first day of rioting. From the San Diego Sailing Center docks, Gerry, Stan, and I saw plumes of black smoke rising from downtown San Diego, even though the worst violence took place in Los Angeles. The rioting erupted when four white police officers who had been video-taped savagely beating Rodney King, a black man, were acquitted, in no small part due to a change of venue maneuver away from liberal Los Angeles courts to a white and very conservative Simi Valley court. Within minutes of the verdict, black neighborhoods in Los Angeles and San Diego exploded. The governor called in the National Guard for the better part of a week.

My life seemed to follow urban unrest. I recalled the other King riot in April of 1968, when my wife and I and our two babies landed back in Chicago after our year in Scotland. As we taxied to the gate at the airport, the pilot announced Martin Luther King Jr. had been shot. By the time we made it through customs, he was pronounced dead—

along with his nonviolent dream. Chicago's West Side erupted in flames. Mayor Richard J. Daley issued his famous "shoot to kill" order. Returning to an increasingly violent America hell-bent on prolonging an increasingly violent war in Vietnam shocked us. For several days Kris and I could barely speak except to recall peaceful Edinburgh, where one day over tea, I had asked a neighbor why there were no police in the vast network of Edinburgh parks. Puzzled, she replied, "Police in the parks, you mean to exercise the horses?"

Now almost thirty years later in California, urban riots raged over police brutality. The same culture clash persisted: black against white, rich against poor, disenfranchised against highly privileged. The American Dream was thrown in a ring to fight for its life.

But not here on the docks of San Diego. Not today. On a long floating dock crowded with empty wheelchairs, disabled sailors from all over the United States sailed off to the starting line of their dream, as oblivious to the riots as they were to their own disabilities.

With binoculars I proudly watched Gerry and Stan head out to the course. Both knew they would die from their disease sooner rather than later. Their lifelong intimacy with death is beyond comprehension for most of us. Gerry no longer can work with carpentry tools, but he can hold the tiller with both hands and steer a course. Stan lost both legs at the hips, but his arms and hands were strong enough to trim the main and jib to perfection. The two of them competed tenaciously around the buoys, as if in hand-to-hand combat with the other sailors.

To see a dock full of empty wheelchairs (some with bags of medicine), motionless as the floating dock gently rose and fell with passing wakes, to see them ignored while their owners sailed, was heartwarming. Not the fuzzy warmth that donors feel at fund-raising banquets where they whisper, "There but for the grace of God go I." The warmth I felt was like the epidural I once received for a knee-replacement operation. First, my legs tingled, then they warmed. The sensation moved up my thighs to my navel, and then, as if my lower body hardened into concrete, I felt nothing. The attendants told me to lift my legs and lie down in the bed, but I just fell over while they chuckled and eased me down. For that moment, before deeper anesthesia and surgery, I was paralyzed and comprehended for real what paraplegia was like. I could only imagine paralysis over a lifetime. Watching the sailors I experienced a peculiar form of envy of those with lifelong disabilities, who knew they had little time to seize the day. These sailors pointed to the San Diego sky, without regard to the bending columns of arsonists' smoke except as they indicated wind direction, telltales that differentiated apparent wind from true wind, the key to sailing to win.

After the King riots in San Diego, the idea of overcoming social and economic disabilities by experiencing sailing motivated me to return dinghy sailing to Chicago's historic neighborhood parks in ghetto neighborhoods that had lagoons and boathouses. And so I dispatched two dinghies and instructors to Humboldt Park's lagoon, where the pavilion and boathouse were boarded up and constantly vandalized. Two days a week, staff invited skeptical young people, many of them gang members, to go for a sail. The results were mixed, but it was a start, a pilot program. Jesse thought I was crazy.

As word spread of the project, I was invited to speak to inner-city groups. The commodore of Corinthian Yacht Club and his wife, who taught at Kelly High in McKinley Park, invited me to speak to the Sea Scouts program they initiated through the yacht club, which provided sailing instruction and regattas on member boats.

Kelly High is on the South Side of Chicago, which has everything no other part of town wants: mountainous garbage landfills, vast abandoned rail yards, a river used as the city's sewer, and Cook County Jail, the largest prison complex in the United States. From its upper-tier cells, inmates can see Chicago's main animal control complex, another sprawling facility where unwanted pets, feral cats, and other trapped animals are brought for possible rehabilitation and adoption but mostly for euthanasia. Harold Washington spent his forty-day sentence at Cook County Jail for failure to file income tax returns back in the 1970s. Every Christmas Day thereafter, he came back to visit inmates. When he became mayor, his public relations advisors tried to talk him out of this tradition, knowing it would just remind voters of his criminal past. But he ignored them.

A few blocks south of the jail on California Avenue stands Kelly High School, a classic example of Chicago Public School architecture from the 1920s and 1930s: three stories of red brick with cream terra-cotta window frames and fascia, a gymnasium on one end, an assembly hall on the other, and a library in the middle with a separate street entrance. Here generations of ethnic immigrants, now mostly Hispanic, have sat behind bolted-down desks and learned the old-fashioned way. No atriums, patios, or landscaped spaces for students to hang out. Instead the masonry fortress occupies an entire city block, sidewalk to sidewalk.

I headed for the assembly hall. One of my public service rules as a pneumacrat was to always go where invited, especially to give a speech. Some sermonic remnant in my Protestant gut aches to preach, even though I am anything but charismatic. In divinity school my homiletics evaluation faintly praised my style as "pleasantly conversational."

I remembered those boring assembly speakers from my high school days: old farts exhorting teenagers to follow their dreams. Now I was one of those old farts and told myself to avoid clichés, especially any reference to young people being "the future of America." I looked out over the audience, fifty kids in sea-foam-green polo shirts and white sailing caps and their families smiling behind them. The Sea Scouts were laughing as they goofed off and told jokes. They knew they had to sit through my speech before their coveted trophies were awarded and refreshments served.

I wanted to tell them of my first sail when I was fifteen at a Baptist retreat in Green Lake, Wisconsin, where I met a girl from Philadelphia named Diana, after the goddess of the moon in Roman mythology. One evening as we walked along the lake, a large catboat was being readied for a sail by the counselors. Even though it was curfew for us, I talked my way onboard. We sailed in a steady wind across that deepwater lake in full moonlight. The boat sailed magically, in full harmony with the wind and water on a chilly June night. While the counselors softly sang hymns, we huddled under blankets and kissed passionately as the moon respectfully turned its back behind curtains of clouds. Diana let me reach under her blouse and feel her breasts. The ecstasy of touching forbidden flesh for the first time was like feeling up the bosom of God, my new invisible friend, all because of the sacred art of sailing.

Of course I couldn't tell that story to the students. Instead I recounted what it was like to sail across the Atlantic, how in storms, we placed our faith in the boat: how sailboats are designed for heavy weather, how the keel, that dense immovable counterweight below the surface, will always right the ship even in a knockdown with mast smacked against the water and sails flat on the sea. I paused for effect then asked what keels these young sailors were attached to that will keep their boats balanced as they sailed through life. I looked out at the audience. They were listening intently. Some parents nodded.

I moved the speech along to the disabled sailing regatta in San Diego amid the Rodney King riots, how the participants ignored the fires and gunshots and hovering helicopters. Society's storms did not faze them. Determined to overcome adversity in their bodies, they adapted their skills. They found the "groove," that angle of heel, adjustment of sails and lines and rudder that combine to move a boat at optimum speed in perfect harmony with the wind and sea. Like an airplane taking off, a fine-tuned sailboat seems to lift out of the drag of the water, above the surface, above gravity, and above the daily concerns of the flesh. The momentary feeling of transcending gravity is a rush. In sailing jargon it is called "airborne."

I took my last pause for effect, and finished with, "No matter what comes along to disable you in life, strive—if only for a precious moment—to be 'airborne.'"

I sat down to polite applause, sweaty palms, and wet underarms.

At the reception after the awards ceremony I shook hands with the honorees. One Hispanic girl named Shelly asked if I owned a boat. She was doing a paper on names people give to their boats and wanted to know mine.

"*Pneuma*," I responded and spelled it out. She had trouble pronouncing it until I explained it was the root word for pneumatic and pneumonia. "It comes from ancient Greek and has three interchangeable meanings: wind, breath, and spirit."

When I started to describe its use in the New Testament, she interrupted, "Oh, that's really cool," and wrote it down on the back of her program. Then she asked for my autograph. I borrowed her pen and with a grateful smile signed with a flourish. She was the only person ever to ask for my autograph.

INDICTMENTS

December 7, 1987.

Six former employees of the Marine Department, Gerald Pfeiffer at the head of the pack, were indicted for corruption by the feds. Charges ranged from taking bribes of $500 to $5,000 from boaters for slips, percentage splits between Pfeiffer and his subordinates, cash solicitations for political campaign events in exchange for boat slips, and expensive gifts and kickbacks from companies doing business in the harbors. A sad day for honest workers in the Marine Department and the park district. All were now tainted. Even though everyone knew months ago that the federal hammer was coming down, the official announcement by the US attorney, Anton Valukas, hit like a sledgehammer. Most disturbing was the repeated pattern of corruption in the harbors. As Barry Cronin wrote, "If convicted, the former harbor chief would follow in the line of harbor officials John Trinka, Anthony Munizo, and Vito Abbananti, all convicted of corruption-related offenses in the late 70s."[1] I knew them all.

Cronin's reminder gave me pause. Four harbor directors in a row over twenty-five years. Would I be compromised and become the fifth? Pfeiffer, too, had been an outside consultant brought in to clean up the harbors only to succumb to the waves of bribery that never stop flooding Chicago's harbor system.

A week or so before Harold Washington died, a boater stopped in my office inquiring about a boat slip. But first he showed me a glossy brochure with pictures of a penthouse condominium in Acapulco next to some marina where I assumed he kept a boat. Instead he explained it was a time share and wondered if I might want to use it for a couple of weeks if I could help him out with a slip in Belmont. When I answered "absolutely not," he quickly added, "It's fully equipped and includes a companion—gender of your choice!" My mouth dropped open. I thought of calling security, but the boater would just say he was showing me a brochure.

Earlier, the owner of one of Chicago's premier restaurants frequented by politicians offered two weeks in a palatial estate on Italy's Lake Como if I would "consider" a slip in Burnham for his son who had just acquired a forty-foot sailboat. A well-connected tour bus owner with city contracts said he would find a job in his company for one of my friends or relatives who might need work.

I wondered what it would be like wired by the FBI.

One day the secretary to one of the newly appointed park commissioners handed me a manila envelope. Inside was a boat slip application with a check for the fee plus ten crisp new twenty-dollar bills that fluttered onto the floor. Thank God, the director of security happened to be there and witnessed it. I called the commissioner, who claimed that he was just dropping off the application of a constituent. After numerous attempts to bring the boater in for an explanation, his teenage son showed up instead. He claimed his father had given him the cash to run errands and somehow he had mistakenly put the money in the wrong envelope. Yeah, right. After telling him his father would have to reapply, I handed him a park district treasury check for the two hundred. He looked at it and asked if he could have it in cash and left very annoyed when I said no. I later believed the incident was a loyalty test set up by the commissioner: if I took the money, I could be trusted to do more favors down the road; if I didn't, I could be punished. Simple as that.

Even after the indictments, bribe attempts were still routine: hundred-dollar bills left on the counter with a wink, gift certificates to Marshall Field's, and even boxes of Fannie May candy with money between layers of chocolates. Nancy Kaszak and I put antibribe procedures in place. Over-the-counter money, whether in my office or in the harbor master offices, was given to me, recorded, and time-stamped on a form identifying the boater. I would personally walk it down to Treasury, where it was deposited in a special escrow account from which a check would be issued to the boat owner along with his application and a stern reminder about the new harbor rules against gifts or considerations. The boater had to reapply on a computer-protected waiting list.

For Chicago's movers and shakers, waiting two or three years for a desirable boat slip was just not acceptable. The smart ones contacted their political connections in the winter ahead of boating season, who in turn called me. Alderman George Hagopian, an opponent of Harold Washington on the city council called, told me what a great job I was doing, and asked if I could please look into one of his constituent's applications. Of course. A week later he called back, and after receiving the bad news that the applicant would probably wait around two years for a slip, he went ballistic, "You goddamned son of a bitch. I know how you got your job, and I'm telling you now I won't rest until you're out of there, motherfucker." I hung up on him but not without a twinge of acid reflux. Congressman Charles Hayes, a close advisor to Harold Washington, had been more civil with his request, but made it clear that if I didn't help his boater friend, he would bring up the matter with Mayor Sawyer. That really worried me; fortunately I never heard anything further.

When political efforts failed, medical excuses for phony disabilities from family physicians and letters from lawyers threatening lawsuits for discriminating against "allegedly" disabled clients poured in. When these too failed, the movers and shakers reluctantly moored their boats in marinas in Wisconsin, Indiana, and Michigan and waited until their applications crept to the top of the computerized waiting and assignment list. I kept a printout on the customer service counter for anyone to peruse and check their number for all boat slip applications and assignments. Transparency was critical to gaining boaters' trust, and a pneumacratic example of the spirit and the letter of the law in perfect harmony.

By late spring only the hustlers, con men, and small timers were left. They flashed wads of Ben Franklins, convinced that when their clout didn't come through, they could always go downtown with that all-purpose squeaky-wheel lube—cash. One such hustler, in a shiny black-leather motorcycle jacket, when repeatedly told at the counter there was a minimum two-year wait for a boat slip, blurted out in pure Chicagoese: "What am I 'sposed to do, keep da boat in my driveway?" A gold navy anchor bobbed along a thick gold neck chain, a thicker linked chain wrapped his wrist. With his right fist around a wad of hundred-dollar bills, he banged on the counter and shouted at one of the clerks.

"Listen honey, I ain't leavin' 'til I get a spot for my boat. So you tell me who I gotta see to get one," said the guy, loud enough for me to hear. The clerk tried her best to explain the new procedures, as did the marine inspector, and then the assistant director, but the boater would not be put off, his feet firmly planted on the principle, if not invented in Chicago certainly perfected here: "Money talks, bullshit walks." When the frustrated clerk apologetically told me that nobody could handle this guy, I told her to send him in. He rolled past her like a bowling ball in the groove for a strike, stuck a pudgy hand, complete with diamond pinky ring, across my desk and shook hands like we were old buddies.

"How you doin'?" he asked.

"That depends," I answered trying to avoid sneezing from his cheap cologne or breath freshener, I was not sure which.

"You da boss, you know, da Harbor Boss?"

I leaned back in my chair and savored the words, the first time I had thought of myself as Chicago's Harbor Boss, a derogatory term always used in the press to describe my jailbird predecessors. Nevertheless, I was the new Harbor Boss.

After a pause I answered, "Yes, I am the Harbor Boss."

As the boater helped himself to a chair and scooted up to my desk, I felt some sort of Mafia ceremony about to take place endowing me with the unalienable right of bosses to reward or punish, deny or dispense favors—the lifeblood of Chicago's political system.

"I bet you know Mickey da Pizza King," he continued, ramrod straight on the edge of the side chair. "His boat down in Burnham Harbor, ain't it. He sez hello, sez you're doing a real good job."

Yes, I knew Mickey. Back when I was selling boats, I met him at one of Ed Kelly's fund-raiser dinners at the Conrad Hilton Grand Ballroom—a must-attend for boat peddlers needing moorings for their customers. Mickey sat next to my wife. After a long invocation by some neighborhood priest from Kelly's "fighting Forty-Seventh Ward," we all stood up for the national anthem as a huge American flag unfurled in front of an air-conditioning duct near the ornate ceiling. Mickey was the first to sit down, and as soon as his slab of beef and mashed potatoes were served, he ate them with his fingers, gravy and all. My wife was so disgusted she swore never to attend another political fund-raiser.

"Well, thank Mickey for me," I said with a yawn to the past. "Now what can I do for you?"

He leaned forward and lowered his balding head far enough that I could see that same fake spray-painted hair on his scalp worn by the Monroe Harbor master. He put his empty right hand on my desk, the other with a wad of cash on his lap.

"I got this problem. I paid lotta money for my boat and got no place to put it. Nobody told me getting a spot in Chicago would be a problem. So that's why I come downtown to see you, boss. You just tell me what I gotta do to get a dock or whatever you call it."

"I believe my staff explained the procedures."

"Yeah, I know all that, but what do I gotta do for you?" he said, his eyelids blinking repeatedly as if to underline whatever offer he was about to make I couldn't refuse.

As I folded my hands on the desk, he did the same except he was holding his wad tightly in his right hand so I could see it. In the old days before Pfeiffer, nothing had to be said; a cigar box would be slid across the desk and when the boater opened it he would see no cigars, just several big bills rolled and rubber-banded. Message understood. I had no cigar box, but a different message. I took a deep breath and with a fake smile looked him in the eyes.

"There is one thing you can do for me. If you can pull it off, I will give you any boat slip in the city,"

"OK, good, now we're talkin'." He was excited.

When he asked what I needed, I answered slowly, exaggerating each syllable for effect, "The Nobel Prize for Peace," and then added, "Now get out of my office."

The guy stood up and stuffed the wad in his pocket. Not insulted, not wiping the smile off his face or calling me names, he nodded acceptance and replied, "OK boss, I'm on it."

He actually thanked me as he left my office. I watched him walk down the hall to the escalator, a swagger in his step, his head held high. I knew what he was thinking, probably muttering to himself over and over as he left the building: "How do I get me one of them *Noble* Prizes?"

While I laughed at such crude bribe attempts, the past and present indictments of the Marine Department were not funny, part of Chicago's sordid political history of which I was now a part. Now it was my turn to ride the reformer's white horse and not be thrown. A prominent Chicago criminal defense lawyer—a friend whom I taught how to sail—called to say facetiously that he had negotiated in advance a plea agreement for me that would be good for ten years.

Chicago reporters, cynical to the core, were no doubt betting on how long it would be until I too was indicted. Ah, Chicago. It is often suggested that the city's motto, *urbs in horto* (city in a garden) be change to "will the defendant please rise." The harbor indictments were minor compared with "Operation Greylord," the early 1980s FBI sting operation of corrupt Cook County judges taking money to fix cases. In all, ninety-two people were indicted: seventeen judges, forty-eight lawyers, ten deputy sheriffs, eight police officers, eight court officials, and one Illinois state legislator. One judge, Richard LeFever, was convicted on fifty-nine counts of mail fraud, racketeering, and income tax violations and received a twelve-year sentence. The worst offender, Judge Thomas J. Maloney, was convicted of fixing three murder trials for bribes. Shocking? Not to a Chicagoan.

In the last half of the 1990s, the FBI conducted another sting operation known as "Silver Shovel," centered on illegal dumping of mountains of construction debris, asbestos, and drums of toxic chemicals in poor minority wards. Cash bribes were traded for city permits. Several aldermen were indicted and convicted, including my friend Larry Bloom, known and respected for his consistent stand for government reform throughout his sixteen-year career in public service. The Hyde Park/South Shore community he served—my community—reeled first in disbelief, and then as facts became known, sank into a constituent coma. How could the "Conscience of the City Council," as he was known, take a $14,000 bribe from a wire-wearing FBI mole? The mole suggested the bribe be officially recorded as campaign contributions from deceased residents. Larry responded, "The more dead the better." This tape shocked good government advocates and my own core beliefs in liberal reform. In a cynical funk, I described politicians as amphibians living a double life in the sea of hypocrisy, occasionally climbing onto a rock principle in the sun.

The press attacked Larry like hyenas around a mortally wounded lion. The *New York Times* ran a long article the day after his indictment, calling Larry "a star member of this city's smallest political club: 'the Squeaky Cleans.'" Steve Neal leaped for his throat and wrote, "He was and is a phony," and concluded, "Bloom is worse than a hypocrite. He's a sellout."[2]

Larry had his loyal supporters, who stood by him to the bitter end, claiming he was a victim of ambitious prosecutors; they decried the fed's use of a convicted criminal as a mole and cited Larry's sixteen years of dedicated service. But Larry pled guilty, the twenty-fourth Chicago alderman to be convicted over the last three decades.

It was through Larry's arranged interview that I obtained my job.

Soon after my appointment, I nervously met with him to find out what he expected of me politically, the obvious thing to do when one gets a plum government job. Jacob Arvey, Chicago's longtime Democratic boss earlier in the century, once said, "There are many definitions of politics: the art of compromise, the art of the possible. But to me, politics is the art of putting people under obligation to you."[3] I felt that obligatory pull like a magnet. I asked what I could do to help him as alderman. He looked puzzled and answered simply, "Bob, just do a good job." He meant it and never called me for a campaign contribution, or to a ward committee meeting, or for a constituent favor.

Larry's public service had inspired me. I wrote a letter to him in prison, one of the most difficult I have ever written. He wrote a sincere thank-you back. But we never got together after his release. Betrayal had struck, not against me, not friend against friend. Something worse: betrayal of the common good he had dedicated his public service to uphold.

Corruption starts in tiny drips, gifts accepted, campaign contributions with strings, then favors. Speaking from experience, there is no immunity from temptation. Fifteen years ago I was late for a lucrative boat sale to a customer waiting at the Chicago Yacht Club. A cop pulled me over for speeding on Lake Shore Drive. Normally I wouldn't care about the citation, except I was already driving on a ticket, which meant automatically being taken to the police station to post bail. From previous experience I knew that would take a couple of hours; I had no time and no cell phone back then to call my customer. When I told the cop my sob story, he handed back my ticket and said, "Anything you'd like to do . . . sir?" The message was Chicago clear. I slipped him ten dollars and drove off, betraying the public interest for my own. I sold the boat for a large commission, which would not have happened without the bribe. My first reaction was euphoria. Back at the boat dealership, I smiled from ear to ear, bragged with the swagger of a ward heeler, and received kudos for my street smarts. But then I sold another boat, this one financed by our bank. The dealership owner told me not to process the title so he wouldn't have to immediately pay back the bank—the dealership desperately needed cash. Knowing my traffic ticket story, the dealership owner thought he could easily drag me into his illegal scheme. The tiny drip was about to become a full-spigot felony. I refused to cover up the sale and was immediately fired. The dealership subsequently went bankrupt. The experience, resulting from my bragging, left a bitter taste, and like Zacchaeus, I periodically tried to make amends.

One Christmas I received two cashier checks from a boater, one for $100 made out to one of my harbor masters, the other for $500 made out to me. Handwritten on his Christmas card: "Thanks for all your help."

What help? I never heard of this boater. His file revealed only that he was on a waiting list for a slip in Burnham. The harbor master only remembered the boater coming in and paying daily fees for a few weekends. Instead of taking the checks to the newly created Park District Ethics Committee, which would launch an investigation of me, I decided to call the boater with a choice: be investigated and possibly convicted under the new harbor rules or donate the money anonymously to the Judd Goldman Adaptive Sailing Foundation. An easy choice for him and the foundation became $600 richer. I like to call my "re-gifting" moral bribery. But no bragging.

Every Christmas I performed a similar re-gifting of bribes. This year, after loading three turkeys, two hams, a box of frozen filet mignons, and a large prime rib roast into my car trunk—all holiday gifts, fresh and shipped via FedEx to me by park district vendors—I drove out of the tunnel under Soldier Field and headed for the Pacific Garden Mission. Gift certificates, theater tickets, and the like can be easily returned, but how do you return a fresh fifteen-pound turkey or a box of steaks from some plant in Kansas City? Every year those looking for favors are told very clearly not to send gifts, but they ship the stuff anyway. Christmas is the season political wise men come bearing gifts.

The Pacific Garden Mission was a storefront soup kitchen on South State Street behind the towering Hilton and Blackstone Hotels on Michigan Avenue. While the hotels offer spectacular views of Grant

Park and the shimmering lake, the Pacific Garden Mission faced their common brick backsides where dumpsters and garbage cans overflow into the alleys where the homeless graze. You could identify the mission by its huge neon cross hanging over the sidewalk with the familiar slogan: "Jesus Died for Our Sins."

When I was a teenager, South State Street was not that great street in the song about Chicago, made famous by Frank Sinatra. South State Street was an infamous sin section lined with flophouses, strip joints, sleazy bars, and whorehouses. In the twenties Al Capone's hotel headquarters—abandoned and torn down now—stood a few blocks south. Now the neighborhood is going upscale with high-rise condos and expansions of Columbia College and DePaul University.

For decades the Pacific Garden Mission provided a unique oasis for the homeless and the hopeless to find respite on mean city nights. Food and a night's sleep were free, but not before required attendance at a radio program produced inside the mission. Called *Unshackled*, it broadcasted an uplifting series of exhortations for street people to find Jesus through testimonials by those unshackled from addictions.

I was sixteen years old when our church youth group spent a Saturday afternoon and evening helping out at the mission. Our new youth pastor thought young people should see firsthand what Jesus meant about feeding the hungry and visiting the sick, "When you do it to the least of these my brethren, you do it to me." Our youth group visited the mission only once. When parents found out, they vigorously objected to any more excursions taking impressionable teens to a sin-soaked slum area of the city. I will never forget that one-day experience of ladling soup into bowls that had to be held in both trembling hands, hearing the gibberish and moaning of the mentally ill, and seeing bandaged new slashes and old scars on expressionless faces, an experience totally foreign to those of us raised in the upward-bound white middle class.

Sitting through the radio program, I was moved, not by the testimonies, but by the heart-filled cries of "thank you, Jesus" from those derided as derelicts and bums by my churchgoing parents. For the first time, the phrase in the Lord's Prayer, "Give us this day our daily bread," spoken in a room reeking of alcohol and stale body odors, rang true and transcendent. That day at the Pacific Garden Mission at age sixteen, my faith turned away from pious habits: praying for material success, believing in the reward of eternal life, and above all avoiding all unpleasantness, which in the mid-fifties, meant avoiding poor black people. At the Pacific Garden Mission, most of the clientele were black, poor, addicted, hungry, homeless, and in and out of prison—the very ones Christians were supposed to serve. That day my church-learned faith became unshackled.

Outside the mission, I joined a caravan of cars with trunks full of food, mostly boxes of unwanted canned goods and dried foodstuffs. While homeless attendants unloaded, givers were ushered inside to a high counter normally used to issue blankets and bath towels. But for Christmastime donors, a female clerk in a white blouse with crosses on both lapels issued receipts for tax purposes. I took mine and later placed it in my basement files, not for tax deductions, but to establish a paper trail in case some ethics bureaucrat or reporter demanded evidence of my re-gifting of bribes. The clerk, eyebrows raised and smiling, gave me a special thanks for the rare gourmet meats, then gently reminded me not to forget the mission after the holidays, when it really needed supplies to get its clients through the harsh Chicago winters. I felt conflicted like an Advent candle burning at both ends. Instead of feeling good about redistributing bribes to the homeless, converting the unethical into the greater common good, I briefly considered quitting my job to work at the mission.

Mid-afternoon, too late to go back to the office, I drove north to Daley Plaza past the towering Christmas tree. Beneath a thick gray sky, like wet plaster troweled down between the skyscrapers, throngs of well-dressed women shuffled in and out of Marshall Field's and Carson's like bag ladies in disguise. Loudspeakers on light poles played "Joy to the World" with static from years of play. I headed over to Lake Shore Drive and snaked my way south, away from the glitz of downtown.

The lake was flat calm and dark gray. Newly planted trees along the shore stood naked and shivering, like those on South State, in anticipation of another winter's night of torture. Past Fifty-Ninth Street and Jackson Harbors covered in ice, I pulled off to the side and watched a couple of fishermen cut a hole with an electric auger. The sound of ice grinding somehow recalled the mission clerk's gravel voice admonishing me not to forget the homeless after the holidays. But realistically I knew I would forget until next year when more unwanted gifts arrived and I reenacted my feeble ritual of putting Christ back into Christmas.

APRIL FOOLS

April 1, 1988.

April Fool's Day saw the last special services directors meeting our boss, Tom Elzey, would conduct. The morning meeting was his token farewell to us directors who headed up Special Services: Harbors, Golf, Concessions, Parking, Soldier Field, and the Grant Park Symphony. With the exception of the Grant Park Symphony, these divisions were called "Special Services" because they did not spend tax dollars; rather they created nontax revenues in excess of their expenses—over $50 million annually, approximately 15 percent of the park district's budget back in the early eighties. "Special" indeed and especially prone to corruption.

Whether resulting from criticism in the press, pressure from city hall, dueling with Jesse for power, or some personal reason, Tom Elzey resigned, leaving the park district for a private sector job in California. The newspapers had pilloried him for ordering two new black Ford Crown Victorias with every available option, one for himself and the other for Tish Martin, Jesse Madison's administrative assistant. They hounded him for hiring cronies whose unknown qualifications he refused to discuss, and made sure the public did not forget his ill-advised decision to remove the fences around the Fifty-Ninth Street Bowling Green.

Since Harold died last November, the press commenced withering fire on Jesse's administration for patronage hiring. In January the *Tribune's* front page story blasted "Parks Patronage Booming," listing all the newly appointed black department heads and their "huge" salary increases over their predecessors in those jobs.[1] According to the story, nothing had changed from the old patronage days of Ed Kelly. Ouch. I read through the lists of new employees with high salaries but did not see my name listed, even though I received a larger salary increase than any of my fellow new hires. More annoying, Bill Recktenwald, the *Tribune's* veteran watch-dog reporter, who wrote the story, interviewed me and knew my salary. The omission so outraged me that I wrote a sarcastic letter to the editor, poking fun at Recktenwald, saying in part:

> Perhaps he misplaced his notes. Perhaps future articles about salaries and hiring at the Park District will include white folks like myself. In the meantime, I am considering a race change operation.[2]

Jesse loved the letter; it took his mind off his tenuous situation, politically adrift without Harold. But he humorously cautioned, "Believe me, Bob, the last thing you want to be is black." The letter certainly did not stop the blistering attacks. His hiring of personal bodyguards was ridiculed, while not mentioned were the frequent racist death threats, which prompted their hiring in the first place. Jesse's request for a four-year contract (standard for all previous general superintendents of the parks) caused additional uproar. Civic groups considered him unworthy. The park board tabled his request, a clear sign of eroding confidence. The interim mayor, Eugene Sawyer, remained silent on Jesse's future.

Adding insult to injury, Tom Elzey had joined Jesse's critics. Under the headline "Aide Jabs Parks Chief," Tom was quoted as saying Jesse's contract request was a "disservice to the public." He said that Mayor Washington never intended Jesse to have a four-year guarantee. (How convenient that Harold couldn't answer this charge.) Tom said Jesse's relationship with Mayor Sawyer had deteriorated, pointing to a mayoral request for a Bears game parking pass for a friend, and how he, Tom, had to get the pass because Jesse "did not respond to the mayor."[3] Amazing how politically explosive parking passes become.

As usual for Tom's Special Service meetings, we were kept waiting in his outer office. We chit-chatted nervously and theorized who would be sent over from city hall to take over for Tom and what other changes would be made. When he finally called us in, we had to bring extra chairs since his spacious leather couch was already piled high with boxes of personal effects. Tom smiled, a rarity, and seemed more relaxed than I had ever seen him. He did not sit in his expensive executive high-back chair, choosing instead to slouch against the windowsill. While brushing lint off his sleeves, he thanked us for our hard work. He announced matter-of-factly that it was his last day. We uttered words of encouragement, mine with tongue in cheek. Then he turned to me and said, also matter-of-factly, "Bob, it's your meeting now."

I assumed some April Fools' joke, aimed at my habit of speaking up at his meetings and arguing more often than not.

"Excuse me. I don't understand."

With raised eyebrows and puzzled expression equal to mine, Tom answered, "You are the new superintendent of special services. Didn't Jesse tell you?"

The answer, which I was embarrassed to give, was no. Jesse did not tell me anything. Last fall, during the finalization of the 1988 budget, a new position of "superintendent of special services" was inserted into the organization chart between Tom Elzey and the cluster of Special Services departments. It bothered me that the position would create another bureaucratic layer between myself and Jesse Madison. The Elzey layer had been bad enough, but to be pushed down another level in a new bureaucracy ripe for political patronage terrified me. I decided to meet with Jesse and nominate myself for the position. Because all the Special Services except for three nine-hole golf courses and some minor food concessions in neighborhood parks were on the lakefront and adjacent to the harbors. I explained my ideas to make them work together instead of the separate fiefdoms they had always been in the past. Golf employees could do landscaping around the harbors and augment the ground crew at Soldier Field football games when the courses were closed, for instance. I offered to take on the newly created responsibility without any additional compensation. Jesse barely listened and turned dismissive—gruff is the word—and didn't even offer to think it over. Embarrassed, I left his office convinced I had made a huge egotistical blunder confusing reform with ambition.

Tom stood up and spoke to the whole group. "This is no joke. Bob is the official new superintendent of special services."

Why didn't Jesse tell me? What kind of crazy agency was the park district? First, its president told me I was not qualified to be harbor director and would not be hired; then Jesse hired me "temporarily" seven months later; and now only one year into the job, I was promoted me to a superintendent-level position without a job posting, interview, test, or even a phone call telling me I had the job.

My puzzled colleagues politely congratulated me, their sincerity underwhelming. Three directors—of Concessions, Golf, and Soldier Field—were either related to, or cronies of, Tom's. The noncrony was the director of auto parking, Marty LaScola, an old-school patronage appointee with one of the most powerful sponsors in Chicago politics, George Dunne, president of the Cook County Board. Marty was quick to tell anyone who would listen how he was director of property at the district when Jesse took over, how Jesse fired him on a Friday afternoon to make room for a Washington appointee, John Grant. On Monday morning Marty was rehired as director of auto parking with a substantial raise. George Dunne had made a call to the mayor on Sunday.

Tom thanked us again and ended the meeting. In the hall Marty grabbed my arm and said, "I knew Elzey was on thin ice," Marty said and then warned me to be careful. "Don't rock the boat," he added. As we filed out of Tom's office, Steve Ovitsky, the quiet, longtime director of the Grant Park Symphony, whispered good luck adding that he would be retiring at the end of the 1988 summer season.

A great way to start off my new position: finding a nonpolitical symphony director, if Chicago could tolerate such a thing.

Just before noon, always a good time to stick my head into Jesse's office before he took off to some luncheon meeting, I popped in while he put on his suit coat.

"Uh, sir, I just received news that I am in charge of Special Services."

He slapped his forehead and sat down in his chair motioning me to sit opposite.

"Bob, I'm so sorry. I thought I told you, but apparently I screwed up. There's a lot on my plate right now. I really apologize."

"It's OK," I replied with every ounce of positive thinking I could muster. "This is a great honor."

"Or great punishment," Jesse interrupted with a hearty laugh.

I wanted to explain my ideas for Special Services, but there wasn't time. Jesse was already running twenty minutes late for a lunch meeting with Mayor Sawyer. But he paused long enough to tell me that there would be no salary increase. "You will wear both Marine and Special Service hats."

"Fine. I did not expect any additional salary."

"Good, because the commissioners made it very clear there won't be any," he answered with another good-natured laugh. On the way out the door, he shook my hand and mentioned one other thing: "You are now officially part of the senior executive staff and will attend all staff meetings beginning Monday morning," he said with a wink.

Back from exile into the inner circle. I left Jesse's office on cloud nine and floated down the escalator to the cafeteria. The word was out. Employees congratulated me as soon as I grabbed a tray. After shaking my hand, one of the landscape designers started complaining about how unhealthy the cafeteria food choices were. No full salad bar or vegetarian entrees. She insisted that if changes were not made, some employees would organize a boycott—for a moment I visualized sixties-style sit-down demonstrations with bullhorns.

"Why are you telling me?"

"Because the cafeteria is part of Concessions and you are in charge," she replied. I apologized that I didn't realize the cafeteria was a concession.

"That's typical of bosses. The bottleneck is always at the top of the bottle."

I couldn't disagree, but she came across so militantly. I put her in her place with some family kitchen humor, how when I was growing up, my mother, intent on pleasing, always prepared two completely different menus for every meal—take it or leave it.

But after lunch I talked with the concessionaire, who also serviced Soldier Field Stadium, where his contract was up for renewal, and was very anxious to please. By the following week, a complete salad bar was added.

HARBOR FIRE

May 17, 1988.

In my new role, I met with Jesse regularly. In one meeting I proposed turning the parking lot by the planetarium into an attended lot. For years it was a hangout for gangs, where the meters were constantly vandalized and ignored (Chicago police were not authorized to write tickets on park district meters). Shell Oil was replacing their small, gas-station cashier booths and selling the old ones for $500, including delivery. One could easily be set on the lot surface, connected to an overhead power line from the Rainbow Fleet building and bring both order and revenue. Jesse was skeptical of my estimate of $300,000 in income the first year, but told me to go ahead. When I boasted everything would be in place by June, he bet against me— and lost. In another meeting I recommended that he terminate the stadium manger, an independent contractor hired by Elzey several months earlier with no managerial experience of any kind, let alone in stadiums. Before I could get into particulars, Jesse held up his hand for me to stop and smiled. "Bob, it isn't that easy. That's a decision to be made in city hall." As I started to protest, Pat Day came in and told me there was an emergency in my office. I immediately ran down the hall where Linda was frantic.

"It's Gloria from Jackson Park Yacht Club on line two. The coast guard station is on fire," she said wide-eyed with concern. I grabbed the phone. Gloria Fallon both managed and lived in the clubhouse right across the harbor from the station. I had known her since my boat-peddling days. Not only was she the yacht club caretaker, but an excellent sailor and rigger who helped me rig several sailboats docked at Jackson.

"There's black smoke coming out of the watchtower, but I can't see any flames yet," she exclaimed.

"Do you see anybody around the building?"

"No, everything seems boarded up. Oh God, now flames are shooting up. I can hear the fire engines."

"OK, Gloria, I'm on my way."

I told Linda to inform Jesse and Al Niemen, then rushed to the station, which is sandwiched between Lake Shore Drive and Jackson Outer Harbor at Sixth-Fifth Street. Flames curled out of the watchtower in the center of the sprawling ninety-year-old wooden structure, U-shaped on the harbor side with large porches on each leg that extend to the water's edge. The indented part of the U contained a large boat room and marine railway. Three steel docks extended into the harbor, one for fueling, and the other two for rescue boats. The station was two stories high, the upper floor built into hipped roofs with eight dormers. The center watchtower, with cupola and widow's walk, extended the entire length of the roof. On the land side, the building's numerous windows looked out onto Lake Shore Drive, about thirty feet away.

The fire department had amassed several engines, snorkels, and pumpers, but no water was forthcoming from the hydrants at either end of the building. Where the hell was the water? The firefighters were standing around the equipment gaping at the growing fire. I got past the police lines with my park ID and quickly found the fire chief.

"Both hydrants are dry—shut off," he said disgusted.

"How can they be shut off?" I asked incredulously.

"You tell me. All the hydrants along the lakefront are park district. Your people shut them off without telling us. We go through this all the time," he said contemptuously. Ironically, when the coast

Figure 5. Jackson Park coast guard station after fire, 1988. (Photo by R. J. Nelson.)

guard abandoned the station in the fifties, the fire department took over the rescue operation and occupied it for several years. They even built a complete sauna for themselves in the basement. You would think they would know where the hydrant valves were or at least have cross-training exercises, but I kept my mouth shut. The chief was summoned by radio to the lake side of the building. A pumper truck designed to suck water out of the harbor was in place but malfunctioned. Twenty minutes passed before they got it to work, plenty of time for the fire to spread relentlessly through the building's upper floor. Intense heat blew out the windows on the watchtower showering the firemen with glass. The chief handed me a fire hat and ordered me to put it on. The fire slowly snaked through the roof in two places.

As the fire spread, I thought of the time and effort spent over the last year obtaining approval to restore the old station. The memos and endless meetings, the bureaucratic skepticism (half the park district engineers wanted to tear the structure down), not to mention find-

ing funds. When both the treasurer and comptroller said no, Nancy
Kaszak determined that $125,000 from the Star Dock Maintenance
Fund could be legally spent on the historic structure. The board approved the project, which was out for bid when the fire struck. At least
no money was spent; the structure was not insured.

Peter Kendall of the *Tribune* arrived and asked the chief how it happened.[1] When firefighters discovered a locked steel basement door
pried open, the chief suspected carelessness by the homeless who
squatted there from time to time. As we talked, the entire one-and-
a-half-story watchtower imploded into a ball of fire crashing down
through the building into the first floor but fortunately not into the
boat room below. The station resembled a volcano spewing ash and
embers out over the water. I organized volunteer boaters and the Jackson Park harbor master to quickly move boats moored close to the
station to safety across the harbor by the yacht club.

Another ten minutes passed before a second lake pumper arrived
and stuck its snout into the harbor; this one worked. With pumps
gushing, firefighters attacked the blaze from both ends of the building. Smoke was so thick they could not enter to search for survivors.
They climbed what was left of the roof and tore it open with fire axes.
Water poured in through windows, doors, and roof until the flames
hissed out. Firemen with oxygen tanks then entered and searched for
bodies. Thank God, there were none. Others dragged hoses and axes
to rip into walls and floors to access hot spots that might reignite.
Waterfalls flowed down the stairs into the basement boat room and
incline railway, streaming into the lake and pushing piles of charred
wood and debris into the harbor.

I sat on an old concrete mooring block and surveyed what appeared
to be a total loss. The fire chief came over and gave me an abbreviated
report from notes in a small notebook.

"Outside walls still standing, upper floor and tower completely
gone, fire burned top down to the first floor before killed. Boat room
and support beams mostly intact. Looks like arson, illegal cooking, or
smoking." The chief closed his book and ordered me not to go inside.

Al Nieman and Luke Cosme pulled up on the grass in a park district car. Al commiserated and put his hand silently on my shoulder. He had spoken out strongly in favor of the restoration project. Luke opined that structurally the old station "beat back the fire pretty good," and actually did the restoration project a favor. Rebuilding from scratch was always easier, according to Luke.

"It will be fine," Al said. "I just might have an idea where we can get more money."

I hoped he was right. This was a chance to do something really special on the South Side lakefront, so long neglected. When Al and Luke drove off, I lingered until the firemen methodically flooded the wooden building before they loaded up and left.

Back downtown I immediately gave Jesse a report. I didn't want him being asked questions by the mayor, the press, and so on, without having all the information. He thanked me and then with a straight face said I was a "person of interest" in the upcoming arson investigation.

Dumbfounded, I asked, "Why I would be investigated?"

"Because you wanted a lot more money for restoration than allocated." When Jesse saw my mouth drop, he giggled, "Just kidding, Bob, just kidding."

A pneumacrat has to learn to take a joke.

SAND TRAPS

June 15, 1988.

Seven thirty in the morning, sunny and hot, a perfect day for golf, but I was not playing. As superintendent of special services I was inspecting all six park courses: South Shore at the cultural center, Jackson Park, Abraham Marovitz on the lakefront between Irving Park and Montrose, Robert A. Black in Warren Park, Columbus, and Marquette in their respective parks. This was my follow-up inspection of Marquette Golf Course. A week ago I toured the course with its incompetent greenskeeper and gave him strict instructions to water the two hundred freshly planted maple trees I had managed to pry out of the Park Reforestation Budget, a major initiative of Walter Netsch and Friends of the Parks. I parked by the first tee and couldn't believe my eyes; the new trees were withered and all but dead. The hoses the greenskeeper dragged out at my insistence were in exactly the same locations and appeared not to have been turned on. Marquette, like most of the golf courses, lacked modern irrigation systems and relied on hand watering.

Furious with the greenskeeper who ignored my instructions, I walked into the starter shack and rapped my hand on the counter.

"Get that greenskeeper and the entire staff out here right now," I demanded of the summer office manager, a middle-aged high school shop teacher who had worked the course for the last three summers.

Last week he convinced me he didn't know there was a greenskeeper, that he had not seen one in his three years.

The course was in appalling condition: sand traps completely overgrown, water hazards choked with invasive weeds, and fairway trees and shrubs drooping down to the ground, untrimmed for years. Half the greens were diseased. Tee boxes were asphalted over with rubber mats for hitting like old-style driving ranges, and drinking fountains, never winterized, sat in muddy pools. Signs and ball washers were missing on most holes, and the connecting paths between greens and tees were dirt ruts. Even though golf nationwide was surging, at Marquette in the last five years the number of rounds played had plummeted, while rounds at all other park district courses had increased.

Driving around the course with the greenskeeper last week was an exercise in anger management. He slouched away from me in the golf cart and wore no park district polo shirt like all the other greenskeepers who proudly showed me around their courses. His shaggy hair had not been cut for a long time, and a dark mustache curled down over his upper lip into his mouth. Unlike his counterparts he displayed no suntan. His file showed he had been assigned to Marquette over twenty years ago, but had used all but six days of his sick time. From the first tee to the last green, he spit out excuses to my questions. On the overgrown sand traps, he insisted he was ordered from "downtown" to leave them alone, even though all the other park district courses' sand traps were well maintained. Regarding the weed infested ponds, his staff had no hip boots; on the diseased greens, no chemicals; on the lack of pruning, a different union was responsible; and the water fountain pipe breaks were the plumbers' fault.

But it was his failure to water the new trees that exasperated me. I had worked so hard to get those trees allocated to the Golf Division. When he grumbled that the water boxes didn't function, I pulled the golf cart up to one and demanded he show me. When he opened it and turned the valve, it released a thick stream of brown rusty water. That did it. I ordered him to fetch every hose available.

"Soak each tree for an hour, then move the hoses. Keep somebody here around the clock to move them. Is that clear?" I had screamed, promising to return a week later. As I drove off I could see him and his staff slowly dragging a hose to a newly planted maple tree.

Now a week later, outside the starter shack, the summoned green-skeeper slowly swung sideways out of a park pickup truck. I placed my hands sternly on my hips. Next to me was Ted Lecesne, the new acting director of golf. With Jesse's permission I had fired the previous golf director, another Tom Elzey appointee, who, like the stadium manager, had no golf management experience and didn't even play golf. After Tom resigned he rarely showed up for work, preferring the local race track instead. He made idiotic decisions—like fertilizing the bowling greens at Fifty-Ninth Street with the wrong product, killing the entire playing surface, which had to be dug up and resodded, costing the lawn bowlers an entire season and the park district tens of thousands of dollars. I wondered if the bowling green was cursed.

Ted Lecesne, on the other hand, knew everything about golf: a scratch golfer, an excellent instructor, and a longtime employee in the Golf Division. I recommended Ted for the director job. Jesse preferred a management professional from outside the district, believing that Ted's long history of doing favors for politicians (free rounds, preferred tee times, and so on) made him part of the problem, not the solution. To me such small-scale favors were minor and certainly not scandalous. I argued that Ted was well past retirement age and could be easily convinced to retire anytime—I had already talked to Ted about the possibility. More importantly, Ted was African American and would help Jesse satisfy the frustration and growing demand from the black community for more executive job appointments in the district. Jesse jokingly asked me, "Are you running for political office?"

"No, sir, but I'm working on a degree from the Arthur Murray School of Political Dancing."

Jesse was finally persuaded, on the condition that Ted be designated "acting director of golf," while a national search for a golf management professional was initiated.

Ted was uncomfortable by my side at Marquette. Raised in Louisiana with the impeccable manners of a southern gentleman, he abhorred confrontation. He preferred to stand behind me while I played son-of-a-bitch big boss as the greenskeeper shuffled up in a long-sleeved, faded flannel shirt, even though the temperature was pushing ninety degrees. His staff lined up haphazardly.

"Why haven't the new trees been watered?"

"We watered them," he muttered, turning red.

"You're lying," I fired back. "Those hoses haven't moved all week." I tore into him in front of his staff of eight workers. I knew it was considered unprofessional to berate a manager in front of his staff, but I didn't care. I yelled and kicked the nearest hose revealing a telltale line of dead grass underneath. Then I turned to the slowly retreating staff.

"Which of you worked overtime moving the hoses? Tell me now or I'll get every one of your time cards and check." The workers replied that none of them were scheduled to work overtime.

I switched back to the greenskeeper who snorted something I couldn't make out, because he had turned completely around. "Goddamn it! Look at me when I speak to you." I shouted, stepping closer, so that we would be face to face. He grudgingly turned toward me but looked sideways. Suddenly, the smell of alcohol overpowered the space between us. It was 7:45 a.m.

"Have you been drinking?"

"Not on the job," he answered, now staring down at the grass. Several employees snickered.

The greenskeeper was unaware that the board of commissioners had just approved a drug-abuse ordinance that required an employee suspected of using a controlled substance—including alcohol—to accompany his or her supervisor immediately to the Medical Department for drug testing. If the employee refused, he or she could be terminated on the spot without recourse. The park district was loaded with drug abusers, and the new ordinance was sorely needed.

"I have adequate reason to believe you have been drinking, and therefore I'm ordering you to accompany Ted Lecesne immediately to Medical for testing. If you refuse, you will be terminated. Do you understand?"

The greenskeeper finally looked me in the eye but only for a moment. Whether from my tongue-lashing or the effects of alcohol, he shoved me hard in the chest, ran to the pickup truck, hopped in, spun the wheels across the first tee, jumped the curb on Sixty-Seventh Street, and squealed away. A perfect script for termination. In fact, his firing would be the first under the new ordinance, a test case that would stick. The greenskeeper did not even show up for his mandatory hearing.

So that everyone could hear I announced that the greenskeeper was terminated immediately. I told Ted to note the time and fill out the papers as soon as he returned to his office. The golf workers stood frozen in place.

"What are you standing here for?" I asked petulantly. "Get to work." But they did not move. Finally one of the younger workers found courage to speak.

"Sir, we can't get to the equipment in the sheds. The greenskeeper has the keys." He explained that all the mowers, tractors, maintenance carts, and even shovels and rakes, were locked up in sheds to which only the greenskeeper had keys he kept in his private locker. Often they couldn't get started until eleven in the morning, because the keys were locked up and the greenskeeper was nowhere to be found. When he failed to show up at all, sometimes for days at a time, they borrowed mowers from neighborhood parks. Unbelievable.

"Show me his locker."

They led Ted and me across the first fairway to a horseshoe-shaped complex of one story buildings marked "Golf." One housed the greenskeeper's office, which faced an outside window with heavy blinds and contained another larger area with lockers, bathrooms, and showers. I was shown the greenskeeper's private locker behind his steel desk, another relic. The drawers were crudely padlocked to hasps bolted through the steel. I shook each one hard, but they would not give. The padlock on his gray enameled steel locker, which contained the keys, also would not budge.

"Is there a bolt cutter around somewhere?"

"No, sir, but I have one at home," said one of the workers. "I can be back in ten minutes."

While he drove home, I gave the rest of the nervous employees my standard speech—that I didn't care if they were precinct captains or had political sponsors. As long as they did their jobs, they would have no trouble with me. I gathered them around the greenskeeper's desk and asked what they needed to transform Marquette Golf Course from the worst in the city to the best. The new trees, the first planted on the course in over twenty years, were only the beginning.

As was apparent with the harbor staff, no one had ever asked their opinions. The suggestions came as fast as I could write them down. A new irrigation system was mentioned by everyone. The soil at Marquette was so poor it needed constant watering, especially the greens, many of which were root bound from adjacent trees. Ball washers were brought up. Like the old harbor buoys, these contraptions were made by hand in park shops with wood paddles, fitted with household scrub brushes that moved up and down in wooden boxes. Frequently stolen or set on fire, only three were left on the course. The wish list lengthened as I wrote on the back of the greenskeeper's May calendar, the only paper on his desk.

When the young man returned with the bolt cutter and with obvious pleasure clamped the jaws on the locker padlock, I stopped him. I did not want him responsible if there were any repercussions. I set the jaws and squeezed as hard as I could, but it wouldn't cut. I held the cutter against the locker, raised my foot, and kicked the arm hard. After three kicks the shank gave way. Inside was a faded park district shirt, an old clock radio, two bottles of vodka in brown bags, and a steel ring of keys. I gave the keys to the young worker, who along with the rest of the staff, quickly left the office. I handed the vodka to Ted to keep for evidence while I cut the desk padlocks like a professional burglar. It was empty except for another half-full bottle of vodka, some golf pencils, tees, and old golf magazines. I handed the third bottle to Ted. Shaking my head, I tore the month of May off the desk calendar. For the entire month of June, there were only two entries, the same for the remaining months to December. Each month, two weeks apart, printed in bold clear letters the entries read "payday." I grabbed the whole calendar and gave it to Ted to place with the other evidence. Then we left.

Of course there were unintended consequences. A week later Nancy Kaszak called me to her office, but this time she was not her usual upbeat self. Wearing a conservative dark business suit, she told her secretary to hold all calls and motioned me to sit down.

"What are we going to do with you?" she asked pressing her lips tightly together. Not sure what she meant I gestured with my hands open. She picked up an Inspections and Investigations incident report marked "Confidential."

"Please tell me you didn't cut a lock off an employee's locker at Marquette Golf Course last week," she continued, moving a pile of papers so she could anchor her elbows and fold her hands.

"This is not about firing the greenskeeper. That was done properly and legally. This is about violating an employee's civil rights," she said very seriously.

"Civil rights?"

"When you broke into that employee's locker, you violated his right to privacy."

"No, not breaking in, breaking out. I 'broke out' the keys that belonged to the park district. The work of the district could not go on without opening that locker."

"Excuse me," she interrupted. "When you cut that lock with a pair of bolt cutters, you violated the employee's constitutional right against search and seizure."

"Oh, give me a break—to use a pun," I said sarcastically.

Nancy normally laughed at my puns but not this time. In her mind this was a serious breach. To me it was common sense.

With deserved pride she told me that in addition to her accomplishments, which included a new disciplinary code, a minority business/women's business enterprise (MBE/WBE) ordinance for fairness in minority hiring and contracts based on the city's ordinance, and the harbor rules and regulations, she wanted to pass a human rights ordinance, outlining rights of employees in the workplace. This ordinance was apparently on its way to the board for approval when the locker incident occurred.

"Thanks to you I had to pull the ordinance until it includes a lock policy that protects every employee's right to privacy." She waved the new version in front of me.

"Right to privacy?" I scoffed. "What about the public's right to the honest services it pays for?"

Nancy shook her hair back. She was way beyond debating me. Her policy allowed supervisors to gain entry into what she called "personal space" *only* in emergency situations. When I asked what "emergency" meant, she answered it had to be life threatening. While I thought of a response, she added, "The unions were up in arms over this, you know."

"Well, of course they were. I'm not against unions except when they defend lousy workers. Wouldn't it be nice if for once unions did something to straighten out its worst members, like sending drunk greenskeepers to AA meetings, for instance?" Nancy facetiously agreed that it would be very nice, but legally irrelevant, and brought the discussion back to padlocked lockers. She read from her proposed ordinance changes:

"Each and every park employee with a personal locker will provide a padlock key or combination to his or her supervisor. Should the need arise for management to gain emergency access, it will be done in the presence of the employee whenever possible, but if not, permission is implied by providing the key in advance."

"Nancy, do you have any idea how many employee lockers are out there? I'm going to guess several thousand."

"That's what computer systems are for. Stop being so difficult."

"I'm trying to use common sense. The action at Marquette is an exception to the rule, and when an exception causes a greater good, it should be the standard by which the rule is judged, not the other way around."

I could hear the echo of Zacchaeus's voice, as I argued spirit against letter of law, but there was no point. Her mind was made up, and Jesse and the board would follow her recommendations. No matter that the workers at Marquette understood the necessity for breaking into the locker—not one complained; no matter that greenskeepers from the other courses thanked me for removing a rotten apple; no matter that the regular golfers at Marquette wrote dozens of support letters, and that the number of rounds increased immediately. The law is the law, and no one climbs above it even if drowning in it. Better to bureaucratically tread water with a minimum of effort than make a pneumacratic exception.

Nancy ended our meeting. I scurried back to my office for a lie down on my newly installed off-white carpet and drifted off into thoughts of sailing, sailing on the Sea of Galilee with the master of exceptions to the law.

Nancy's "human rights ordinance" was passed by the board a month later. Memos were sent to all employees to provide locker keys to their supervisors, who had authority to use them in cases of emergency. Three file boxes of duplicate keys with every kind of tag and tie imaginable were delivered to my office. The boxes were marked with the various Special Services divisions. Some of the keys had employee names attached. Others had already lost their makeshift tags during transport. I picked up one huge bunch tied together on a string marked "Soldier Field" and counted fifty keys. Odd, there were only a dozen workers at the stadium. Did each worker have four lockers? Parking had hundreds of keys. Apparently each garage manager decided to include keys to every locked door, cabinet, cash register, and closet, as well as piles of customer car keys from lost and found drawers. Golf included keys to all the golf carts. In the Grant Park Symphony box were keys on souvenir violin key rings and a note from the musicians' union steward, asking if lockers only used during performances had to be included under the policy. I forwarded it to Nancy.

Rich Tinker returned from lunch in the cafeteria and told me, "Everyone is talking about 'Admiral Nelson's Lock Policy.'" One clerk from Planning asked him if she had to give a key to her apartment. Rich picked up the box of keys from Harbors and after counting them said some were missing. "You know they aren't going to give up all their keys," he said. "Nobody wants the boss poking around in their private stuff."

"I know, I know. It's a stupid idea like the ban on long-distance calls," I responded defensively.

He dropped the Harbor keys back in the box and gave it a theatrical kick.

"After all this, I bet you never break into a locker again."

I looked him straight in the eye to see if he was serious or just playing straight man. He knew I could not care less about the scuttlebutt echoing through the building. In my best Clint Eastwood impression I answered, "Watch me."

Speaking of unintended consequences, a month later on a Friday afternoon I received a certified mail notice from the Ethics Department of the county clerk's office stating that my ethics filing statement known as a "Statement of Economic Interests" had not been received by the deadline. Therefore I was being fined fifteen dollars payable by the fifteenth of the month. If missed the deadline, I would be fined one hundred dollars a day and risk "forfeiture of office or position of employment."

But I had filed the same day I received the form, two weeks before the deadline. I called the county clerk's office and was told, "We do not question whether or not you sent it, only that our records show it was not received; therefore you must pay the fine." This is why the world hates bureaucrats. I marched into Nancy's office. Somewhat testy, she said she would look into the matter when she had time, adding, "The ethics ordinance does not allow for appeal or arbitration; you have to pay the fine."

I refused and demanded she take the bumbling county clerk to court if necessary. As evidence I showed her time-stamped copies I personally made of my "Statement of Economic Interests," in which all eight answers to the questions of conflict of interest were "none." Nancy was not impressed. I continued to steam.

"Nancy, the questions on the form should not ask how much money or how many gifts a person receives and from whom, but how much is given away and to whom." She gave me a blank stare.

"Do you know the story of Zaccheus? He was a chief tax collector for the Romans who climbed a tree to see Jesus."

"Where are you going with this?"

"He gave away half his wealth and promised to restore fourfold to anyone he may have defrauded. That's ethics in government. Ethics are not about conflict of interest, but about self-emptying. The form should be a list of an employee's giving." Nancy smiled and reiterated she would look into the matter.

At a staff meeting two weeks later, Nancy, to my surprise, announced a change in the city's ethics ordinances: ethics statements were not to be mailed to the city clerk but personally submitted to the office of the president of the park district board, whereupon a printed and dated receipt would be issued. The president's office would be responsible for delivering the statements to the county clerk on time and would keep a permanent record of those submitted in case of any questions. Looking directly at me, she ended by saying a memo would go out to all park employees.

"Nancy, will this new procedure apply to previous cases like mine?" I asked, the moral fire in my belly now a smoldering ash

"Absolutely not. There is no way for the law departments of all governmental agencies in Chicago and Cook County to determine what errors occurred. To investigate each case would create more bureaucracy and not be cost effective." She tapped a pencil on the table, her signal it was time to end discussion. But I persisted and, again, protested my fifteen-dollar fine. My fellow execs had had enough and told me to pay. Al Nieman pulled fifteen dollars out of his pocket and pushed them across the table. The ensuing laughter shut me up.

After the meeting I asked Rich Tinker to drive me over to city hall and wait outside of the county clerk's office. There was a long line. When my turn finally came, I suppressed my righteous indignation. I thought of paying in pennies but pulled out three five-dollar bills instead and paid my "ethics non-compliance fine." The clerk issued me a receipt and, noticing my disapproving glare, lectured me on the importance of rules. The gold cross around her neck almost compelled me to lecture back on Jesus's attitude toward the bureaucratic Pharisees and their rules, but I looked at my watch instead. Rich had been circling city hall for almost an hour on park district time, or was it my personal time?—another ethics violation for sure. I mumbled thanks and exited the building.

WULKY

June 23, 1988.

In 1988, Chicago experienced an unusual drought that began simultaneously with the extensive tree plantings in parks and showed no sign of abating. Indeed, that summer would set an all-time heat record with forty-seven days in the nineties and no rain. It affected all the Special Services except Auto Parking and Concessions, which boomed as people flocked to the lakefront to cool off. Due to cloudless skies and high evaporation rates, the lake level dropped nearly three feet.

Soldier Field Stadium, a totally exposed concrete bowl, retained so much heat that newly planted natural turf would not root by the beginning of the Bears season. A fire department tugboat was enlisted to cruise up and down the thirty miles of coastline, drenching new park district trees with its massive pumps designed to extinguish warehouse fires on the Chicago River. Record drought covered Chicago like a hot tin roof. Kids played on park dust where there should have been grass and opened fire hydrants all over the city to cool off.

The year before, ironically, it had rained so much the lake level swelled to an all-time high. Mayor Washington established a blue ribbon "Shoreline Commission" to deal with the real possibility of massive flooding on sections of Lake Shore Drive after the underpass at McCormick Place had filled with six feet of water, closing the drive for several days. A huge berm, costing over a million dollars, was shaped just south of McCormick Place to protect the drive. When the lake level reversed, previous concerns about stone revetments crumbling and causing flooding along the lakefront had been replaced by worries the drought would kill thousands of newly planted trees, a key reform initiative of Jesse's administration to reverse the years of neglected landscaping. The cost of tree replacement would be astronomical.

Reflecting the rarity of drought in Chicago, the park district with its 550 parks and hundreds of thousands of trees and plantings had only two water tanker trucks, and even if it found money to buy more, manufacture and delivery could not occur until next winter.

Just before noon the entire executive staff and all department heads assembled outside the building for a press conference to explain plans for saving the trees. Four television crews hoisted their truck-mounted antennas into a scorching sky and set up cameras. While we waited for Jesse to announce emergency steps, reporters stuck microphones into the face of any official who would talk about the crisis. A reporter from the *Tribune* recognized me and asked what the new Harbor Boss was going to do about the drought.

"I have ordered all boaters to stop at their local churches before coming down to the harbors," I replied dryly.

The reporter started to write down my comment, then said, "No, seriously."

"Seriously, we will do two things. First, all of our boat slips have water spigots for filling tanks and washing. By stringing boat hoses together to reach shore, harbor staff will water any and all trees around harbor perimeters. Second, the harbors will pay for the fuel for the fire boat."

The reporter jotted it all down, completely unaware of the person standing next to me, Bob Wulkowicz, the unknown star of the news conference. I might have ignored him too if I didn't know him. Short, pear-shaped, with a paintbrush mustache and hair parted down the middle, he looked like one of the seven dwarfs, his personality a mix of Dopey, Sneezy, and Grumpy. Everyone called him "Wulky." To see him next to a freshly planted linden tree by the podium, you assumed he was some patronage landscaper standing by to clip and groom the shrubbery for the television cameras.

But Wulky was no party hack; he was an inventor, personally hired by Walter Netsch to solve problems through innovation and invention. His job title, "electronics designer," was nowhere on the organization chart, as he too was brought in as an independent contractor. Netsch discovered Bob at a series of community meetings in Lincoln Park where a project to enlarge and lengthen the on-ramps to Lake Shore Drive at Fullerton and Belmont was hotly debated. At those points Lake Shore Drive hugs the lake. The original 1940s design (when traffic was a fraction of present-day numbers) elevated the highway every four blocks so pedestrians could cross under the traffic for access to the lakefront—another legacy of Chicago's "forever open, clear, and free" tradition. The Fullerton overpass was so steep, that motorists zooming north over them could not see cars entering from the short on-ramps on the other side. Serious accidents had occurred regularly at these merge areas before the city and state decided to solve the problem by lengthening the on-ramp.

But community groups like Friends of the Parks vigorously objected because the new wider ramp would cut into the narrow park land between the drive and the lake edge, eliminate more than an acre of green space, and cost millions of dollars. Wulky devised a simple system of warning lights and signs positioned on the upside of the overpasses that blinked a warning to slow down when cars were entering the on-ramps on the other side. His system worked so well, he was later presented a "Presidential Design Award" at the White House by President Ronald Reagan.

Bob was a genius and pure Chicagoan. He grew up in a tough part of the South Side, a neighborhood made famous by Chicago writer Stuart Dybek, a close childhood friend of Bob's. Dybek's classic Chicago short story collection, *Childhood and Other Neighborhoods*, contains the autobiographical story "The Long Thoughts," about two teenagers hanging out in the streets, walking around the outside of

Cook County Jail shouting conversations with the inmates in the middle of a snowy January night. It presents a moving glimpse into the antisocial nature of a budding genius (Bob Wulkowicz) rejected by the adult world.[1]

He dropped out of Catholic high school and landed a full scholarship at the Art Institute. At age twenty he suddenly gave up an artist's career to become a journeyman electrician and worked on the electrical wiring of the tallest building in the world at the time, Sears Tower. Because of his skills, he rose to supervisor and was frequently consulted by the builders. He redesigned significant parts of the electrical system, saving Sears millions of dollars. Bob told me that designing the miles of conduit and woven wiring was his work of art, better than anything he could have created as a painter. Beneath all the brilliance, he exhibited a mystical side as he described his experience:

"The view from the top of Sears Tower was spectacular. I remember one moonlit night I was up there alone trying to figure out some electrical problem. Suddenly a bank of thick clouds formed a giant powdered doughnut around the building at the same level of the floor I was standing on. I experienced this mystical moment, a desire to walk off the tallest building on the planet onto the top of a cloud. I became disoriented and actually held on tight to a girder until the cloud moved on. I'll never forget it."

Wulky stood beside me as Jesse mounted the portable podium next to the new linden tree. It was suffocating hot, like being inside the mouth of a panting dog. Wulky stepped to the curb of McFetridge Drive, the street that separates the park district from the Field Museum. At the corner a bright orange dump truck made the turn toward the podium. Wulky signaled the driver to keep coming. The district had hundreds of dump trucks, and Wulky designed an ingenious way to convert them temporarily to water tankers by welding a valve through the tailgate. Attached by hose to any fire hydrant, they could be quickly filled with thousands of gallons of water. But that was not all. Wulky's real invention was getting the water from the dump truck to the trees through a device, made of ordinary plastic tubing the thickness of a sandwich bag perforated with tiny holes, which he called "a tree sausage." These plastic tubes could be easily coiled around a tree and filled from the dump truck in a few seconds. Over several days the "tree sausages" dripped water into the soil around the root balls. The plastic tubing cost only pennies.

On Wulky's cue the dump truck, groaning under the water's weight, started to move toward the podium. Just as it gained momentum, a police officer stepped in front of it and signaled the driver to stop. Apparently no one told him the dump truck was part of the press conference. The driver slammed on the brakes, which would have brought the truck to an easy stop if filled with dirt. But with water, the braking turned its cargo into a rogue wave, which curled over the truck cab and cascaded through the windows, temporarily submerging the driver, then onto the hood in a huge splash. The hapless police officer was knocked down and deluged. Laughter rippled through the crowd as Jesse suggested the Police Marine Unit direct traffic the next time. A park executive standing behind me commented, "Only a Polack would use a dump truck to water trees." Luke Cosme turned around and glared.

When Jesse introduced the inventor of the "tree sausage" to polite applause, Wulky first explained his passion for trees, describing them as "gossamer engines." If he had time he would have lectured, as he did to me once, that trees live in societies far superior to our own, that they tolerate us, not the other way around. Thankfully he only explained his invention. The staff and press gathered around the linden tree where Wulky had coiled several of his plastic tubes. The dump truck, now half full of water, carefully parked parallel to the curb. Wulky connected the plastic hose to the gate valve in the truck's tailgate. He turned it on and water filled the entire tree sausage coil in less than two minutes. Then he shut off the valve and tied the end of the sausage in a knot like a bag of goldfish and dropped it on the ground.

The press dutifully snapped pictures and asked questions. Cameras zoomed in on the plastic coils that slowly trickled water into the root ball of the tree. Not exactly front page news, the "tree sausage" press conference ended after a few minutes.

It ended because Jesse wanted to get away from reporters. The evening news barely mentioned "tree sausages," and the following day's newspapers again blasted Jesse for patronage hiring with only short articles on Wulky's invention in the back pages.[2]

Wulky invented like Ben Franklin, who never patented any of his governmental inventions, believing their benefit belonged to the common good of the people. Franklin invented the four-sided street lamp with removable glass panes replacing the fragile and very expensive handblown glass globes. His maritime inventions included watertight compartments for ships, engine propellers, and weather forecasting. He advised ship captains to carry thermometers and measure temperatures at various depths to determine sea currents, he financed the first manned air balloon flight in France, where he also suggested the concept of daylight saving, which the French adopted. He invented the public lending library, believing knowledge must be loaned for free to the people. Franklin's famous statement, carved in stone above the entrance to his library, the first public lending library in the nation, "To pour forth benefits for the common good is divine," rings as true now as it did in the eighteenth century. He also believed top government officials should serve without pay and bequeathed all he earned as president of Pennsylvania to funds for artisans and back to the public treasury. Ben Franklin was a pneumacrat and so was Bob Wulkowicz.

I can almost hear old Ben standing next to the tree sausage pleading for more inventors in government. For those who looked closely, Divinity could be seen pouring forth benefits from a dump truck full of water.

Wulky volunteered to help me improve the harbors in any way he could. I asked him to analyze costs of the old steel buoys designed in the 1940s and fabricated by park ironworkers in various park welding shops. There was no consistency in design or fabrication; each shop made them differently. Some floated one foot off the water; some three feet; some had pad eyes for boat mooring lines directly on top of the buoy, others on two- or three-foot steel stems. A few were made of heavy gauge steel, but most were made from thin sheet metal (whatever was left over from other jobs) that dented and punctured easily. No foam floatation was injected into them, which meant over time they rusted, developed pinholes, and sank.

There were two thousand steel buoys throughout the harbor system, with Monroe floating more than one thousand. Each fall, the buoys were detached from their anchor chains, lifted onto barges, transported to shore, loaded onto trucks, and taken to various storage facilities on the lakefront. Because they were all different shapes and sizes, they could not be uniformly stacked; they were loaded and unloaded into piles causing more dents and damaged seams in addition to those sustained from boats running into them during season. "Sinkers" were taken to the ironworkers for repairs over the winter.

In early spring, the buoys were loaded back onto trucks and taken to park district paint shops to be power washed, wire brushed, and given a fresh coat of cheap and always available yellow traffic paint. Finally, they were stenciled with numbers corresponding to harbor locations, loaded on trucks for the third time, returned to their harbors, transferred onto barges, and placed back into the water. It was incredibly inefficient.

Wulky documented a maintenance cost of $300 per buoy or $60,000 annually, not including buoys stolen from the winter piles by scrappers or numerous legal settlements over damage to boats by the buoys' steel edges and center rods. For years boaters, including me, had complained. My first new boat was moored in Monroe and by the end of the summer was full of gouges and chips on both sides. Boaters moored there referred to the problem as "Monroe Measles."

I asked Wulky to work with Rich Tinker and Luke to invent a "Chicago buoy." First, they scoured boat supply catalogs finding buoys made of plastic, with swivels, and foam filled, but too small, designed for boats less than twenty feet to use on inland lakes. Unlike small lakes where wave action rarely exceeds one foot, Chicago's harbors experience two- to three-foot storm waves. Chicago needed a stout buoy designed for its unique conditions.

That fall Wulky, Luke and I met at Belmont when the work crew unloaded buoys, stripping them of tires, laundry baskets, old life jackets, cushions, pieces of PVC pipe, sail bags filled with rags—all the things boaters used to prevent damage to their boats.

"Gentlemen, the district invented the star dock; it can invent a proper buoy," I said.

They nodded in agreement and waded into the pile of buoys with measuring tapes, pads and pencils, and pocket knives. They scraped away rust from the dents and creases in some of the "sinkers," then looked at what boaters had tried as solutions to hull damage. One in particular caught Wulky's eye, a reinforced steel wheel covered with canvas over a rubber cushion clamped onto the buoy shaft. It was bent like a pretzel. The force required to bend the steel surprised him. "A boat did this?" I assured him the sharp bow of a boat rising up a wave and coming down on the steel wheel had the force of a coast guard icebreaker.

Wulky asked what features boaters wanted. A boater from the Monroe Harbor Advisory Council pointed out that you could barely see the yellow-painted buoys at night, which was one reason they were run into so often. Why didn't the buoys have reflective tape? We made a list of features:

Harmless to Boat Finishes
One Standard Size for Easy Stacking
Lightweight
Durable, High Impact Strength
Foam-Filled and Unsinkable
Permanent Finish, No Annual Painting
White and Visible at Night

Luke looked at the list. "That's a tall order. How much time do we have?"

"I want new buoys for the spring of 1989."

"Spring? Oh no. Maybe a year from next spring, what with testing, bidding, and all the rest. Two years is more realistic."

I couldn't wait two years. My honeymoon with the boaters was

Figure 6. Rich Tinker holding newly invented "Chicago buoy" amidst old buoys, 1989. (Photo by R. J. Nelson.)

over. The harbor advisory councils wanted results, not promises. And since almost a third of Chicago's boats are on mooring buoys, a new boat-friendly one would go a long way to show the boating community that the park district was serious about improving their harbor neighborhoods.

Wulky called the Army Corps of Engineers and found out where they obtained commercial buoys: Smith Roylan, in northern Wisconsin. Wulky noticed it manufactured a type of buoy for marking wing dams on navigable rivers, very similar to the floating markers in swimming pools, only much larger and more substantial: high-impact white plastic, waterproof foam filled, and two feet long by a foot and a half in diameter but floated horizontally. Bob suggested, "Why not tip one on end, weight it somehow, insert a shaft with swivel on the bottom and a pad eye on top?"

Smith Roylan enthusiastically assigned an engineer to the project. All the dam markers needed was a thicker skin and swivel hardware, the weight of heavy anchor chain being sufficient to keep them vertical. I gave the engineer my list including a two-inch strip of light-blue reflective tape for night spotting. By spring 1989, one hundred prototype buoys were delivered in uniform stacks. The cost: $85.00 each. Luke verified Smith Roylan's test data and groups of buoys were anchored in all harbors and performed flawlessly. The boaters loved them. The following winter, two thousand were ordered. "Chicago buoys" have now been in service for over twenty-five years at a great cost savings both to the district and boaters.

Smith Roylan gave me an extra prototype buoy, a gift I never reported on my ethics statements, though by the rules for gifts, I probably should have. The buoy hangs from a pipe in my basement, the closest it will ever get to a lake or other body of water. Its blue reflective strip glows in the dark when I turn off the lights, a metaphor, perhaps, of public service in Chicago's "blue space": chained between deeply grounded anchors and vessels on the surface, tethered strong to ride out storms, and useful only for a period.

MOVING ON UP

Thanksgiving 1988.

I was just getting comfortable with my newly decorated office when a memo from Jesse dictated that the Marine Department had to move. Nancy Kaszak's Law Department, located next to Marine on the third floor, had hired so many reformers there was no space for desks let alone cubicles and conference areas. Marine and Special Services was moved one floor down to an area formerly occupied by the secretarial pool. As computers were introduced into more and more departments, the old typist and file clerk pools had become obsolete. Not even patronage clout could save jobs from new technology. My spacious office became a conference room, which I was allowed to use—when available.

My new space was next to the ancient single-file escalators that rattled incessantly. The outer office space was about the same size as upstairs, but my office was reduced to a small box, half the size of my former office. Built out of plaster board without ceiling or soundproofing—a large cubicle really—it was never quiet. But what a view. On the front side of the building, it faced the Field Museum of Natural History across McFetridge Drive, with the downtown skyline in the background, a great improvement from the crumbling backside of Soldier Field. The move was a depressing change at first, but then came its silver lining: its proximity to the general superintendent's and com-

missioners' offices at the end of the hall. They, and all the VIPs coming to see them, had to walk by my office, where, when I needed to,
I could easily snag them like the fishermen in Jackson Park Harbor
snagged coho salmon swimming in to spawn.

The new space lacked a customer service counter, so I was assigned
a park carpenter, Paul Ziltz, to build one. For several years, prior to
being transferred to Soldier Field, Paul worked in the South Side Carpentry shop, across the street from the University of Chicago's trade
shops, where he often lunched with university tradesmen, especially
the "angel carvers," Swedes in their seventies who repaired and re-
finished the university's wooden statues and carvings. My favorites
included ten human-size wooden angels defying gravity on massive
beams holding up the Divinity School library ceiling, their wings
spread ready to fly down to students' shoulders with holy inspiration.
When I worked at the University of Chicago, I too spent more than
a few lunches with the Swedish angel carvers to hear stories of my
grandparents' homeland and, more importantly, as respite from bureaucratic chores.

The week before Thanksgiving, Paul Ziltz met me with a tape measure, index card, a pencil behind one ear and three more in his shirt
pocket. He was tall, somewhat overweight, with a full head of gray
hair and a salt-and-pepper beard. What looked like heavy dandruff
on his shoulders was actually sawdust he brushed off only at the end
of the day. I could smell this "carpenter's cologne" as he extended his
tape measure along the floor. He wrote down a couple of measure-
ments and asked if I wanted the old customer counter moved down.

"No, too narrow, and those old oak teller-type windows look like
something out of *It's a Wonderful Life*," I answered.

The new counter would be twenty-four feet long, allowing several
boaters to be serviced at one time with plenty of space for literature,
forms, newsletters, and so on. Paul informed me that rules dictated
I could have any color countertop I wanted as long as it was gray—
mouse gray. What better color for a huge bureaucracy?

Paul finished the counter the day before Thanksgiving. On Thanksgiving morning, when the building was deserted, I filled my tool bag with measuring tape, level, drill, and picture hangers and spent the morning in my new space. I placed enlarged laminated photos of the harbors on the counter, along with information about not only the Chicago harbors, but the surrounding harbors as well, and blueprints and renderings of new projects for boater comments. On the pillars and walls, I hung nautical charts of Lake Michigan, Chicago's lakefront and river system, and some historic pictures of the harbors under construction. On my cubicle office walls, I hung my iceberg photos so they could be seen from the hall. After hanging and assembling everything, I placed a new coffeemaker at one end of the counter, made a pot, and then walked up and down the hall to view the results from every customer angle. Paul told me I was entitled to a department sign, but none was needed; the nautical décor made it obvious.

When Harold Washington died, I feared for the political worst and being replaced by Mayor Sawyer. But instead, after two boating seasons, the Marine Department, even though physically down a floor, was moving up. After the indictments, the board was anxious to speed up improvements in the harbors. Walter Netsch and I met frequently to discuss modernizing the facilities. Walter, a would-be Daniel Burnham, proposed a multimillion-dollar master plan to upgrade all the harbors at once The great architect was surprised when I disagreed, preferring incremental improvements in all eight harbors. In the meantime a new harbor in the Turning Basin would be planned and another for Thirty-First Street, to show boaters the future. "Walter," as he now insisted I call him, bought into my thinking, which pleased Jesse as well. For once, he and Walter agreed on something.

Perception of the harbors was moving away from scandal and corruption. After months of negotiations, the city council abolished the odious 50 percent mooring tax. I testified humorously, "The last time there was a harbor tax in this country, the country changed hands." The park district agreed to collect back taxes owed through 1987, and for this service the Marine Division would receive a 10 percent collection fee. Many boaters, still unhappy with the deal, sailed to other harbors around Lake Michigan, but it didn't matter. There were hundreds on the waiting lists waiting patiently and honestly to take their spots. With the tax on the ash heap, I campaigned successfully for a 25 percent increase in harbor fees to establish an ongoing "Harbor Improvement Fund" (approximately $1.5 million annually). Approved unanimously by the park board, it gave the harbor director discretion to decide which harbor projects the money would be spent. After all the scandals, their action was a large and humbling vote of confidence.

The board also approved a new harbor water taxi service in Monroe with six proper harbor tender boats. This new service would shuttle people to and from their boats in a timely and safe fashion. It was a hard sell convincing the board that the government could run a water taxi service much better than private operators, a string of whom had failed because the season was so short and the cost of an adequate fleet didn't add up to profitability. The current operator made money on selling boats not the taxi service. He made Pfeiffer a silent partner, who in exchange for alleged kickbacks on boat sales, arranged slips for the buyers. When I became director, the scam disappeared and suddenly the taxi service, which was really a loss leader, deteriorated. Instead of proper boats, the taxi service used three used ski boats, with limited hours of operation, expensive tickets, and only one pickup station in a harbor one and half miles long and with over a thousand boats on moorings. Boaters waited hours for pickups and complained bitterly. The operator, whose contract extended through the 1988 season, had the balls to ask me for an extension of his contract with a huge increase. That didn't happen.

My solution: charge every boater in Monroe a hundred-dollar annual fee for unlimited service for two; additional guests would pay a modest fee. Four pickup stations would be established, and weekend service would operate twenty-four hours a day. Additionally, one season parking pass in the underutilized Monroe underground garage adjacent to Monroe Harbor would be provided—something I could offer, since as superintendent of special services I was in charge of auto parking.

Figure 7. Two of six new water taxis in Monroe Harbor, 1989. (Photo by R. J. Nelson.)

Boaters, as well as commissioners, were skeptical. A class action suit was planned by some boater-lawyers in Monroe who argued the fee was a hidden illegal tax. Only the jaw boning of Bill Parks, commodore of the Chicago Yacht Club at the time, and one of my closest advisors, dissuaded them. If Bill had not intervened, my plan would have been tied up in court for years.

With some hesitation the park board passed the plan, and I purchased six boats from a company on Long Island, Crosby Yachts, which for generations had built sturdy harbor tenders in use from Maine to Fort Lauderdale. Their only drawback was limited seating capacity on fiberglass benches molded into the hulls. The center cockpit areas were open but coast guard safety regulations prohibited passengers from standing there. I called several Crosby customers to ask how they got around this problem. An old Yankee captain in Marblehead, Massachusetts, suggested Igloos, the commercial fiberglass ice chests used on fishing charter boats. Because they were large, they came equipped with seats molded into the tops. As long as they were bolted down into the cockpit sole, the coast guard certified them for

Figure 8. The nation's first disabled-accessible dock and fishing platform with wheelchair ramp that automatically adjusts to lake levels, designed by Fred Hunt and installed in 1991. (Photo by R. J. Nelson.)

additional seating. But the best feature of the Igloos—they hold lots of ice. Prior to the new taxi service, passengers had to buy ice at the Chicago Yacht Club gas dock and carry it, often after waiting an hour or more, to their boats (the yacht club only offered fuel and ice as a service and was happy to let me take over the ice operation; they ultimately closed their gas operation as well). In my plan the tender drivers could sell ice to passengers just before they boarded their boats. "Real good money there," the captain had confided. The Igloos added eight coast guard–approved passenger seats per boat and, in the first year of operation, produced over $16,000 dollars net profit on ice sales. The $100 fee plus visitor revenue paid off the cost of the boats in three years. The common good for Monroe Harbor was served.

More improvements flowed: wrought iron fencing to replace barbed wire, a comfort/harbor master station in Burnham, restoration of the old coast guard station in Jackson, and the hiring of a prestigious engineering firm to plan a new Millennium Harbor in the Turning Basin, and floating docks in several harbors. The new docks included a large dock for disabled boaters and fishermen that automatically adjusted its ramp angle to changing lake levels as required by federal rules for wheelchairs; it was the first such dock in the United States.

Pneumacracy was working. I had been Harbor Boss for less than two years—but two full boating seasons—and the blue space world entrusted to me experienced real repairs. The press, instead of focusing on scandal, switched to positive stories on the changes. My basement files now included positive clippings.

As I gathered up my tools and headed home for our family Thanksgiving feast, I looked forward to the end of long holiday weekend. I wanted to be the first in the building on Monday morning and to stand behind my new counter and personally serve the first customer.

FOG BOWL

December 31, 1988.

Jesse finally fired the stadium manager. Reports of all-night partying, unauthorized catering bills from the stadium concessionaire, drug paraphernalia in the manager's private bathroom, condoms and panties under the couch cushions, and piles of beer bottles and party food remnants on the fifty-yard line—a major violation of the Bears' contract—were given to Jesse either by me or anonymously. The manager rarely showed up during office hours and skipped required meetings. When he did show up, he always dressed in suit and tie—never Soldier Field uniform shirts—and strutted around like a drum major during games. He never properly scheduled stadium staff, who had to guess which shifts and days to work. Marine clerks had to process the stadium payroll based on handwritten notes. He caused major problems for the Bears, like failing to communicate practice times to visiting teams. On one occasion the Miami Dolphins were refused access to practice. Miami's coach complained bitterly to the NFL, a mess Jesse and I had to smooth over. And in June, Kay Brett called me to her office and dangled five full pages of long-distance calls made in one month all over the United States by the manager, almost all of them, like drug transactions, lasting less than a minute.

At midnight one November night, Harold Krezinsky, longtime fleet manager for the park district called me: "Got an anonymous tip about your stadium manger. He took a Soldier Field truck, number 143, and parked it on South Indiana at Twenty-Ninth Street. My source says his girlfriend lives there." Taking vehicles home for personal use was absolutely forbidden. I instructed Harold to tow the truck to one of his warehouses while I waited for the manager to report the truck missing. It took three days for him to tell me. When I revealed the truck had been towed on my order, he accused me of racial discrimination and doing everything possible to get him fired—the latter accusation being the only time I remember him telling the truth. On December 28, Jesse terminated him and I moved temporarily into the stadium office the next day, forty-eight hours before the famous playoff game with the Philadelphia Eagles. Amazingly, the press, which crawled all over the stadium looking for story angles, never exposed the scandal.

Jesse appointed Jimmy Duggan, who reported to me as acting stadium manager. A lifer in the district since age eighteen, he was a perfect choice. He worked his way up from the mail room to a supervisory position in landscaping. Widely respected, Jimmy knew everyone and had excellent people skills. But because so much could go wrong on game day, especially a packed playoff game, I moved in to help Jimmy and his staff any way I could.

I arrived early. Freezing wind off the lake whipped around Soldier Field so hard that quarterbacks practiced short passes only. Bears weather, perfect for smash-mouth football. A half hour before he opened the gates to the south parking lot, Marty LaScola, director of auto parking, came in for coffee. He pulled off his wool Bears cap and lit a cigarette. The new ordinance that Kay Brett feared, forbidding smoking inside all park facilities, had passed, but Marty didn't care; he tested the rules and me every chance he got. He pulled off fur-lined mitts that reached halfway up his arms, unzipped his worn and faded Soldier Field jacket, and fell into the leather sofa along one wall of the stadium office.

"Chief, you gotta do something about handicapped parkers. They're killing me out there. Last game I set aside three hundred spaces, and we ran out in the first hour."

"There can't be that many fans with disabilities."

"No shit. The lying motherfuckers somehow get handicap stickers and tags, so we have to let 'em in."

Marty had complained before but never to such an extent. Three hundred spaces? Not only was the abuse disgusting—fans taking advantage of a law that had nothing to do with them—it was perfect for an exposé by the press of my management. I could see the headline: "Stadium Chief Blind to Handicapped Parking Abuse, Ignores Complaints from Staff." I imagined a reporter asking how I could manage a disabled sailing program across the street in Burnham Harbor with woefully inadequate parking and allow hundreds of fans with fake handicapped tags to park next to the stadium entrance. Paranoid perhaps, but I had to get ahead of this one.

"Marty, finish your coffee and tell your staff not to open the gates until I get there."

The south parking lot was one huge expanse of cracked and broken asphalt with no lanes, wheel stops, or lines. Besides Bears games it was used for CTA bus driver tests, police maneuvers and practice chases, and occasional carnivals and exhibits connected with McCormick Place.

On Bears game days, Marty assigned a platoon of temporary staff to marshal the hundreds of cars, vans, and motor homes that poured into the lot. Tailgaters were directed toward the temporary washroom areas near the harbor. All others, depending on who they knew, were sent near south, mid-south, and far south almost to McCormick Place a half mile away. Those with handicapped plates or tags were directed to an area closest to the stadium in compliance with the federal ADA law.

Marty told his marshals assigned to the disabled area to take a break, and we proceeded to stop cars flashing handicap tags. I instructed every driver (all males) to roll down his window. Marty was clearly uncomfortable. He knew a lot of these guys and gladly let me do the talking.

"Excuse me, I am the superintendent here, can you please tell me who is handicapped in this car?" I asked politely. In almost all cases, there were three to five able-bodied passengers who looked at each other bewildered, having never been asked this before. If one wise

guy said he was handicapped, I asked him the nature of his disability.
And when he stumbled to lie, I read off a statement prewritten on an
index card: "This is a warning: if you attempt to park in the handicapped section again, an assigned Chicago police officer will ticket
and tow your vehicle. The fine is $500.00 plus impoundment and
storage fees."

I made that statement up. The police had no enforcement interest
inside park district lots. It would take an act of God to get one of
the dozens of cops standing on Waldron Drive, the street outside the
south parking lot, to do anything, let alone tow a car. They were much
too busy directing their clout-heavy buddies to park on the sidewalks
in front of the stadium. At a subsequent game, I tried to stop this time-
honored practice and voiced my concern to the captain in charge.
His response was immediate: "I don't give a fuck who you are. This
is a public street, and we control public streets. Now get lost." Later,
Marty, who knew the captain well, warned me to lay off or the cops
would start checking every car coming into the lot for minor infrac-
tions and bring traffic flow to a halt. In clout language, he whispered
that my own car might "disappear" if I pushed the matter. After that I
moved back to my office and left Jimmy to deal with the cops.

When I asked each scammer who owned the car, the answer was
always the same: "My car is in the shop so my sister, father, mother,
uncle or friend let me use theirs." After an hour of stopping fakers
and sending them as far south as possible, those still in line could see
the jig was up, pulled out, and headed south. By kickoff, instead of
three hundred cars in the disabled section, we counted sixty legitimate parkers.

My toes were frozen by the time I walked back through the turn-
stiles where off-duty cops frisked every fan for concealed alcohol.
A locked room for the contraband was waist high in bottles, flasks,
water bottles—even baby bottles filled with booze. By game's end, it
would all disappear.

In the manager's office, I poured a cup of coffee wondering what
else would go wrong. There were plenty of tradesmen on standby:

plumbers for clogged toilets and bursting pipes; skybox elevator repairmen; electricians for the scoreboard, PA systems, power feeds, and
backup generators; ironworkers to level the goal posts both before the
game and at halftime per NFL rules; refrigeration and air-conditioning
repairmen; telephone repairmen and computer geeks; paramedics
with three full-service ambulances; X-ray technicians for player injuries; park district lawyers to witness fights and police brutality allega-
tions when disorderly drunks were removed from the stands; an army
of Andy Frain ushers and supervisors; concessionaires and skybox ca-
terers; health inspectors; fire department inspectors; liquor license inspectors; FAA inspectors (to prevent small planes from flying over the
stadium); press photographers and TV cameramen demanding sideline credentials; and NFL referees measuring yard markers, sidelines,
and the height of the grass.

Police bomb-squad officers with dogs were stationed throughout
the games. There were lots of bomb threats deliberately kept secret. If
the Bears were losing in the third and fourth quarters, the bomb threat
calls came in, usually threatening to blow up either Coach Ditka or the
Bears' owners. The dogs dutifully sniffed everything from the locker
rooms to the labyrinth of rooms beneath the stadium. In a few hours
Soldier Field was transformed from an empty tomb to a noisy city of
seventy thousand people. A real bomb would turn it into a real tomb.

As I sipped my coffee wishing it were laced with a generous slug
of Kahlúa, a boy in a wheelchair and his father came into the office. I
recognized them from the parking lot line where they received a legitimate space. But the father was angry. A friend gave him two tickets,
but they were located in one of the upper-tier seating areas, not accessible. (Only fifty seats, twenty-five in the front rows on either side
of the field were wheelchair accessible.) When the father wheeled his
son to the ticket office, he was told they could do nothing. The father
demanded to see someone in charge and was directed to me. One look
at the young boy decked out in a Walter Payton jersey and Bears hel-
met and parka and holding a football he hoped to get autographed by
a player or two moved me to find seats for him and his father.

The game was sold out so the only place to seat them was behind the south end zone, a largely unused oval space originally designed for Olympic track events. There, on raised platforms behind the goal posts, the Bears band played, and photographers and TV cameramen set up for touchdowns and goal-line stands. From there, with a little luck, the boy could see the Bears make a touchdown up close. The father sighed with relief as Jimmy and I personally accompanied the two down the ramp to the south end zone. But then Bears security guards stationed at the bottom refused to allow access. "No credentials, no entrance."

A heated confrontation ensued. One guard pulled out his radio and called a Bears administrator who arrived in a flash. Without even looking at the boy or his dad he got in my face, shouting that park staff had nothing to do with seating. While we were toe to toe arguing what the contract said, the boy scrunched up in his wheelchair to see the game over the heads of the guards. But he couldn't see, so he reached down and released the brake. The chair started to roll down the ramp. The father grabbed the chair as it bumped into my calves and pulled it back.

It was my turn to get in the administrator's face: "You know, I think this is a story the *Chicago Sun-Times* and *Tribune* would like to cover. A nice human interest story, don't you think? Jimmy, go find one of those reporters and see if there's interest and ask one of the photographers on the sidelines to take a few pictures."

The administrator blustered but backed down, announcing he would file an official complaint to Jesse Madison. Reluctantly he told his security people to let us in and disappeared up the ramp. We borrowed an extra folding chair from the bandstand and set it up for the father next to his son's wheelchair. I ordered a stadium staffer to get hot dogs and whatever else the two wanted to eat—at no charge. Meanwhile the Bears were driving close to the goal line. The boy was so excited. His wheelchair was less than twenty feet from the goal posts,

Back at the office, three young men, fundamentalist Christians judging from their John 3:16 signs, were waiting. Now what? One of them handed me a copy of a federal district court's ten-page decision upholding the right to display religious signs at sporting events.

"Have you see this court order?" he asked defensively. I answered that I had, that religious signs were no longer an issue at Soldier Field. The Bears had dropped their initial opposition when the court order, which held that the potential harm in denying fans their ability to display their signs substantially outweighed the harm to team owners who wished to deny such displays, was issued.

John 3:16 signs pop up like computer ads after every extra point and field goal kick. Fundamentalist Christians raise these signs to fulfill their evangelistic mission of spreading the gospel. What better way than to flash a classic Bible verse across millions of television screens?

The signs do not offend me, any more than religious players who, after making a touchdown, drop to their knees and give token thanks to God; although it would be nice when they miss the touchdown pass or fumble, or deliberately hurt another player, if they dropped down and prayed for forgiveness. Maybe a golf cart outfitted with a portable confessional should be parked on the sidelines.

Fundamentalists take Jesus's Great Commission to preach the gospel to the whole world very seriously and have become expert at using mass media—combining scripture with secular rights of freedom of religion and speech—for free. In evangelical minds if twenty million football fans are watching the extra point kick in a close game and see John 3:16 for just a second or two, that is more than enough time for the subliminal power of the Holy Spirit to do its work. If, during the ensuing commercial, just one couch potato goes to the bathroom and grabs a Bible instead of a *Penthouse*, fundamentalists believe they have succeeded.

Why John 3:16? Because it's the perfect advertisement. It divides the Christian faith into three easily remembered phrases: "For God so loved the world, that he gave his only begotten son, that whosoever believeth in him shall not perish but have eternal life." Talk about a sales pitch for switching to a brand name to get a big reward!

The Baptist church, in which I grew up, made us memorize the keystone verse. As a questioning teenager, I balked at the idea that for a pitifully short time on earth, believers received blissful eternal life. It made no sense when the hypocrisy of those believers, including my own, permeated their daily lives. My skepticism led to seminary. While some students expanded the core phrase into elaborate theological systems, mine contracted. I let go of the personal valet belief in God's presence, substituting a presence only discovered through suffering alongside movements for justice and peace in the secular world. I easily lopped off the eternal life reward system and later snipped off the only begotten son phrase—that ancient notion of human sacrifice to appease an angry God. That left "For God so loved the world," an incomplete clause requiring completion by the believer and moral involvement in that world. If asked to sit in the end zone and raise my placard of faith to the television cameras, my sign would read: "For God So Loved the World, We Can Do No Less."

I told the young men, "You may raise your signs anytime during the game. Just don't block another fan's view." They blessed me and made their way to the end zones. As soon as they left, Marty came in out of breath. "Chief, you gotta get out on the field and see this." We rushed out to the thirty-yard line.

Heavy fog off Burnham Harbor eased down deck by deck onto the field, shrouding the players in a bone-white cloud. I stood next to the yard-marker official on the thirty-yard line. During a commercial time out, he looked at me and asked, "Hey, ain't you one of them turf toads?" referring to the first exhibition game last August when the new "Prescription Athletic Turf" (installed in June to replace the old indoor-carpet surface) failed to root due to the drought and extreme heat—as if Soldier Field had been left on a stove all summer. When a runner or receiver made a cut, huge chunks of sod would roll up. It was so bad that between plays Al Neiman, the groundskeeping staff, Jimmy, and I ran out onto the field and put the many pieces of jelly-roll sod back down. While fans laughed and cheered us on, the TV commentators dubbed us "turf toads." Our head groundskeeper, Ken

Mrock, was quoted, "It was like playing on a throw rug over a wooden floor."[1] Before the next game, the sod was completely replaced with three-inch-thick sod slabs trucked in from Tennessee. Being so heavy it held together, but it cost a small fortune.

"Yeah, I was the head turf toad," I joked as a TV cameraman moved out onto the field of play, his equipment useless from the fog-bound sidelines. Officials could not whistle plays they could not see, and when the ball was punted, no player was assigned to catch an unseen ball. Commentators borrowed stadium radios and moved down on the field as nothing could be seen from their positions. This would be remembered as "the greatest game *never* seen."[2]

The fog poured in during the second quarter, refused to move on until after the game, and scooped every other sports story. Perhaps it was a political omen foretelling the foggy interim before the Chicago mayoral election while I stood all but blind on the political sidelines.

I have sailed in fog numerous times, not only around icebergs in Labrador, but on Lake Michigan: off course on the way to Charlevoix, slamming into the boulders at Fisherman's Island and waking my family to put on life jackets while I pushed the boat off the rocks with a boat hook; then crossing the north-south shipping channels that bisect the lake, hearing the ominous engine noise from freighters, but clueless as to how far away they were or whether we were on collision course; hearing the big ship foghorns in the Straits of Mackinac, one after the other, staying away from them by grabbing on to a channel buoy until the ships' wakes stopped rocking our little twenty-five-foot sailboat, and then, using chart and compass (long before GPS), heading for the next channel marker to do the same. In the straits of Chicago politics, with my handheld moral compass, I did the same.

D-DAY

On April 24, 1989, Richard M. Daley, handily defeated Mayor Sawyer. The atmospheric change at the park district was palpable. "Green flu" spread through the district, and everything slowed down. Autographed photographs of Daley, kept in closets for years, appeared centered on office walls. Machine patronage workers started smiling again. Board meetings were short. All my projects were put on hold—except one, the formal presentation of the Goldman family gift of three Freedom 20 sailboats to the park board. I was so glad the partnership between the park district and the Goldman Adaptive Sailing Foundation was established during Jesse's watch. It gave him a real lift.

Petty bureaucratic harassment also spread. My requisition for two file cabinets was returned by the assistant Property Department director, a Daley supporter who knew me well but claimed he couldn't read my signature. When I asked him how he knew it was mine if he couldn't read it, he warned, "Don't mess with me. You might regret it." Two weeks later I received two beat-up file cabinets. Half the drawers wouldn't open, and the other half had no file separators. I sent them back and bought used ones in perfect condition from an office supply store. When I ordered a newly appointed Soldier Field assistant manager to give me a report on his duties, he told me to go fuck myself and talk to his sponsor, a high official in state government. I let him slide to avoid a confrontation that could only end badly.

The question of what would happen to Jesse Madison was on everyone's mind, especially the press, which mentioned Daley's possible choices for a replacement as they attacked Jesse's five-year record in the parks. Less than a month after the election, Steve Neal, then political editor of the *Sun-Times*, suggested several possible replacements (including Ed Kelly) and then wrote a scathing attack on the liberal supporters of Harold Washington, specifically the Friends of the Parks, which he called "Fakers of the Parks." He wrote, "Parks 'watchdogs' are really Madison's lapdogs."[1] He also ranted against the "nonqualified flunkies" Jesse hired. Oddly I was the only one mentioned by name. My sarcastic response letter to the editor, labeled by the *Sun-Times*, "At Least 'Flunkie' No Criminal," was published a week later.[2] I decided to throw a small "Lapdog and Nonqualified Flunkie" surprise party for Jesse at the end of a workday in the executive conference room. I invited about twelve of his staff appointees who were vilified in the press for one thing or another. Over the weekend I purchased, then carefully hid, bottles of alcohol and mixers in cabinets. Pat Day, Jesse's secretary, scheduled a fake emergency staff meeting on a Tuesday at 4:45 p.m. The look on Jesse's face going from frown to smile when he saw us with drinks held high was priceless. After pouring one of his own, he said to me, "Bob, you realize it's totally illegal to have alcohol in this building." Frankly, it had never occurred to me, but when I assured him no flunkie in the room was qualified enough to leak the event to the press, he laughed heartily, a laugh not heard for quite a while.

We talked frequently. Jesse grew up in Memphis under Jim Crow segregation. His mother was not allowed to try on a dress in the local Sears store, even though his father worked there as a shipping clerk. At seventeen he left for Chicago, only to experience Jim Crow, Chicago-style. At one point he worked for Saul Alinsky's Organization for a Better Austin. When I told him I had worked for Alinsky's Fight Organization in Rochester, New York, one summer, we exchanged high fives. Like his mentor, Harold Washington, Jesse felt the same burning desire to change machine politics from the inside.

During one of our talks, Margaret Burroughs, founder of the Du-Sable Museum of African American History (the first in the nation), longtime park commissioner appointed by Harold, and the closest thing to a saint in the black community, popped in. She always called me "Admiral." Once, when she said she would ask the board to raise my salary, I replied that I would work for nothing I loved my job so much, but if she told the other commissioners, I would say she had Alzheimer's. How she laughed. Like Harold and Jesse, laughter carried her through dark times.

Everyone knew Daley's election sealed Jesse's fate. Daley did not want to be the one to fire the first black head of the park district, so he left Jesse to twist in the wind until he resigned. At a December 1989 press conference, Jesse confessed that he was not receiving "implicit or explicit" support from Daley, adding that he understood a new mayor needed his own man in the job. He resigned.[3] In an earlier in-depth article in *Chicago Magazine*, Jesse was quoted as saying, "Anybody who thinks the Park District is not a political entity has got their head in the sand. My challenge is to make it a professional organization that operates within a political system."[4] I was an early example of Jesse's efforts at professionalizing the district, and I have no doubt that had Harold Washington not died, Jesse would have succeeded in that challenge.

Loyal staff threw a farewell party for Jesse at the Cliff Dwellers Club overlooking Grant Park and the lake. What an appropriate scene, not to mention the irony that all his staff were now political cliff dwellers waiting to jump or be pushed. We celebrated good times, and at the end "roundtabled" as we did at executive meetings. When it came to my turn, I said, "My definition of a friend is, no matter how much you want to, no matter how hard you try, you can never get rid of a friend."

BATMAN

April 1990.

After Jesse's resignation rumors and gossip ruled the park district, anticipating Daley's imminent broom sweeping. The *Tribune* listed five Madison-appointed executives, including "harbors and marinas honcho Robert Nelson," to be swept out in the housecleaning to come.[1]

The next day I received a call from one of the local racetracks to interview for a well-paying management position. Obviously they were convinced I would be swept out very soon. Concerned about my tenuous situation and curious, I got my hair cut and interviewed, which went well; they proposed a second meeting with the track owner. We set a time for a few days later while I mulled it over. I wondered if Zacchaeus was ever asked to manage the Coliseum in Rome and what advice he might give. His silence was a clear sign. There was no way I could work for a racetrack. Gambling on horses running around in circles? Where's the common good? I told the racetrack people I was not interested and waited.

Not wanting to be tagged with replacing the first black park superintendent with a white person, Daley chose another African American, Robert Penn. Penn had credentials. He served as head of the Buffalo, New York, parks for a couple of years and, more importantly, held a series of political positions. Investigated by a grand jury in 1975 regarding corruption issues in Buffalo, he was never charged. What public official has not been investigated? More recently he had formed his own consulting company serving minority businesses.

When I read he was a Vietnam veteran, an infantry captain with two Bronze Stars, three Crosses of Gallantry, a Purple Heart, and the army Commendation Medal for Valor, my heart raced. While he was being repeatedly shot in Vietnam jungles, I was burning my draft card in Central Park. Surely this decorated true hero would be told of my antiwar past. Bye-bye "harbors and marine honcho." Not only that, Bob Penn and his family moved into a house on my street.

As the new general superintendent was moving into Jesse's old office, the "Batman" incident exploded. Alvin McRoyal moored his boat in Fifty-Ninth Street Harbor for many years. He was the first boater I encountered at Fifty-Ninth when I started making unannounced harbor visits in 1987, when getting to know boaters in their harbor neighborhoods was my highest priority. Every weekend and many evenings, I visited each harbor to talk to boaters on their turf, which convinced me to establish "harbor councils." It was what the sixties were all about and what I was still about—Power to the People and all that. Like other grassroots organizations, the councils would be of great assistance pressuring the board to spend money on harbor neighborhoods.

Alvin McRoyal, a short, thin man in his sixties with a smoke ring of white hair and matching goatee, sat shirtless on a park bench. Despite his age he displayed a muscular chest with a long zipper scar from open-heart surgery. When I introduced myself, he looked surprised to see a white man in the harbor after dark. He told me I was the first harbor director to bother coming to "Chittlins Harbor," his term for the only all-black harbor in the system. The facilities were a mess. Dock gates were wrapped haphazardly in rusty barbed wire. The docks lacked enough outlets, so boaters bundled household extension cords down the main piers across the perimeter sidewalk inside a plastic pipe duct-taped onto a fence and fed through a side window of a toolshed to the fuse box. This temporary wiring was dangerous and in violation of city building codes. But, typical of black areas on the South Side, city inspectors didn't seem to care. The tool-shed was sheathed in corrugated metal, its sagging roof rusting away under multiple layers of peeling paint. Converted into a tiny yacht club called Museum Shores, it housed a small meeting room and two bathrooms, which it shared with park users who picnicked around the harbor in large numbers. The landscaping around the building was overgrown, and every inch of sidewalk pavement and curbing was cracked and crumbling.

Alvin was convinced the South Side harbors had been neglected due to racism; I could not disagree. Even though all the harbors were in states of disrepair, none was as bad as Fifty-Ninth Street, with Jackson Inner, also mostly black, a close second. I listened to Alvin for about an hour and dutifully wrote down his complaints, particularly his antipathy toward Joe O'Malley, the assistant marine director. He accused Joe of "corruption," giving special favors to boaters who promised not to complain. When I left Alvin that night with a promise for improvements and a plea for patience, he warned, "I don't have no kind of time," pointing to the scar on his chest.

The next day I confronted Joe about Alvin's accusation. Before I could finish, Joe interrupted and suggested I look into McRoyal's thick boater file, adding that on several occasions the other black boaters in Fifty-Ninth Street pleaded with him to get rid of the "McRoyal pain in the ass."

At first reading, McRoyal's boater file showed nothing unusual. He lived in the Hyde Park area, had owned an eighteen-foot runabout, the kind used for waterskiing, named *El Diablo*, since 1975, and had transferred from Jackson Outer to Fifty-Ninth Street in 1983. But halfway through his file was a 1985 memo from Security regarding a motor home McRoyal parked in the harbor parking lot next to his boat. It recommended creating an ordinance "to prohibit the parking of motor homes in our Parks."

Joe explained that Alvin and his girlfriend lived in the motor home all summer, which they hooked up illegally to boat outlets and occupied three precious parking spaces. McRoyal refused to move it because, as he wrote to Security, "there ain't no law against parking it there." He was right. Joe confirmed that no ordinance was ever proposed prohibiting motor homes in the harbors. He blamed Gerald Pfeiffer, who, not wanting to be labeled a racist, just ignored the issue, as he did another more sensitive issue involving a powerful South Side alderman.

When Rich Tinker conducted a complete audit of Fifty-Ninth, he discovered an old wooden powerboat with no name, registration, title, and no permit. Rich traced it to Alderman William C. Henry, a flamboyant South Side machine pol. "Big Bill" denied the boat was his, even though he used it frequently for parties and political entertaining. The night before it was scheduled for impoundment it mysteriously sank at its slip, spewing oil and gasoline into the harbor.

Salvage companies insisted on proof of ownership before touching it. With pneumacratic skill I convinced a scuba dive group to raise the vessel as part of a "harbor cleaning" public service. The boat planking was so rotten that the boat disintegrated in the raising process and had to be trucked to a landfill in pieces. As for "Big Bill" Henry, he was indicted in 1990 for corruption, but died in 1993 before his federal trial could be completed.

Sensing my ambivalence about Alvin's situation, Joe asked point blank what I was going to do about the motor home. He seemed to be testing me. Would his new boss, the liberal reformer, follow through with a new ordinance? Or would the fact that McRoyal was black and lived in my neighborhood cause me to persuade the first black administration in the parks to overlook the problem? In short, would racial politics trump doing the right thing for everyone in the harbor?

"Joe, how many other motor homes are there in the harbors?" I asked, remembering seeing two in Burnham and one in Montrose on my walk-arounds. Joe didn't know, so I instructed him to interview every harbor master about any and all motor homes and produce a written report.

That evening I stopped at Fifty-Ninth to see McRoyal's thirty-eight-foot motor home, which did indeed take up three parking places with two extension cords leading to boat outlets on the dock near his boat. After taking a few pictures, I knocked on the door. There was no answer and no one on his boat. A boater in the next slip gave me an earful about McRoyal's volatile personality and constant complaining about the rules. Did I notice the motor home was parked over the storm drain? I was told that some nights, McRoyal removed the cast-iron cover and flushed the motor home's thirty-gallon holding tank. The drain was for rain- and storm-water runoff, not sewage, and emptied directly into the harbor. While motor-home parking was still technically legal, dumping human waste into the harbors was not. I thanked the boater for the information and put a note on the motor-home door for McRoyal to call me.

Joe O'Malley's report tracked down those motor homes I had seen in Burnham and Montrose, and two others in Diversey. All were owned by fishing charter captains, who preferred the mobile homes to the cramped living quarters on their boats. All the captains were white, which would offset any "racial discrimination" charge McRoyal might claim if motor homes were made illegal. I asked Nancy Kaszak to formulate an ordinance banning them. A check on all the other municipal marinas in lower Lake Michigan revealed that none allowed motor homes. I brought McRoyal into my office and formally ordered him to move his motor home based on illegally dumping sewage. At the same time, Joe informed the ship captains to move theirs out immediately, which they unhappily did.

Alvin McRoyal absolutely refused. Instead he circulated a petition among Fifty-Ninth Street boaters to keep it, but all refused to sign. The motor-home ordinance was enacted in the winter of 1988, and that spring McRoyal's motor home was towed out by Chicago police—not once, not twice, but three times. Each time he paid the city's tow and impoundment fees and immediately drove it right back to the harbor. He refused to pay park district fines, then wrote a series of strange rambling letters accusing me, Joe O'Malley, Rich Tinker, and Jesse Madison, of corruption and bribery. To Madison he wrote, "I feel like David up against Goliath but I feel good."

He copied handwritten manifestos to the mayor, investigative reporters, the FBI—everyone he could think of who might stop the conspiracy against him. His file grew thicker with my carefully written responses to his wild charges, transcripts of independent hearings, and numerous logged telephone threats—all the time-consuming things that government officials, especially pneumacrats, are forced to do, keeping them from important work.

When McRoyal refused to pay his fines for 1988, his 1989 boat permit was revoked; when he refused to remove his illegally moored boat that summer, it was impounded and chained to a dock; when he appealed his impoundment, an independent hearing officer ruled against him; when he deliberately removed the drain plug in the hull in a bungled attempt to sink the boat and sue for negligence, Rich Tinker quickly pumped it out and dragged it to a sandbar; when ice began to form in the harbor and he still refused to move the boat, it was towed.

In April of 1990, having received no further letters from McRoyal nor a new mooring application for *El Diablo*, I forgot about him. Bob Penn had just moved in, and I was preoccupied with meeting the new administration players. I didn't give McRoyal a second thought until he showed up one afternoon at the customer service counter dressed in old work clothes spotted with antifouling boat-bottom paint.

"You're too busy, right?" suggested my secretary, who for three years had endured abusive calls from McRoyal and wanted to get rid of him as soon as possible. "It's OK," I answered and walked to the counter. McRoyal slapped several Polaroid photos down on the counter like playing cards.

"You damaged my boat. What are you going to do about my boat damage," he said forcefully as I glanced at pictures of scrapes and gouges on his boat that could have happened in any number of ways. I answered, "That's a legal matter."

The next thing I knew I was laying dazed on the floor, my mouth full of blood. I heard McRoyal screaming he was going to kill me while staff shouted for Security. Even without my glasses, which were broken and halfway across the room, I saw Rich Tinker leap across the counter and tackle McRoyal. He had sucker punched me. I had fallen backward, hit my head on my secretary's desk, and then landed semi-conscious in a heap. Everything from my neck up throbbed with pain. Joe and Linda told me to lie still. The room was spinning as Security raced up from the lobby and subdued McRoyal. The police arrived a few minutes later and handcuffed him. He kept screaming.

"Go ahead and lock me up. I have nothing to lose. I'm dying. I'll be back and next time with a gun." By this time I was helped up into a chair with a handful of paper napkins against my mouth. My jaw was swollen, and my teeth were loose on the left side. Blood oozed both inside and outside my cheek. He had hit me hard enough that my teeth cut through the cheek from the inside. Staff wanted to call an ambulance, but I refused, preferring to be driven. A clerk found my broken glasses and tucked them in my suit pocket as Rich Tinker drove me to Grant hospital. X-rays of my jaw showed it was not broken, but I received seven stitches in my left cheek.

The next morning, as soon as he was released on bond, McRoyal telephoned the first of a series of death threats, which Andrea, one of my staff clerks, wrote down verbatim: "Tell Nelson he's going to see me every day for the rest of his life." That afternoon, he appeared at the counter again, somehow slipping past Security. He announced he had a gun, which freaked out everyone. I was rushed out of my office to a room in the basement until the police arrived and arrested him again. Even though he had no gun, I was furious. How could he get past the security desk? No one knew. I asked Security to check McRoyal's background and was horrified to discover he had served prison time for "assault with a deadly weapon."

That evening, my wife and I went out to a Hyde Park restaurant for some clam chowder—about the only thing my swollen jaw could manage. By the time we finished, it was dark. As we were leaving, McRoyal suddenly appeared out of nowhere and planted himself in front of us. "I know where you live, and I'm going to kill you," he growled. The man was deranged.

"Calm down, Alvin," I managed to reply. We hurried to our car and drove home looking anxiously in the rearview mirrors. Once inside Kris insisted I call the police. "There's nothing we can do until he actually commits a crime" was their reply. So much for crime prevention! I stayed up that night peeking through the window blinds, listening for cars, and crouching whenever one drove by.

The next morning, after carefully looking up and down the street and around the house, I quickly drove to the office. The McRoyal affair was hardly something I wanted to bother the new general superintendent with. What would I say: "Mr. Penn, I know you were nearly killed fighting in Vietnam, but I was punched in the mouth by a black boater and you need to do something." So I made a beeline for Nancy Kaszak's office. Like everyone else in the building, she was aware of the assault, but was too busy preparing to brief Bob Penn on pressing legal matters.

"Nancy, I'm worried that McRoyal will go postal. He has a long criminal record, you know: assault with deadly weapons!"

"That's not good," she said sympathetically, arranging a stack of files and binders on her way to meet with the new park superintendent.

"And outside a restaurant last night he threatened to kill me. Kris was there too. The police said there is nothing they can do. I think it would be prudent to assign one of our security officers to me for a while until McRoyal cools off. Security will need your OK."

She did not agree. "While you're in the building there's no problem, but after working hours, no."

I was not surprised. The new administration, sensitive to all the bad publicity Jesse received for hiring personal security guards, put a hold on anything related to "body guards." Instead the Law Department agreed to press charges against McRoyal and assign one of its lawyers to assist in the case. I was very surprised when the Cook County District Attorney's Office agreed only to a misdemeanor assault charge. The case dragged on into the summer.

On a quiet morning as I was typing up my résumé (Bob Penn requested them from all executive staff), I heard a bullhorn booming

Figure 9. "Batman" outside park district headquarters protesting general superintendent Robert Penn, 1990. (Photo by R. J. Nelson.)

outside. There on the sidewalk, standing on top of an overturned wooden box and dressed in a Batman costume complete with black mask, flowing green cape, and tights, was Alvin McRoyal, his girlfriend dressed as Robin at his side, ranting about corruption in the harbors and naming me as the Joker he would take down. Employees from all four floors crowded at the windows to see Batman, who periodically jumped off his box with arms outstretched and cape fluttering.

Penn of course wondered what the hell was going on and consulted with Nancy. She determined McRoyal had every right to play Batman as long as he didn't attempt to enter the building, or have the volume on his bullhorn so high it interfered with the business of the district. Just before noon Batman attempted to come to my office and was arrested. By three o'clock in the afternoon, he had posted bail and was back in his cape, bullhorn blasting. He was arrested again, this time with a stern written warning from the new general superintendent, which I appreciated, but which infuriated Batman.

Two days later, Batman returned with a large cardboard sign with stick-on letters that read "Robert Penn, The New House Nigger." A TV news truck pulled up, and a reporter began interviewing Batman—no wonder Pfeiffer had avoided McRoyal. I snapped a Polaroid picture and put it in Batman's ever-expanding file, which would be copied over and over as various new appointees of Penn requested information on the "Batman Incident." What an embarrassing first interaction between the superintendent of special services and Mayor Daley's new park district administration.

Penn never talked to me about Batman directly. Instead his new assistant and lawyer, Colette Holt, told me on his behalf, "handle it yourself." This meant monitoring the frequent comings and goings of Batman, alerting Security, and producing more reports, which were never discussed. Penn was too busy carrying out Daley's housecleaning. Amazingly, while my fellow Madison appointees named in the *Tribune's* O'Malley & Gratteau, Inc. column either resigned or were fired, I survived. I briefly thought of demanding a printed correction. I not only survived but was still included in executive staff meetings and remained on the influential budget committee. As summer came to an end, so did Batman's flourishes on the sidewalk. The death threats stopped shortly before his trial on the misdemeanor charge of "assaulting a public official."

The park district's lawyer, the Cook County assistant state's attorney, and I waited outside the crowded old courtroom over an hour for the jury to come in with a verdict. "It shouldn't be much longer," the state's attorney, a young man just out of law school, assured us. "This is a slam dunk." We could see Alvin sitting in the third row with a huge green oxygen tank on wheels next to him. Throughout the trial he never removed his breathing mask except when testifying against me, pausing dramatically and all too frequently to gulp oxygen as if it were malt liquor. But now, waiting for the jury's decision, it was turned off, and he was joking with his young girlfriend.

"In the matter of the *People v. Alvin McRoyal*, assault on a public official, how does the jury find?" The jury foreman, a young black man, stood and cleared his throat:

"Not guilty."

McRoyal jumped to his feet and shouted, "Amen." He flashed me a fiery look as he packed up his oxygen tank—still turned off—and swaggered out of the courtroom. I felt a sharp pain in my chest, not from fear of what he might do next, but from losing faith in the justice system. What were the jurors thinking when they deliberated? There were the police reports, the hospital stitches, and the eyewitnesses. The evidence could not have been more overwhelming. What reasonable doubt did they find?

The young state's attorney was also stunned. As the judge dismissed the jury, thanking them for their public service, the attorney followed them out into the hall. Part of his job was to find out why the jury failed to convict. He returned with not-unexpected reasons.

"This happens a lot when you have eight black jurors and four white. They voted along racial lines. I'm sorry," he said shaking his head while he snapped shut the clasp on his briefcase. It didn't help that the judge (also black) would not allow any of the incidents that led up to the assault to be used as evidence. All those letters and manifestos and his Batman routine might have swayed the black jurors, but none of it was allowed in.

"The black jurors said there were two factors: his public defender convinced them you provoked McRoyal, and more importantly they didn't believe your eyewitness."

"What? The eyewitness, my secretary, was a few feet away when he hit me."

The state's attorney sighed and explained that because my secretary was a carry-over from the Ed Kelly administration, the jurors believed she would say anything I told her to say in order to keep her job. They knew how Chicago clout worked. My mouth dropped. The state's attorney continued:

"The jury saw Mr. McRoyal as a long-term harbor resident treated badly by the government."

Of course. Those who don't get their way blame the government. Blame those who erect stop signs while dreamy Cadillac ads show luxury cars speeding down desert roads with the words "Live without

Limits." Blame those who have to tell customers they are not always right. Public servants are despised and rejected, called "desk jockeys" and "paper pushers," and considered inferior. Even Saint Paul, in his letter to the Corinthians, listed church workers in order of importance: "first apostles, second prophets, third teachers, and then workers of miracles, then healers, helpers, administrators, and speakers in tongues." Administrators were second to last only in front of worshippers whom no one could understand. When professionals, like police officers or teachers, make mistakes, they are suspended and assigned to administrative or desk duties and are known in the department as "desk donkeys." Public servants are considered screwups unable to obtain real employment, referees and umpires, tolerated for the sake of order and rule enforcement, but hated just the same. It is no accident that referees and umpires are dressed in black-and-white stripes like criminals.

The state's attorney looked at his shoes patiently waiting for my diatribe to end before shaking hands and leaving. The courtroom turned very noisy as the judge retired to his chambers while bailiffs and clerks prepared for the next case. The park district's attorney said it was pointless to appeal. I was sure he was right, but that didn't assuage my feelings about injustice.

I walked outside for some fresh air. Strong off the lake, wind stirred up dirt on the sidewalk at Thirteenth and Michigan. I turned my head away squinting and saw the viaduct at Sixteenth Street like a funnel collecting the dust. It was at that viaduct a military roadblock was set up to stop protesters during the 1968 Democratic Convention. I was there. From a swirl of litter around a sidewalk planter, I thought I recognized the voice of Zacchaeus.

"Now you know personally what injustice feels like. If you're going to be an effective pneumacrat, you have to relish the ironies of public service. Rejoice and be glad in them, for they reveal the difficulty of repairing the world. You could have easily made an exception and allowed Batman his motor home, which your predecessor chose out of expediency. Yet his exception did not advance the common good, which all exceptions must do. Instead you changed the rules, an exception in itself."

"But if the jury couldn't determine right from wrong, I failed."

"Precisely. You failed on a personal level. Individual failure is the natural goal of life. The flesh fails, the mind fails. Death is the ultimate proof that everyone fails."

"My thinking is becoming so negative, what with all the political changes, and now this."

"Another excellent point. All the great principles are given in the negative: the Ten Commandments, the inalienable rights of your Declaration and Constitution and its insistence on separation of powers and checks and balances, the Hippocratic oath to do no harm, the Pledge of Allegiance to one nation indivisible, all the movements from antislavery, antisegregation, antiwar, antiapartheid, and conscientious objection—do I need to go on?"

"You're encouraging me to think negatively."

"Absolutely. Thinking negatively means you can never be disappointed by human cruelty and betrayal. Isn't that what all spirits of the law are about?"

Before I could respond, Zacchaeus added that the occasional sucker punch in a pneumacrat's mouth is a good thing. "They knock one's ego down a notch or two." And then the voice faded into the wind.

Back at the office, Rich was seething at the verdict and after closing my office door quietly said there was a group of guys at Fifty-Ninth Street that would make sure McRoyal never bothered me again. This hint at some kind of physical intimidation was as shocking as the verdict. I warned him under no circumstances should he pursue the offer. Word of the verdict quickly spread through the building. Colette Holt took the time to stop in and say she was sorry I did not prevail. She urged me to sue Batman in civil court, where rules of evidence are different and a personal injury award would be almost certain. I was grateful for her gesture, but I had never sued anyone in my life and was not about to start. Using the law for personal satisfaction, let alone monetary gain, was not my thing.

One morning in April, Rich came into my office with what he called the best news of the year: "Goliath got him after all. Batman died of a heart attack today." Rich wanted to celebrate McRoyal's ultimate verdict, but I couldn't. For the four years of trouble he caused, I never thought of him as a mortal enemy, more a demented old man. Yes, he made threats against my life, but they were not real. He staged his narcissistic world in a play with several scenes: David fighting Goliath, Batman exposing the corrupt park district and assaulting me, the Joker. If he really wanted to kill me, he could have easily shot me at the service counter.

I will always remember my encounter with Alvin McRoyal as a play suspending my disbelief in order to be emotionally moved deeper into the ironies of public service.

PAUL MCCARTNEY

July 29, 1990.

Two days before the final concert of Paul McCartney's "World Tour" was to be held in Soldier Field, a logistics meeting took place in a sky-box above the south end zone as a gigantic stage formed at the oppo-site end of the field. Robert Penn presided. For Penn, Jimmy Duggan, and me, this was our first concert in the stadium. Bears games were our only guides. The McCartney concert carried us into unchartered waters—international waters—for this was a major international event: McCartney's final concert before his retirement. (He would change his mind later, of course.)

Tickets sold out in an hour. All the skyboxes were rented almost immediately, in many cases by groups of total strangers who divided up the cost of the twenty seats in each. But still, the demand for tick-ets was insatiable. On the promoter's suggestion, common in the rock concert world when concerts sell out, Bob Penn authorized over two thousand seats with minimal or blocked views. These too were gobbled up immediately. I had an idea for increasing seating: convert the NFL film and broadcasting booths to seating areas. These booths on the fifty-yard line, empty except at Bears games, afforded excellent sight lines to the stage. By using folding chairs we could add another three hundred seats. Bob Penn approved my plan. By the logistics meeting, all three hundred tickets were sold.

Bob Penn sat at a conference table, his back to the skybox windows, and somewhat nervously started the meeting. Hundreds of thorny details had been worked out, the two most difficult being fireworks to be fired off inside the stadium during the finale and the Bears' objections to use of the natural grass field for seating only a month before football season. In the middle of the table were stacks of blueprints, stage plans, permits, procedure manuals, and a bound copy of the Bears' lease opened to the section on the exclusive rights of the district to use the stadium, including the Bears' skyboxes, for nonfootball events.

Penn had barely opened the meeting when the Bears administrator strongly voiced his field concern: if it rained (as was forecast), the field would be trampled into a muddy mess. He doubted the park district could restore the playing surface for the first game in September and demanded the field seats be removed. The administrator, a former park district PR officer, was the Bears' attack dog, always looking for chinks in the lease, which was more favorable to the district than the Bears. For instance, the parks received all concession and parking revenues, worth millions annually, a percentage of ticket and skybox sales, and free use of two skyboxes, one for the general superintendent and one for the commissioners. In most NFL stadiums, such revenues go to the team owners.

The administrator was always complaining about something: security, the outdated scoreboard, inadequate washrooms, anything that might possibly be grounds for breaking the lease. But it was the grass playing surface that he criticized the most. If Kevin Butler missed a field goal, it was because the field was not level. If the grass was slippery from rain, it was our fault for not covering it; if the ground froze in December, it was our fault for not heating it. Even though an underground heating system was proposed to the Bears—at no charge when the old artificial surface was replaced by grass in 1988—they refused, testifying at a board meeting that the system, developed in Sweden, was unproven.

"The field seats have all been sold. They can't be removed," said Bob Penn.

Doubts that the district could get a muddy field ready for football season made Jimmy Duggan bristle. No matter what damage there might be, he and his staff would have it in perfect condition by the first kickoff. In his calm and earnest voice, Jimmy asked everyone to look out the window at workers pushing huge rolls of a special filter cloth designed to cushion the blows of thousands of dancing feet while allowing the grass to breathe.

"Here is a sample of the cloth," he said handing a foot-square piece to the Bears guy, who barely glanced at it before passing it to the fire chief sitting next to him.

"This filter cloth can cover the field for three days without damaging the grass, and there will be an extra layer placed in the aisles. Even if it rains, the cloth will protect the field, and it will be in perfect condition by the first game."

At this point the Bears administrator abruptly left the room. Bob Penn turned the discussion away from the grass to fireworks, a contentious issue for historic preservationists. But the fire chief expressed no problem with the fireworks, pointing out that the city used to hold its Fourth of July fireworks shows in Soldier Field where the rockets were fired from the fifty-yard line. (My dad took me to one of those shows.) The chief's only request was access to two water standpipes in the area where the fireworks would be set off for two pumper trucks. With all issues settled, Bob Penn adjourned the meeting, the last before the concert.

At ten o'clock on the night before the concert, Jimmy and I conducted a final walk-through of the stadium and stage areas. While we had spent two months worrying about mounting a mega-concert in a stadium built just after World War I, the stage pros were used to such venues. They arrived five days before the event in sixty semis packed with equipment. They brought diesel generators the size of house trailers to power the light and sound extravaganza. Hundreds of stagehands, electricians, and craftsmen descended on the playing field and constructed the stage and lighting system that extended from the north end zone to the twenty-yard line, all in less than forty-eight hours.

We walked around the stage and then up the tunnel to the play-ers' locker rooms. Under the north stands, the tunnel widened to the width of a two-lane road, the visitors' locker room on one side, the Bears' on the other. The utilitarian locker rooms were built of cinder-block with steel doors. But the McCartney staff had transformed the ugly space into an English village streetscape with facades of cottages, artificial shrubbery, flowers, and grass. Red imitation cobblestones ex-tended nearly half a city block with mannequins of English bobbies, gardeners smoking pipes, and British bulldogs and terriers. At the en-trance to the Bears' locker room, the steel doors were covered to rep-licate a palace gate with red kiosks on both sides and palace guards in full dress including beaver hats. Our mouths opened in amazement.

"The Bears brass would shit their pants if they saw this," Jimmy exclaimed and then snickered, "but they won't; the 'suits' never come back here."

The locker room, a space about forty by forty feet with open player lockers around the perimeter walls, was transformed into an English pub. Not scenery made to look like one, but a real antique English pub interior with ornate walnut paneling covering the players' lock-ers. The carpeted floor was covered with wood planking and sprinkled with sawdust. There were billiard tables and dartboards. Most spec-tacular of all, a long turn-of-the-century bar of carved English walnut with working Guinness and Harp taps, racks for glasses, and bottles of every imaginable British gin and single-malt scotch on glass shelves took up an entire wall of the locker room. Polished brass rails and an-tique chandeliers adorned the bar and lighted brass sconces gleamed against the varnished paneled walls. It even smelled like a British pub as if the walls and floor were sprayed with ale. The entire pub had been shipped from England for the tour.

"Would you like to see Paul's dressing room?" asked the production manager. He opened the door to Coach Ditka's game day office and ushered us in. What was formerly another bare space about twelve by twenty feet with an old metal desk and a few chairs was now as ele-gant as a Buckingham Palace sitting room. The walls were paneled in white with inlaid mahogany trim; the floor covered in white carpeting, oriental area rugs, and a Victorian sofa and chairs. Two magnificently carved tables, one with a book on Chicago, the other a linen-covered serving table with sterling silver candlesticks, tea servers, and flatware.

"When Paul and Linda arrive, their favorite foods will be waiting on this table," we were properly informed.

A large mahogany armoire dominated one corner where a production assistant was hanging clothes—suits, gowns, jeans, and casual wear for the fabled guests. One wall was outfitted with a white marble fireplace above which hung a signed portrait of Queen Elizabeth. As we considered bowing, the production manager flipped a switch. Unbelievably, natural gas flames licked and enveloped artificial logs. The fire quickly took the dampness out of the room and somehow filled the air with a faint smell of lilac. When Jimmy asked where the exhaust pipe for the fireplace exited, the manager smiled. "Outside, mates. Don't worry—we have your fire codes covered."

We were invited into the control room, actually the room where trainers for the Bears tended to injured players. Instead of bandages and buckets of ice, it was filled with electronics, light boards, monitors, and radios buzzing with worker conversations. Jimmy and I shook hands with the staff, and made one final inspection of the filter cloth on the field. Everything was coming together, or so we thought.

An hour before the concert, Daley's appointed president of the park board, Dick Devine, summoned Jimmy and me to the commissioners' skybox, presumably to get an update on the weather and condition of the field. Thundershowers had been pounding the stadium all afternoon. Underground drainage system pumps sucked as much water out of the turf as possible, but 90 percent humidity kept the field very wet. In a few minutes, the stadium doors were supposed to open, and patrons would rush to their assigned folding chairs on every square inch of the playing field. We were very worried that the turf would become the muddy mess the Bears administrator had predicted.

We walked to the commissioners' box down the corridor on the west wall of the stadium with windows overlooking the southbound lanes of Lake Shore Drive. Superintendent Penn had also been summoned. We could see the crowd gathering outside the gates in the narrow space between the stadium and Lake Shore Drive (before it was later reconfigured), separated by a line of waist-high concrete barriers. The crowd grew rapidly as more and more patrons funneled from both the north and south ends of the stadium to the west-side entrance gates.

"Why aren't they letting the people in?" demanded Devine.

Bob Penn said nothing. I explained that severe thunderstorms required McCartney's private jet to circle Midway airport for over an hour, thus delaying the dress rehearsal an hour and a half.

"The promoter won't let anyone in until after the rehearsal," I added.

"There are too many people jammed into that space. Call the promoter right now and get those gates opened," said President Devine.

But we couldn't call the promoter. He and his staff had their own radios on a restricted frequency. I told Jimmy to contact Soldier Field staff to find the promoter and give him one of our stadium radios. Five minutes passed. Jimmy's assistants couldn't find the promoter but were informed by concert security hired by the promoter that the gates would not be opened until Paul McCartney finished his rehearsal. Basically we were told to mind our own business.

A livid Devine, Penn, and I looked down on the swelling crowd. Not only were three or four thousand people pressing in from the north and south, large numbers of patrons were crossing Lake Shore Drive from remote parking areas on the other side. This was dangerous but not unusual and occurred before every Bears game. When a traffic light on Lake Shore Drive at the north end of the stadium stopped southbound traffic, fans scampered across the six lanes, and climbed over the Jersey barriers before the light turned green. But unlike a Bears game, where all the gates were opened two hours before kickoff, the gates were closed. The crowd was backing up onto the drive. Cars screeched to a halt to avoid hitting concertgoers, who pushed against those in front of them into the stadium wall and closed gates. Slowly and dangerously people compacted against stone walls and steel gates.

"Gentlemen, we are getting very close to a tragedy out there," exclaimed the president, his voice quivering. I too was concerned, being well aware of Cincinnati in 1979, when gates were not opened and eleven people were crushed to death at a Who concert.

We watched waves of flesh press against the stadium wall and heard people screaming: "Open the doors," "Stop pushing," and "We can't breathe." In a matter of seconds, the glass inside the steel grated windows flanking the gates was broken from futile attempts to get in. Then we heard desperate shrieking as more and more patrons crossed Lake Shore Drive and pressed against the crowd to avoid the traffic bearing down on them. At that point police blocked the traffic with squad cars, but it was too late. The crowd mass was too large with those in the rear pushing, unaware of the effect on bodies up against the stadium. To keep from being crushed, some patrons jumped onto the shoulders of those in front of them.

The president clenched his fists. "Get those goddamned gates open *now!*" He literally pushed me and Bob Penn toward the elevator. Knowing the elevator would take too long, Bob and I bolted down the emergency stairs, two and three at a time, to the main floor. We ran as fast as two middle-aged men wearing suits and ties could run. At the first closed gate, we heard muffled screaming and pounding on the twelve-foot-high steel doors. Thank God, those old doors opened inward. If they had hinged outward, there would be no way to open them against all those compressed bodies.

"As superintendent of special services, I order you to open up now!" I screamed at the event guards by the first gate. They looked at me suspiciously and did nothing.

"*Now!*" Bob Penn screamed in a powerful voice, far more authoritative than mine. The security guards hesitated. I notice two of them were part-timers used at Bears games. I pointed at them. "You know who we are. Open the gates." That did it. They unlatched the steel doors, which swung open hard from the tremendous force of compressed flesh.

Amazingly there was no stampede or panic, only relief from the pressure. Some patrons fell down gasping for breath. We ran to the next gate and the next. Once guards and ticket takers saw the first few doors opened, they followed suit. Dozens of patrons had to be helped in and seated until they could catch their breaths. In a few more seconds, they might have been asphyxiated. Bob Penn and I walked all the way around the stadium concourse just to make sure all gates were opened. "Welcome to the park district, Mr. Penn," I offered, but he didn't bother to even look at me.

I radioed President Devine that there were no injuries. "OK," he replied coldly. Bob Penn returned to the skybox while I made my way to Jimmy's office, where I collapsed on the couch shaking, not ordinary shaking from adrenalin and all the running, more like biblical fear and trembling. Had fans been crushed to death, I could only imagine the consequences—investigations, terminations, criminal charges, lawsuits, and trials. How could I face the sobbing stares of loved ones in courtrooms? Forget about being blamed in the press; I would blame myself for the rest of my life.

Thankfully the storms had passed. McCartney's "final" concert ended in perfection. I joined my wife and family in one of the converted NFL boxes for the last few numbers, punctuated by spectacular fireworks. Thousands of satisfied fans, holding mini-flashlights and swaying in waves, turned the stadium bowl into a galaxy of stars swirling beneath the city's skyline. When the concert ended, seventy thousand delighted fans quietly exited into the summer night as teardown crews swarmed the stage.

An hour later, Kris and I, with Jimmy Duggan and his wife, Shirley, were seated in a huge white party tent erected in the north end of the stadium for a late-night dinner party. Tickets were issued by special invitation only. Security was tight for the fifty or so guests; our credentials were checked repeatedly along the red-carpet entrance to the tent.

I was worried. Jimmy and I and our spouses were the only public officials invited, not even Mayor Daley, Superintendent Penn, or President Devine—just us. When word leaked out, I would catch hell for this violation of protocol. I had asked repeatedly for their invitations but was firmly denied by the production manager, "Sorry mate, that's the way Paul wants it."

While sitting at white linen–covered tables with expensive flowers and English sterling silver flatware, sipping champagne from crystal flutes, Kris dug her nails into my arm and whispered, "He's coming our way. Oh my God, and Linda's with him."

Paul McCartney and his beautiful wife, Linda, made their way through the elegantly set tables, shaking hands and talking casually to each guest. When they arrived at our table, we stood up and shook the famous hands. I introduced Jimmy and our wives. Paul smiled genuinely, disarming our nervousness. With a wink he said he knew who we were.

"I know you worked very hard to make all this happen, and I am very grateful," he said with such sincerity, it made me blush.

"You know, I love Chicago. It reminds me of Liverpool where I grew up and the spirit of the people there. Chicago has that same working-class feel to it," he said with a wistful look, as if fame and fortune frequently tempted him to forget his working-class roots. Perhaps that's why he only invited us stadium workers. "That's so much a part of my life, you know."

I fumbled for words and mentioned my English bricklayer grandfather on my mother's side. He asked if I knew where he immigrated from. When I confessed I didn't, he responded, "He sounds very Liverpool." Then Jimmy spoke of his Irish working-class background to which Paul responded, "You see. That's what is so great about Chicago; it's so mixed up."

"Chicago is a great city," I agreed, clearing my throat. "Some say it is the center of the universe."

McCartney laughed at my clumsy hyperbole. He introduced Linda to Kris and Shirley, and they chatted briefly. Our brush with fame was over. The ex-Beatle and his wife moved on to other guests, but not before looking over his shoulder. "Thanks again for making our final concert come off so well."

If he only knew!

In July of 1992, two years later, I drove to Montrose Harbor, the sunroof and back windows open, so cool air would waterfall across my thinning hair and down the back of my neck. It was eight o'clock on a Sunday morning, early enough to avoid the hordes of tourists and lakefront users that gridlock the drive by mid-morning. Montrose Harbor rippled calmly. Boats tugged their mooring leashes like dogs begging for walks. Sails climbed masts for the day's yacht club regatta while fishermen lined the horseshoe promenade, some sitting on overturned buckets and milk crates, casting lures or tying worm-baited poles to harbor railings. They sported sweat-stained baseball caps or Asian-style straw hats to ward off the rising sun. Most had walked over from the poor neighborhood of Uptown hoping to catch a bass, lake trout, or a mess of perch to take home for dinner. Some preferred the piers that jut out into the lake to minimize wave action in the entrance.

One of my proudest achievements stands on those concrete piers, two white, cone-shaped towers with red and green stripes and harbor entrance lights on top that frame the city skyline to the south. Photographers love the framing effect the towers provide. They replaced old and rusted steel-girder towers plagued by vandals who easily climbed up and smashed the navigation lights. The new Corten steel cones cannot be climbed and are covered with a special coating that prevents graffiti from sticking. I had plans to install identical ones at Belmont, Diversey, Burnham, and the south harbors—one harbor each year.

The Montrose harbor master was not scheduled until ten o'clock that morning, but his Whaler patrol boat was tied up and, as part of my routine, I checked it out to make sure it was clean and in good order. Then I walked into the Corinthian Yacht Club, which smelled deliciously of bacon and eggs, sausages, and pancakes. I stood in line with the members, loaded my plate, paid, and sat down with the early risers. One sailor was reading the *Tribune* and asked if I had seen it. "You might want to read about yourself," he said and handed me the front page, the lead story being, "Best Seat in House? You Can't Touch It," by Ray Gibson and Mark Caro, two of the *Tribune's* outstanding investigative reporters. The article, first in a three-part series, chronicled the multimillion-dollar abuse schemes of ticket brokers who held back tickets to popular events until prices rose for big profits. I was only mildly interested until I reached page two where half the article was about the Paul McCartney concert two years earlier:

> Even public venues are not immune to the politics of tickets . . . tickets were made available for more than 2,300 Park District employees, commissioners, their friends and other Chicago-area politicians, according to recently released district records and interviews.
>
> In true Chicago tradition, plenty of McCartney tickets were left for those who had clout. "The high and mighty started inundating the Park District for tickets,' said Robert Nelson, the district official who coordinated the concert, "Everybody wanted tickets."
>
> Nelson and Park District General Superintendent Robert Penn delivered. William Daley, a banker and the mayor's brother, bought seats from Nelson, according to Park District records.
>
> . . . Penn had already permitted the promoter to add an additional 2,460 seats beyond those specified in the contract and Nelson had also permitted more seats to be added in the days before the concert, records and interviews show.[1]

I bit my lower lip to keep from screaming. Three months earlier, Ray Gibson began filing dozens of Freedom of Information Act requests regarding the concert: all records, letters, memos, phone call logs, bills, ticket manifests, contracts, and so on. Answering his queries became so time consuming, I called him. "Mr. Gibson, come over and I'll tell you everything you want to know," I said, which seemed to surprise him, as if he assumed I had something to hide. But over he

came, and we went at it for a couple of hours. I freely admitted to adding three hundred seats before the concert. Providing more access and
more revenue was one of my proudest achievements. When I offered
to take him over to the stadium to show how I converted the empty
NFL film, radio, and press booths, he was not interested. He said he
would only believe me if I provided him with records of the users'
names. "Ray, that was two years ago; I don't remember their names."

"You didn't keep records of them?"

When I answered that no records of ticket buyers are kept, he
sneered, apparently convinced I was lying.

"Who else obtained those prime seats?"

I explained that many were sold to young people from park programs, guests of commissioners like Dr. Burroughs and President
Devine, others to park employees who had worked on the concert. I
freely admitted my wife, daughter, son, and I paid for four seats.

He interrupted suddenly. "What about the twenty tickets for Bill
Daley? Who used those tickets?"

"You'll have to ask him. I never talked with nor met the mayor's
brother." That was true. Superintendent Penn asked me to hold the
tickets, which were picked up by a messenger who paid for them with
a check, as I remembered. My spotty memory made him all the more
suspicious.

The interview dragged on. No matter how hard I tried, even dragging up my chaplain background and studies in ethics, I could not
convince him that my use of the NFL film boxes was altruistic. At one
point, when he wanted to know how many complimentary tickets
were handed out, I thought I could win him over.

"None," I answered proudly. "Nobody got in free, not me, my
family, Superintendent Penn, Bill Daley, or Mayor Daley—if he was
even there. I honestly don't know. During the contract negotiations,
I had argued successfully that 'no comps' be stipulated so that traditional political favors of free tickets would be eliminated."

Because Ray Gibson dutifully wrote this quote down, I naively assumed I would find it in his story. Foolish me. Anything that might

have indicated honesty or simple helpfulness by a public servant doing his job was not the point of his story and therefore excluded.

I handed the *Tribune* back to the boater who asked facetiously if I could get him tickets on the fifty-yard line to the Bears-Packers game. I smiled to conceal a deep sigh, finished my breakfast, and headed out for a routine inspection walk around the harbor. Except for some overnight litter, everything looked in order. I got back to my car and drove to Belmont. Rich Tinker was there getting ready to do boat inspections. He also asked if I had seen the *Tribune* article and then added with all sincerity, "No good deed goes unpunished."

More than a good deed, it was a pneumacratic exception to sky-box rules that would become a standard. All future concerts in Soldier Field added seating in the NFL boxes. What irony. The delicate balance between the press and public service can get out of whack so easily; no wonder the two distrust each other so much.

The only recourse for a public servant after such an article is to compose a letter to the editor. Mine was not published until a month later, and then next to a complaint letter about replacing park district meters with attended fee parking at Lincoln Park Zoo, another one of my innovations based on the success at the planetarium.[2] Perhaps the juxtaposition was just a coincidence.

GOLF DOME FROM HELL

December 15, 1990.

The "golf dome," another one of my lakefront initiatives, should have been erected yesterday in a vast unused parking lot at Wilson Avenue. Packed with cars during summer, it emptied in winter except for steady streams of drug dealers and their customers. Winter drug dealing, shootings, and constant vandalism would have been driven out by an inflatable golf dome overflowing with golfers hungry for an indoor driving range in winter. Instead, rolls of fabric air chambers laid limp, barely inflated and still attached to concrete-and-steel anchors. Yesterday I begged the Chicago Plan Commission to defer their vote against it, but the vote was predetermined by Mayor Daley. He killed the dome.

Two years ago two young African American investors came to me with the idea when no one else in the park district would even talk to them. Now they can't understand why it was stopped a few days before the grand opening. They had obtained all the permits from the park district. Park lawyers opined it did not have to go to the city's Plan Commission for Lakefront Protection Ordinance approval because it was not a permanent building and not on city property. But at the last minute, the city's lawyers disagreed and claimed jurisdiction, requiring Plan Commission approval with one additional strange condition: that the structure obtain a building permit each year, since only when inflated did it become a building. (Chicago's code did not cover inflatable buildings; the golf dome was the first test.)[1]

At the Plan Commission, I passionately argued that domes were admired and found up and down the lakefront: the Museum of Science and Industry with four domes, including a new one built in the last decade; Shedd Aquarium; Adler Planetarium; Navy Pier; and just north on Evanston's lakefront, the exquisite Baha'i Temple. All were aesthetically pleasing. The only difference was that the golf dome was temporary, like portable offices and classrooms throughout the city. More importantly, it would eliminate a dangerous, drug-infested meeting ground, generate revenue, and provide instruction for kids in our junior golf and disabled golf programs. I ended by saying, "Compromise, we know, is the art of politics. But I think expansion is the art of sustaining our principles. A principle is expanded, i.e., the Lakefront Protection Ordinance, in order to embrace a new idea. And when a principle is expanded to embrace a new idea that results in a greater public good, then it should be expanded."[2]

But my testimony was ignored. The eyes of the plan commissioners glazed over during my impassioned speech. Friends of the Parks, which had approved the project in March, reversed its decision and urged the commission to kill it. Yuppie cliff dwellers in the high-rises a quarter mile away from the site had complained it would ruin their lake view. Their letters, petitions, and angry phone calls flooded the mayor's office, upsetting Daley. Lakefront liberals, an essential part of his voter coalition, were not to be pissed off over some "blimp on the lake," as opponents labeled it. What a shame. What a great project. What a financial loss for two nonpolitical black entrepreneurs. What an incredible mess for which only I could be blamed. "The Golf Dome from Hell," I called it.

Construction fences were gone. The parking lot returned to drug business as usual. I counted five drug buys taking place as two cops drove by ignoring the transactions. Why should they risk a gun battle in a remote section of the park where nobody cared what happened in the dead of winter? Press coverage of the project's rise and fall was

accurate but gave the impression of a giant boondoggle benefiting in-
siders, not the public. That hurt, but I had to move on. As the voice
of Zacchaeus kept reminding me, "If you don't fail working for the
common good, try, try again."

My actual destination that freezing morning was not the golf dome
site but the wedding ceremony of Gerry and Kathleen Thomas, old
sailing friends from the Columbia Yacht Club. When they discovered
I served as a former chaplain, they asked if I would marry them. I
had performed about a dozen such ceremonies for couples like Gerry
and Kathleen, who didn't fit into traditional religious molds, but who
wanted a symbolic act to formalize their marriages: on a lakefront
beach at dawn, in a sculpture garden, under a waterfall, or in this case
in the simplicity of an apartment in Rogers Park. I considered my role
somewhere between priest and justice of the peace.

Gerry buzzed me in. As soon as I took off my coat, Kathleen
handed me a cup of steaming coffee. "You look like you could use a
little something in it," Gerry said with his wide smile. "I'm fine," I answered, trying to put the Golf Dome from Hell out of my mind. While
Kathleen excused herself to prepare food for some thirty guests, many
of whom I knew from Grebe Shipyard days, Gerry showed me around
the spacious 1920s apartment. The living room was set up with folding chairs facing away from the handsome fireplace and toward the
hallway, the couple thinking it would be easier for the bride to enter
from the adjacent bedroom. I suggested we turn the chairs around and
build a nice fire as backdrop for the ceremony. "You mean to remind
us what hell marriage can be?" Kathleen quipped. Gerry and I hauled
wood from the back porch and built a crackling blaze, which would
reduce to small flames and glowing embers by the time of the ceremony. It would be simple and relaxed. No giving away of the bride,
no bridesmaids or groomsmen, no professional photographers, taped
music, or videos—just simple vows exchanged before a warm hearth
and close friends.

The guests arrived, stamped snow off their feet, and piled their heavy coats in a bedroom. When everyone was seated, Kathleen, Gerry, and I stood before the fireplace. My homily or "charge" was not a sermon, more like a love letter, like Saint Paul's famous love letter to the Corinthian church so often read at weddings. I had been writing and rewriting my letter for over thirty years. In one very personal sense it was a love letter to my wife about our own marriage. In spite of all we had been through, we never stopped believing that love once found cannot be lost.

"Kathleen and Gerry, I require and charge you both, as you will answer to those who love you, especially those who will take your love as their example . . . to know deeply and intimately, as deeply and intimately as you know your own selves, that marriage is neither legal contract nor social requirement nor religious institution; know that marriage is but a symbol, a very fragile symbol, of the power of love in this world.

"As you exchange vows and promises, you commit yourselves to the most profound of divine principles which is this: belief in love cannot be lost. The proof of love's power to transform despair into joy, hatred into harmony, and even war into peace, begins when two people, face to face for a lifetime, unite in that love which bears all things, hopes all things, endures all things.

"You are therefore charged to *be* in love. When the world gives you the choice between standing in line and falling in love, take the risk and plunge. Whether romantic, pragmatic, intense, detached, or highly principled, be immersed in love like agates in a mountain stream polished smooth with age. For immersion in love is the essence and ground of our being.

"You are charged to learn the language of love, both the language of the body and the language of the mind, that language so often unspoken between a husband and wife, yet recognizable and memorable in those surprise moments of discovering new depths in one another; that language distilled by poets, like this poem, 'A Decade,' by Amy Lowell:

'When you came, you were like red wine and honey,
And the taste of you burnt my mouth with its sweetness.
Now you are like morning bread,
Smooth and pleasant.
I hardly taste you at all, for I know your savor;
But I am completely nourished.'

"Gerry and Kathleen, you will be completely nourished when you discover your partner to be far more important than yourself.

"You are charged finally and reverently to give away your love. Give it freely and without reserve, not only to friends and family who expect it, or to children who require it. Bestow your love on those who have no expectations, on those who are powerless to demand, on those who cannot and will never ask. For by giving love away you prove its power and complete that sacred circle symbolized in the wedding ring: for God is love and God so loved the world, we can do no less. Amen."

As the charge ended, I immediately started thinking about the golf dome fiasco, reminding me that the opposite of love is betrayal, in that case a bureaucratic betrayal. The project did not die; the city, my city, killed it. It is one thing to love a partner for better or worse, quite another to love a city. In marriage there is a union, a mutual love with deeply believed vows. But when you truly love a city, the city takes no such vows. Those coffee mugs sold to tourists with a line drawing of a heart and the city at sunset that say "Chicago loves you" are lying. Nelson Algren knew better. In his famous prose poem *Chicago: City on the Make*, in the chapter, "Love Is for Barflies," he wrote, "And Chicago divided your heart. Leaving you loving the joint for keeps. Yet knowing it never can love you."[3]

The city grabs your love and does not love back, demanding instead a prenup agreement governed by rewards and punishments. The city cares nothing for dreams and desires. It provides necessities and luxuries, but never out of love. As it rewards hard work and luck, cunning and success, with money and power, it also punishes with failure, loss of reputation, and worse. But never does it bestow love on those who proclaim theirs. And if you fall out of love, your only choice is to divorce and move away. Love it or leave it. The city, an immovable kingdom that rules by a secular form of divine right, will not move. Those subjects who mistakenly lavish their love on its elected monarchs are merely fooled into loyalty for what they think is the common good, when it is for the good of the rulers that we are required to love our city . . .

Kathleen tugged my elbow and whispered they were ready to exchange vows. I stepped back as they faced each other. A second marriage for both, they put aside any sadness from the past as they entered the symbolic zone and beamed at each other. The beam is always the same, so intense it paralyzes any attempt at gesture. I have never seen a bride or groom use hand gestures while repeating their vows. They stand straight and solid leaning toward each other like a gothic arch. Their eyes reflect a momentary glimpse into the ideal of love itself, and as minister I have the pleasure of seeing that glimpse up close, like peeking into the raised chalice of wine as it transubstantiates into divine presence.

And then Kathleen's and Gerry's ceremony was over, the symbols put away, replaced by champagne and applause. While Gerry put another log on the fire, Kathleen motioned me into the kitchen. She handed me the license to sign. In the blank for title, I wrote "M.Div." for master of divinity and handed it back. She looked at my scribbling which made the v look like an r, and asked jokingly, "Is that 'marina director' or what?"

On that note I took my leave. My role of secular priest ended, and I was tired. A blast of wind off the lake returned my soul to cold reality, to the city's impersonal world of principalities and powers and players with long knives against my paper shield of wedding vows. It does not matter what happens. I will always love Chicago.

MBE/WBE

February 4, 1991.

Colette Holt, Bob Penn's assistant superintendent for external affairs, was my favorite member of Bob Penn's administration. Tall and beautiful with straightened black hair coifed perfectly down to her shoulders, she was a lawyer with a sharp and ready wit, and a passion for public service. She loved to tell stories about her father, one of the legendary Tuskegee airmen in World War II. A very good negotiator, she served as Penn's lightning rod.

She wanted to see me regarding compliance with the "minority business/women's business" ordinance put in place last year. These ordinances were enacted after a city audit showed that 94 percent of city contracts were in the hands of white contractors. A park district audit had found the Marine Department noncompliant in purchases from certified minority-owned and women-owned businesses. And Larry Cain, the new contract compliance officer in purchasing, had told Colette that I was "not cooperating." What he really meant was I refused to route supplies of Marine materials and services through questionably legitimate minority business/women's business enterprise (MBE/WBE) firms he was connected with who charged higher prices than traditional marine sources, all of which were white owned. From the first day he and I met (when he bragged that he was a Harvard Law School graduate), I smelled a rat. He used his Ivy League pedigree to develop schemes certifying phony MBE/WBE

companies. I tried to avoid him and his increasingly frequent inquiries into Marine business contracts. I didn't think Colette was aware
of his scheming; she simply wanted to make sure there was compliance with the statutes.

Colette's door was open, and though she was on the phone, she
waved me in with a full arm sweep and a smile. She covered the
mouthpiece with one hand and said, "Admiral of the fleet, what are
we going to do with you?" While talking with some alderman, she
handed me a spreadsheet on harbor expenses and contractors.

She hung up the phone and swiveled her chair toward me. "We
have a problem of compliance in the Marine Department, Admiral.
All your vendor companies are Caucasian owned," then she added
deadpan, "Is that why all the boats out there are painted white?" I
laughed and assured her that boats came in several colors—including
black—that the boat I sailed across the Atlantic was black, that during
the American Revolution warships were painted black so as to be invisible to the enemy.

"Sort of like slavery," she shot back.

"Very funny," I replied and then returned to noncompliance. "Did
you get my memo on the Marine Department's outreach efforts?" I
asked referring to my lengthy defense of repeated attempts to find minority marine contractors and suppliers.

"Yes. Unfortunately, except for the harbor uniforms and fuel contracts, none of it complies with the ordinance guidelines."

"I understand, but the marine industry is small, specialized, and
all white owned. There's nothing I can do about that. But I do have a
question. Most of our supplies come from two local businesses which
are owned jointly by husband and wife, whom I have worked with
for over fifteen years. They are legitimate joint owners who set up
their businesses as equal partnerships. Why can't a legitimate fifty-
fifty husband-and-wife-owned business qualify as a 'women's business
enterprise?'"

Colette theatrically exhaled a sigh big enough to rustle papers on
her desk. "Because the ordinance specifies 51 percent ownership and
control by minorities or women."

"But Colette, in these Chicago-based mom-and-pop marine businesses there's only a one percent difference. One percent!"

"That doesn't matter. Fifty-one percent is the legal requirement. I suggest you talk to these couples and convince them to change their incorporation documents to fifty-one–forty-nine and become certified minority business enterprises. As you say, it's only one percent."

"I already suggested that. One of the couples who took over the business from parents were insulted. For two generations they have proudly operated as a fifty-fifty family business and aren't about to change. The other couple, who by the way have substantial contracts with the US Army for armored personnel carrier rigging components, told me to get lost. Both couples are my age and started their business in the sixties when equality was far more important than certification as minority owned. Do you see what I'm getting at?"

"I see perfectly, and it's an interesting argument I've heard before. Nevertheless, to comply with the law they have to change, not the law."

"What you are saying is they are being punished for believing in equality."

"Oh, please. Equality of opportunity is not a problem for them."

"I totally agree, but I'm not arguing on their behalf. I'm arguing on my behalf as Marine Director trying to operate in the best interest of the public. These two businesses are honest, efficient, and cost effective. You are demanding the letter of the law while they embody its spirit. Can't there be exceptions?"

"No, the courts have ruled repeatedly on the side of MBE/WBE ordinances. Look, the ordinance doesn't say that every contract has to be with a minority-owned firm; it only requires a percentage of your total expenses, 25 percent MBE and 5 percent WBE. So go find some certified contractors to reach those percentages. You can do it, Admiral."

But I couldn't. I had scoured every distributor and manufacturer of marine supplies nationwide and all, including companies capable of making our new buoys, were white owned. There was no way to be in compliance unless I played games with the compliance officer in Purchasing.

"Don't I at least get credit for the golf dome concession and its legitimate African American owners?"

Colette shook her head. "Don't you mean blame and embarrassment to the district?"

"I admit it turned out badly, but not until the last minute when a bunch of white people killed it. I worked for two years to get that MBE enterprise operational, and in spite of kickback rumors, it was all above board."

"Fine, right idea, wrong procedure. You violated the Lakefront Protection Ordinance."

I threw up my hands. Before I could shift the discussion to Larry's shenanigans, Colette's intercom buzzed. She excused herself for an urgent meeting with Superintendent Penn. She told me we would continue our conversation later then slipped into Penn's office through an adjoining door.

I walked back to my office, sat down, and put my feet up on the desk. Another confrontation between the spirit of a perfectly good law and the absurd rules made to implement it. I switched focus to Larry Cain. He was dangerous. If I was not very careful, I could easily get into deep trouble. One authorization to purchase supplies through one of his dummy corporations at inflated prices would make me a co-conspirator. Resisting was not easy. He buttonholed me once or twice a month. I did take notes on our discussions, meetings in the cafeteria, and phone calls. If he ever directly discussed payoffs or kickbacks, the FBI would have been my first call. But I didn't have to call. On July 24, 2000, Mr. Cain was sentenced to twenty-seven months in prison for bribes and kickback schemes from various park district contractors, in part to support his cocaine habit.[1]

"LAKEFRONT'S SMALL WONDER"

June 3, 1991.

According to baseball rules, three strikes and you're out. But in spite of the Batman saga, McCartney party, and golf dome embarrassments, Mayor Daley and his handpicked park general superintendent still retained me as superintendent of special services and senior official on the new park district team. Today was the grand opening of the first new harbor building in Burnham Harbor in forty years. While Mayor Daley declined my invitation, Bob Penn not only agreed to christen the new building, but when I asked if Jesse, who was responsible for most of the work and permitting, could also be present, he had no objections.

The structure stands two stories with boater and public washrooms, patios and harborside benches, laundry and showers, a ship's store concession, and a tower-like second-floor office for the harbor master. The *Tribune*, noting its presence among the gigantic structures around Burnham's perimeter—Field Museum, Shedd Aquarium, Adler Planetarium, Meigs Field terminal, McCormick Place, and Soldier Field Stadium—called it the "lakefront's small wonder." The writer, M. W. Newman, wrote, "Perhaps the biggest surprise about this cheery lakefront addition is that it emerged from the Chicago Park District. The parks have an architectural heritage they seldom have been accused of living up to in late years."[1]

The approval process for that "architectural heritage" on Chica-

Figure 10. From the left: unidentified, Robert Penn, Jesse Madison, and the author at the Burnham Harbor building dedication, 1991. (Photo by Kris Nelson.)

go's lakefront was excruciating. The Burnham station took four years, beginning with a design by Bill Latoza and Eric Davis, with Walter Netsch looking over their shoulders. They designed it in wood to blend in with other historic harbor facilities, the coast guard stations in Jackson Park Harbor and the Turning Basin, both on my schedule for restoration. While boaters demanded practical things like more showers and laundry facilities, city planners insisted on less pitch in the roof. Friends of the Parks wanted no building at all, but relented when Netsch showed that two current structures, the condemned harbor master office shack built as a toilet building for the Century of Progress in the thirties and an ugly toilet/fish-cleaning "Charter Boat Headquarters" building, would be torn down. He convinced Erma Tranter, executive director of Friends of the Parks, who wanted a much smaller building, that it was a two for one.

But after she joined the consensus to build it, the park board almost killed the project anyway. In the fall of 1989, the Burnham station was up for board approval when, as the *Tribune* recalled, "the commissioners turned their wrath on Robert Nelson" and Commissioner Anthony Bass ridiculed the proposal, calling it a "White Hen Pantry for the Rich." The building included a mini–convenience store, which was partially funded by monies left over from a construction project in long-neglected Garfield Park. Bass said that the transfer violated a federal consent decree ordering the parks to rectify the neglect of parks in poor neighborhoods.[2] Ironically, this was the same argument Jesse used to fund the restoration of the coast guard station in Jackson Park Harbor, which would reopen in 1992.

After the design was approved by three different agencies and funding from five different sources was Scotch-taped together by Jesse before he resigned, the $564,000 contract was publicly bid. The low bid was awarded to Firehouse Construction Company, and controversy immediately raged. Firehouse was nonunion. The principals, Bill Boardman and Dave Sullivan, were ex-employees of US Steel and, when it closed, activists in the battle over lost pensions and benefits. They were also products of the sixties and lived communally with their families in an old firehouse on east Eighty-Seventh Street, which was also their shop. Dave had been heavily involved in Students for a Democratic Society (SDS) and was arrested in a famous Ohio demonstration against the Ku Klux Klan and was successfully defended by attorney William Kunstler, the famous defense lawyer for many activists, myself included, during the civil rights and anti–Vietnam War movements. None of this was known when the contract was awarded, but when word leaked out during construction, all hell broke loose. Immediately the unions cried "union busting," even though Firehouse had contractually agreed to pay its workers union scale, a normal provision in such rare cases in Chicago. The unions found other ways to fight: physical threats, slashed tires, stolen materials, and other forms of harassment. For instance, when the appointed time came to seal the high-voltage electrical cable feed in concrete, which required a city inspector to be present for the pouring, the inspector mysteriously didn't show up and the truck full of hardening concrete had to be dumped next to the harbor and hauled away at considerable ex-

Figure II. "Lakefront's Small Wonder" building, 1991, with sailboat and sailors from the Goldman disabled sailing program. (Photo by R. J. Nelson.)

pense to Firehouse. Death and arson threats were so common, Bill and Dave slept on army cots inside the framed-in building with loaded handguns under their pillows. I looked out for their interests as best I could, hiding expensive building materials in Soldier Field Stadium until they were needed. In spite of the harassment, the building was finished on budget, on time.

The building received a prestigious award from *Architectural Record*. The press did its job, not spreading government happy news, but chronicling the city's unique, ever-evolving lakefront. And fully disabled-accessible public bathrooms were added. The small wonder of Burnham became the focal point of Chicago's busiest harbor neighborhood.

After the christening ceremony, Bill and Dave showed me a bronze sculpture of a sailboat welded into the wrought iron main gate, which they explained was a gift. Not designed from a generic model, the boys from Firehouse had cast a replica of the sailboat I had to give up as a condition for taking the job of director of harbors. I was moved.

A COAST GUARD STATION RESTORED

August 12, 1992.

After thirty years of abandonment, neglect, and a devastating fire, the flags on the Jackson Park coast guard station waved proudly. The building was restored to its 1907 original design. The widow's walk and lookout tower, once manned by rescue sentries, now offered tourists a panorama of the harbor and Jackson Park. At night the tower and grounds were illuminated with lights built into the eaves. A hundred-year-old tall ship, on loan from its charter company, was moored at the gas dock for the reopening celebration. Additionally, one of the Monroe Harbor water taxis sat halfway up the marine railway leading into the boat room.

The careful historical restoration reflected the new purpose of the Jackson Park Harbor Station, as it was officially rededicated. Harbor master offices in Fifty-Ninth and Jackson Harbors were combined; its new fuel facility replaced the EPA-cited, old, leaking facilities in those harbors. Fully accessible public washrooms, boater washrooms with showers, laundry facilities, and a ship's store were added as well. The original second-floor apartment was completely made over so that a harbor master could live there, like the caretaker, Gloria Fallon, at the yacht club, and deter vandalism, which had been a huge problem around the south harbors. An intimate little restaurant with indoor and harborside porch seating invited neighbors and joggers to stop in

Figure 12. Jackson Park Harbor Station after restoration, 1992. (Photo by R. J. Nelson.)

for a meal. The fueling facility extended out from the restaurant, with the idea that the restaurateur could offer discounts on either food or fuel to attract boaters from other harbors. Not since Sharky's, a shrimp joint between the Chicago Lock and Navy Pier, was demolished, was there any place on the lakefront where a boater could dock and buy fast food. The rest of the second floor was converted into a meeting room/mini–maritime museum with photos of the Columbian Exposition and the early days of the harbors.

The ceremony was fabulous. While Mayor Daley was invited only to decline, hundreds of people showed up, including the original station master's daughter, who lived there most of her childhood. She brought thick albums of pictures showing much of the station's history. Superintendent Penn and I gave speeches. Jesse (not present this time) and Al Nieman were applauded for finding the $700,000 plus from consent decree escrow funds, which Commissioner Bass supported this time. Luke Cosme told lakefront history stories.

But the real luminary was former park district architect Bill Latoza. Trained as a restoration architect (Bill had worked on the Statue of

Liberty restoration), he researched the original blueprints and drew up the restoration plans. Unfortunately, Bill abruptly left the district in late 1990, largely because of this project. All park district architects belonged to a union with strict work rules. Bill was ordered to work on more pressing projects, but he broke the rules. He often stayed after hours, not to mention spending countless hours at home working on the project. For his dedication he was punished with a written reprimand from his supervisor, also in the union, a common relationship in most departments at the district. No wonder so many young professionals, who idealistically enter public service only to be reprimanded for their "above and beyond" contributions, leave for smoother waters.

Other conflicts with unions emerged on this project. When an outside contractor excavated the area for the underground fueling system, the backhoe operator was about to remove an ailanthus tree, no more than two inches in diameter, growing out of cracked concrete, but was stopped by a union representative who insisted only union park landscapers could remove the tree. I happened to be there at the time and argued, but to no avail. I asked when a union landscaper would cut the tree down and was told, "Maybe this afternoon, maybe tomorrow. We're real busy." Fuming, I waited until the workers broke for lunch, drove to my house only three blocks away, retrieved my trim saw out of the garage, drove back, sawed the ailanthus off at the pavement, cut it into short pieces, and stuffed them into my trunk. When the contractor's men returned and asked what happened I said, "The landscapers must have come and removed the tree." Not wanting to hear the shouting between the contractor and union rep as to who removed the tree, I got the hell out of there hoping no one saw me putting the weedy branches into my trunk. The excavation resumed and was completed by the end of the day.

My standing with unions at the district had become tenuous at best. The realization that they were targeting me sank in. There were too many confrontations like over the Firehouse Construction contract, which I had nothing to do with but the union believed I had engineered. In Golf, I replaced the old farm tractor mowers with state-of-the-art hydraulic riding mowers that can adjust heights of fairways and roughs at the flip of a switch. I did not realize the old farm tractors, because they had a cab over the driver, required union "chauffeurs" to operate at a much higher pay rate. The head of the chauffeurs' union filed a grievance over the subsequent loss of twenty-eight summer chauffeurs. (In golf season, politically connected laborers were chosen to operate the old tractors at a much higher rate of pay—another patronage perk.) The director of labor relations worked out a compromise by finding ten additional summer chauffeur jobs in various parks where the old tractors were donated; but in the eyes of the union, I deliberately eliminated eighteen jobs. I wondered if my union confrontations were reaching Mayor Daley's ear, especially after my confrontation over gifts of flowers to my secretary back in February.

"Flowers for the Harbor Boss," a messenger announced as he delivered a long white box embossed with a gold rose and tied with gold ribbon but no card. At first I thought it was for my secretary, who received flowers almost every day from her boyfriend, but they were addressed to me. Inside were a dozen long-stem roses, but instead of fragrant red, white, yellow, or vermillion roses, they were brown, dry, and dead. Tucked under the roses was a copy of the "Leap Year Edition" newsletter from Union 46, which represented most park district workers, including all harbor staff.

The lead story in bold print was entitled "This Could Be You":

A young woman who works in the Ad Building on occasion receives flowers from a special person, her boyfriend. This action, of course, makes the woman feel happy and good about herself, and adds some color and change into an overcrowded, under-ventilated, dirty office environment. It lifts employee spirit, and helps with the overpowering morale problem that engulfs the entire Park System.

I read on and realized the article was about my run-in with my secretary. Not only did I tell her to stop her boyfriend from bringing flowers, I insisted any flowers received must be taken home the same day. I found the story's description of my "dirty office environment" amusing as ironically it was cleaned daily by the same union's employees. How then could it be dirty? The half-page item ended in bold print: "We'd like to recognize Mr. Nelson for the way he treats employees. Roses are not permitted in his department, but thorns would be more appropriate anyway."

As I finished reading, I glanced at my secretary sitting at her desk, her back to my door, busily shuffling papers and surprisingly grabbing the phone when it rang before any of the other office staff, something she rarely bothered to do. Our five years together had come to this: an exploited peasant and evil lord of the manor morality play. Naturally the newsletter left out three years of disciplinary actions against her. In response to each one, she filed a grievance, complaining she was singled out for punishment because she came from a previous administration—the same argument used in reverse at the Batman trial. Each grievance led to a hearing. She lost them all except one— known as "the case of the long-stem roses."

About six months earlier, she found a new boyfriend, a park gardener who worked in the district's nurseries growing flowers and plants for public gardens throughout the city. He would select elaborate bouquets of flowers, especially roses, and deliver them to her at the Marine Department office, often three times a week. Not only did she and her boyfriend act like lovebirds in this desktop garden, secretaries from other departments came by every day to gape at the flower arrangements, talk, and gossip. The other clerks in my office began complaining.

One day the president of the park district board, Dick Devine, very annoyed that he was unable to get through to me by phone, stopped me in the hall and in no uncertain terms told me to "straighten out the phone problem in my office." After that embarrassing incident, I called her in and told her the flower deliveries had to stop. When I issued her a written reprimand, she naturally filed a grievance. Since other clerks received flowers and were not disciplined, the union cited the incident as a clear case of discrimination.

I was the one officially reprimanded because I could not produce a written "flower policy" applicable to all staff. My hands were slapped hard, and a copy of the reprimand was placed in my permanent file along with the Marquette lock policy.

The next day I issued a one-sentence flower policy: "Flowers may be received during office hours but must be taken home the same day."

Remembering Zacchaeus's suggestion to enjoy ironies, I took scissors out of my desk and trimmed the long stems of the dead roses, arranging them to look full in a waterless vase. Then I moved the flowers to the middle of my desk, so that my secretary would see the dead blooms, no doubt wondering what retaliation was coming that would give her cause for another grievance. Indeed her position hung by a union-made thread. Ultimately I managed to transfer her out of the building, where she bounced from park to park and finally out of the park district completely. In Chicago parlance such moves are called the "dance of the lemons."

That afternoon as staff were leaving I made sure I left first, carrying the vase of dead roses per the new policy. Not only did I have to create the rule, I had to follow it to the letter, which was exactly how unions operate. How Zacchaeus must have laughed.

But at today's grand reopening, union problems faded away while newly planted flowers bloomed. At the end of ceremonies a beautiful bouquet of red roses was given to the station master's daughter to a steady round of applause. The station soon became a very popular place, used extensively by neighborhood groups for meetings and parties in the boat room and outdoor patios. The restaurant was featured on Channel Seven's "Top Ten Best Restaurants in Chicago" list. Both the *Sun-Times* and *Tribune* printed extensive stories. Like the Burnham building, the project received another *Architectural Record* citation, as well as the Hyde Park Historical Society's Paul Cornell Award for historic preservation.

As I joined guests taking turns climbing up to the widow's walk to take pictures, I remembered one of my favorite Emily Dickinson poems:

The Props assist the House
Until the House is built
And then the Props withdraw
And adequate, erect,
The House supports itself
And ceases to recollect
The Auger and the Carpenter—
Just such a retrospect
Hath the perfected Life—
A past of Plank and Nail
And slowness—then the Scaffolds drop
Affirming it a Soul—

For me, becoming a pneumacrat was the perfected Life. To bring access and new life to the Jackson Park Harbor Station, at the intersection of green space and blue space, was not just the achievement of restoring a public building. Dedicating its future to public use affirmed my soul that roamed Chicago's lakefront and always will.

A REPORTER FALLS OVERBOARD

On March 24, 1992, I received a hand-delivered note from President Devine that read: "What are we doing about this? Please answer ASAP." Attached was a copy of a letter he had received from Dick Kay, the political editor for NBC Channel Five News. Kay demanded that his boat mooring in Monroe Harbor be renewed. It had not been renewed because Kay had refused to pay two fines: for not having a state of Illinois registration and for failure to display his harbor decal for the 1992 season. Dick Kay included a threat: "Please forward my renewal application. Failure to do so will result in legal action." His letter, printed on NBC Channel Five stationery, rambled on about how his boat, being federally documented, superseded state registration, how he was on "assignment in Washington" for most of last summer and didn't have time to stick on his harbor decal. I called Rich into the office and told him to bring Dick Kay's boater file.

"Did I do something wrong?" Rich asked perplexed.

"No, I just have to explain to President Devine why we are being threatened with a lawsuit by the political editor of NBC Channel Five. You might say this is a little sensitive," I said handing him Devine's note.

Dick Kay's file contained over twenty letters, reports, memos, and fines over the last five years plus numerous Freedom of Information Act requests, the sword of Damocles investigative reporters hang over public servants' heads. Dick Kay was a delinquent—paying his mooring fees late each year, always with some excuse or protest.

In 1987 when he protested the city's 50 percent mooring tax by refusing to pay, the city's corporation counsel wanted to prosecute a high-profile example and ordered me to withhold his mooring permit. While Dick Kay never knew this, I refused and turned the matter over to Nancy Kaszak.

After much research on the legal independence of the park district from the city, she concluded it was my decision whether or not Kay could have his mooring renewed, not the city's. So I gave Dick Kay his mooring back, not because he was political editor of Channel Five, but because hundreds of other boaters also refused to pay the onerous city tax. My consistent practice in all cases was to ignore the city's attempts to enforce it. As a pneumacrat I believed fines should be imposed to maintain order, not used as punishment, and authorities should impose them only after going the extra nautical mile. Because the city had no way to enforce it, the tax was eventually eliminated, and Dick eventually skated, thanks in large part to me.

Dick Kay loved to circumvent harbor rules. For instance, he documented his boat with the US Coast Guard in order to avoid sales tax. Documentation of vessels is a USCG licensing and mortgaging system designed for commercial ships and extended to yachts larger than twenty-five feet decades ago, probably through lobbying by luxury boat manufacturers. It was a system that superseded state titling and was important for banks, because the coast guard physically held the boat titles and all liens were "documented" by the federal government, saving the banks time and money searching for titles. By documenting with the coast guard, smart boaters with large boats could avoid state registration and therefore state sales taxes.

But in 1989, the Great Lakes states closed the loophole and jointly required state registration in addition to federal documentation. The state of Illinois, ironically using the Freedom of Information Act, demanded from me the names and addresses of all Chicago harbor boaters to cross-check against state registrations. Bingo! Illinois collected millions of dollars in unpaid sales taxes. The Chicago boating community lampooned me as a traitor for turning over the names even though the law gave me no choice—the names were subpoenaed. Even if they hadn't been, I still would have turned over the lists, because in this case the spirit and letter of the law were in sync. Documentation unfairly allowed the rich to avoid sales taxes while those who could only afford boats smaller than twenty-five feet—the vast majority in Illinois—paid when they purchased their boats.

When I was hired, Dick Kay invited me to be the featured guest on his half-hour television show, *City Desk*, to talk about harbor corruption and my ideas for cleaning it up. Because of his attacks on Jesse's administration I was wary, but Dick explained there would be two interviewers, himself and Ron Magers, the local ABC affiliate news anchor. I knew Ron from Grebe Shipyard, where he purchased and stored his boat. With Ron, I knew the interview would be balanced, and so I agreed. But when I arrived for the taping, Ron was not there. In his place sat Barry Cronin of the *Sun-Times*.

"Where's Ron Magers?" I asked while a technician wired me with a microphone.

"Oh, he couldn't make it," said Dick with a shrug while the director counted down the last few seconds to airtime. I was tricked. For a half hour, under what seemed like police interrogation lights, two of Chicago's toughest reporters tried to make me look like a political hack: repeatedly they asked if I would sell political fund-raiser tickets like my predecessor, who demanded boaters buy many tickets (at $10 to $500 each) in order to keep their slips.

"No," I said repeatedly. As part of Harold Washington's reform movement, at least at the park district, fund-raiser ticket sales were banned, so I never asked an employee, a boater, or anyone else to buy one. Nor was I ever asked to buy tickets. Forcing lower level employees to sell tickets with veiled threats about their jobs if quotas were not met caused incredible corruption. Political employees are easily tempted to trade favors for ticket purchases to make their quotas while their political bosses conveniently look the other way.[1] When Cronin and Kay got nowhere with ticket questions, they turned to the appalling conditions of the harbors, for which I enthusiastically explained my five- and ten-year remedy plans. While the program ended well, I never trusted Dick Kay again.

In the summer of 1988, we met by chance at Monroe Harbor. Furious that a one-hundred-dollar fee, which he considered an illegal tax, would be charged for a new water taxi service, he threatened that if I went through with my plan to replace the privatized water taxi service with a government-run service, he would personally "expose all the corruption" in the harbors. "Not only might I organize a class action suit, I will tie you up with FOIA [Freedom of Information Act] requests and do investigative reports you don't want to see on TV!" he shouted outside the harbor master's office.

"If you stop the water taxi idea, you will stop a great service for boaters in Monroe," I shot back, reminding him that I had moored my own boats in and operated businesses out of Monroe for a dozen years and knew the problems and solutions a lot better than he did. Dick would not listen.

Instead in March of 1990, still looking for corruption, he filed FOIA requests regarding federal and state grants for improvements to the launch ramps and related facilities. Instead of forwarding his requests to the new FOIA compliance officer, I decided to send him everything he asked for directly, as I had nothing to hide. When the Law Department found out, I was reprimanded for not going through channels, even though I had followed the spirit of FOIA.

"You're not going to give in to Dick Kay?" asked Rich.

"Is that what you think?"

"I think you are too soft sometimes. Here's a guy who flouts the system, does everything to get out of paying, accuses me of singling him out for inspections, and gets away with it just because he is a TV reporter. He's full of shit," said Rich, his sonorous Bahamian voice rising an octave or two.

"Speaking of shit, you're forgetting his 'overboard discharge' fine. He paid that one."

In August of 1988, Rich was doing routine sanitation inspections of boat toilets to make sure they did not discharge waste overboard, both a federal and harbor ordinance violation. Dick Kay's large sailboat, which he had purchased in Florida, had two toilets, both of which discharged directly into the water. In Florida and other coastal states, waste discharge into the oceans is allowed—but not in the Great Lakes. He was fined fifty dollars and informed by letter that he had to convert his overboard discharge system to a holding tank or his mooring would be revoked.

In September he marched to the Marine office counter and launched one of his tirades, refusing to pay. Because he had bought the boat in Florida, he argued it was grandfathered regarding overboard discharge. "It's not my fault the boat was built that way," he thundered, insisting there was a conspiracy against him because of his political commentaries. He announced he would file yet another FOIA request for every toilet inspection report on every boat in every Chicago harbor for the last five years. At that point I came out of my office and motioned him inside. In a firm voice, I told him to calm down, sit down, and write out a check for the fifty dollars if he knew what was good for him. He did not like my tone.

"I'm not paying until I see that every boat has been inspected. Furthermore, you have no right to board my boat. That's a violation of my rights to privacy and search and seizure protections of the US Constitution."

I sat quietly as the red in his face accentuated his gray-and-white beard. A big man, overweight and sloppily dressed in a worn tweed jacket too tight to button, he looked totally different from his persona on television. Arguing with him would go nowhere, so I tried a different tack.

"Dick, let me ask you something. While you were out at the counter loudly protesting your fine for dumping human waste into Chicago harbors, did you notice all the park district workers, department heads, and others walking by in the hall?"

"So what?"

"Well, how long do you think it will take one of them to find a telephone and call Michael Sneed's gossip column in the *Sun-Times*? I think you know that if Sneed files a FOIA request, I will have to produce the inspection report showing that your boat dumped feces out of not one but two toilets into Lake Michigan. Do you really want your name in the paper for illegally dumping shit into Lake Michigan?"

For a few seconds, he stared at me like a deer caught in the headlights. The game was up, and he knew it. Without accusing me of blackmail or some other conspiratorial nonsense, without another disparaging word, he pulled a checkbook out of his tweed jacket, leaned one elbow with its shiny leather patch on my desk, and quietly paid his fine.

"That was a fine, fine, day," said Rich, very fond of puns. I assured him that Dick Kay, with similar coaxing, would pay his current fine, and predicted (correctly) that President Devine would be relieved and impressed with the fair and thorough way we had handled it. Before Rich left my office, I asked him to calculate what Dick Kay and his FOIA requests had cost the district in employee hours and dollars. About an hour later, he handed me his calculation. The total came to about $9,000, triple what Dick had paid in mooring fees and fines over the years. Citizens don't care about such things, but I did. What really bothered me was my inability to convince Dick, as I couldn't convince Ray Gibson, that he was wrong in his cynical assumptions about public servants. Five years had passed since my appearance on *City Desk*. In spite of our numerous interactions, he never asked a follow-up question about selling fund-raiser tickets. How interesting that both Kay and Gibson never pursued my involvement in false ticket stories or any political involvement I may have succumbed to. That was too bad because the answer would have been negative: in my tenure at the park district, there were no requests for donations to candidates, no pressures to attend ward committee meetings or any political meeting, and no summons to city hall political operatives. He wouldn't have believed me anyway. Perhaps that's why I imagined Zacchaeus to be my invisible friend. He always knew the truth.

TAGLINE CONTEST

March 31, 1992.

All new administrations mold perceptions of their reform, both for the general public and their inherited bureaucracies. Painting park benches a different color is a good example. Jesse's administration repainted the old forest-green benches beige. Bob Penn's changed beige to black. But when both discovered the cost of painting the thousands of park benches throughout the city, the repainting was limited to a few in high-profile areas, especially when neighborhood advisory councils made it clear there were far more urgent painting needs in their field houses.

One of Bob Penn's attempts to change perceptions involved a tagline contest. He and Dick Devine wanted to replace the old tagline printed at the bottom of all interoffice memo forms which read in quotes: "The Only Reason You and I Are Here Is to Serve the People of Chicago." The memo announcing the contest stated:

It's been confirmed . . . it's time for change. Take the time to think about what working here at the Chicago Park District means to you in terms of the public we serve. Ideas should focus on commitment, dedication, something humorous, something serious or "something to make you go hmmm!" This is an opportunity to immortalize yourself in CPD history!

"Who thought this up?" I asked Al Nieman at one of our routine get-togethers after hours. Al was the "go to" guy in the district when there were problems or trouble. His knowledge of every aspect of the parks was encyclopedic, and he knew how to get things done. Al, a carryover from the Kelly administration, was so good both Jesse Madison and Bob Penn retained him as their "special assistant." Most of the time, Al cruised all over the city, park to park, crisis to crisis, project to project. If you had a problem, you could call him anytime day or night.

He read the memo quickly with a tight-lipped smile. He knew which Penn underling thought up the idea but would not tell. Instead he picked up on the last line of the contest. "I thought you wanted to 'immortalize yourself' at the park district. Here's your chance."

"Very funny, but there's nothing wrong with the old tagline: 'The Only Reason You and I Are Here Is to Serve the People of Chicago.' It's a moral imperative from an unidentified speaker, like some moral voice or hovering spirit." I didn't mention that I attributed the tagline to Zacchaeus—Al would suspect I was mentally unbalanced.

Al rolled his eyes while sifting through his pile of messages on scraps of paper, napkins, and hunks of cardboard, requests people handed him wherever he had traveled that day. "It's only a contest, for God's sake. You win twenty-five bucks and get your picture taken with President Devine."

"Twenty-five bucks and a picture? That's nothing but a door prize. Public service should not be trivialized. The old tagline doesn't do that. It's in quotes . . . 'The Only Reason You and I Are Here . . .'"

"Are you through? I have calls to make," he said picking up a phone.

"No. I'm going to write a rebuttal against the contest in favor of keeping the old tagline."

Al put the phone down, leaned back in his chair, and rubbed his puffy eyes. "I would think carefully before you do. Superintendent Penn is very serious about changing the park district image and improving morale. This is not the time to rock the boat . . . Mr. Marine Director."

To Al, taglines were minor details in the scheme of things, import-ant only to keep public relations directors busy and out of his hair.

"Al, I have to stand up for what I believe."

When Al realized I was dead serious, he paused and advised, "Sometimes it is better to sit down on one's beliefs. They stay warm that way." Then he picked up the phone, dialed, and gestured for me to leave him alone.

After three drafts of my rebuttal, Al's advice took hold: if President Devine added his name to the damn contest, it must be important. I played around with a few new taglines, but they all came across as sar-casm. With a sigh, I deleted them stroke by computer stroke until the screen was blank and decided not to mess with the top bosses.

Several weeks later, from only a handful of entries, the winning ta-gline was announced: "Pride in Our Parks." Maybe it referred to the lions in Lincoln Park Zoo, I mused. The winner was the secretary to the commissioners, for God's sake. Along with the announcement was a directive to use up the old memo forms before switching to save ad-ditional printing expense. The memo gave me an idea. I checked the Special Services supply cabinet and discovered less than twenty of the old forms. I immediately headed down to the basement print shop where all park programs, posters, calendars, stationery, and myriads of forms and reports were printed. Three ancient presses, army sur-plus from World War I, clattered away, reeking of inks and solvents that a small exhaust fan in the outside wall did little to remove. Lubri-cants dripped out of the worn-out machines onto pieces of cardboard on the floor. The place was dimly lit by old single-tube fluorescent lights. Ink-stained shelves were jammed with paper and poster stock in several colors and sizes.

I never saw an exposé in the press about these print shop workers hanging around doing nothing. With five hundred parks and the cen-tral administration needing printed information daily, they were con-stantly working. The shop was so overloaded, it worked double shifts every day. If you needed something printed in a timely fashion, you'd better ask nicely.

"Do you have any of the old memo forms left?" I asked after sincerely complimenting one of the clerks on the amount of work turned out. She did not speak—too difficult to shout over the noisy machines. She pointed to a shelf with several reams of memo forms. I held up eight fingers. Without replying or asking me to fill out the usual requisition form, she quickly filled a box and slid it across a worn-through Formica counter, then disappeared behind one of the growling presses. Eight reams at five hundred forms per ream. As one who wrote as few memos as possible, four thousand would last until retirement.

DALEY'S UNDERGROUND RIVER

April 15, 1992.

Chicagoans were glued to their televisions as Mayor Daley declared a state of emergency. Police cordoned off the entire Loop. Most downtown building basements, some three and four stories below ground, as well as utilities vaults flooded. All power was out. Firemen rescued hundreds of stranded workers from elevators. Huge diesel-powered pumps placed everywhere sucked Chicago River water out of buildings into the streets, now whitewater rapids flowing into the storm sewer system that emptied right back into the river.

A contractor rehabilitating the Kinzie Street Bridge accidentally drove pilings through the roof of one of the railroad tunnels running under the river. Now abandoned, the tunnels were part of a sixty-mile system that a hundred years ago carried coal and other goods to Chicago's buildings from rail terminals along the river. Now the tunnels are only used to route electrical lines and communication utilities. As millions of gallons of water poured into the punctured tunnel, the hole increased in size as the force of the vortex collapsed more of the old brick walls. Attempts to plug the whirlpool with barges of stone and bricks failed. In a desperate measure, mattresses were thrown in by the dozens only to be sucked down instantly with no effect on the torrent. Additional pumps installed around the Loop only increased the flow velocity, enlarging the hole even more—to at least ten feet in diameter. Three floors of valuable records under city hall were submerged. The Art Institute's extensive collections stored underground were endangered and frantically relocated.

The park district underground garages in Grant Park under Michigan Avenue, part of my Special Services responsibility, began filling with water. When the garages were built in the sixties, some railroad tunnels that ran parallel to Michigan Avenue were blocked off with cinder-block walls intended to keep rats out of the garages, not millions of gallons of pressurized water. The walls quickly collapsed. At an emergency meeting, one park engineer, Arvin Modi, spoke to the impending catastrophe. With his outstretched hands palms down, he explained that the garage was designed to take weight and pressure from the top down. Then he turned his hands over palms up demonstrating, "Not from the bottom up." If water reached the ceiling of the lower level, the force would collapse the entire garage system under Michigan Avenue from Randolph to Van Buren Streets, into a three-story-deep pile of rubble.

Urgent calls to the mayor's office were ignored. The top brass assumed we at the district were worried about parked cars. Emergencies of every description were reported continually on television—except the impending catastrophe in the parking garages.

Until engineers figured out a way to plug the river tunnel, pumps were the only temporary solution. If the water level could be kept below the lower tier ceiling, the garages would be fine. But there was not a heavy-duty pump to be found in Chicago. The city had commandeered every industrial pump with more brought in by city trucks from Milwaukee, Indianapolis, and Detroit. Al Nieman and an army of park engineers worked the phones. Al finally located two heavy-duty electric pumps in Dayton, Ohio. Without hesitation he chartered a plane and flew them into Midway.

By midnight, park district electricians had them hooked up with two-foot-diameter discharge hoses snaking up the garage stairwells out onto Michigan Avenue. The murky river water was within a foot of the ceilings when everything was ready. Al gave the signal. The force of so much water discharging caused the hoses to whip like giant snakes, while spitting geysers of water half a block, cracking a bus windshield, and knocking down pedestrians. I, along with dozens of park workers, wrestled the rubber pythons to the street until they could be cabled to utility poles. The spectacle reminded me of the "turf toad" fiasco in Soldier Field. Wulky, who sat bouncing on one of the wriggling hoses like a Jell-O Buddha, absurdly suggested we convert the garage to an underground harbor with a "tunnel of love" back to the river.

After a couple of hours, the pumps lowered the water level to three feet below the ceilings. The garages were saved, with water damage only to the ventilation and electrical systems. Only a dozen or so cars were total losses; there would have been a lot more if the Loop had not been evacuated earlier.

The cleanup and restoration of Chicago's Loop would cost hundreds of millions of dollars. At a news conference after the breech was plugged and rebuilding of the tunnel infrastructure was completed, Daley inadvertently admitted the city was liable and later the courts agreed, but amazingly he suffered no consequences politically. Michigan Avenue did not collapse, but Mayor Daley's carefully sculpted image as the great city manager was questioned. He had to shift the blame

After a brief investigation, he concluded that "individuals were responsible, not the city," and fired a career public service professional, John LaPlante, along with a tunnel inspector named Jim McTigue. In fact, as newspaper reporters discovered, McTigue had warned his bosses about driving pilings in the river so close to the tunnel system. The fault was Daley's, who as part of his initiatives to reform the city's bureaucracy, combined two city departments without clear lines of authority regarding the all-but-forgotten tunnels.[1]

LaPlante and McTigue were scapegoats. Scapegoating was an ancient Old Testament ritual in which, on the holy Day of Atonement the sins of the Israelites were figuratively placed on the head of a goat that was then released into the wilderness, never to be seen again.

McTigue, however, refused to wander in the political wilderness and sued the city to get his job back with benefits and lost pay. While it took years, he won. John LaPlante, a quintessential highly respected public servant (until the great flood), retired quietly, choosing not to file a lawsuit, though he too surely would have prevailed.

At the same time, a different underground torrent flowed into the park district: privatization. Instead of reorganizing existing departments, with entrenched bureaucracies, Daley favored replacing them with private management, the theory being more efficient service at lower cost. He was not alone. Privatization became popular at all levels of government. Even in the Iraq and Afghanistan wars, private companies were given traditional military operations, including combat.

At the park district, the Golf Division was first to go. I was appointed to the committee that selected the winning bidder, Kemper Sports. But like so many Chicago-style contracts, after the initial award, negotiations took place, and the requirement, which I had insisted on, that the bowling greens at Fifty-Ninth Street also be maintained by the golf management company, was quietly eliminated. Golf had always maintained the bowling greens, which are identical to golf greens and adjacent to Jackson Park Golf Course. Maintenance by Golf made sense and cut costs. But out they escaped from the contract, thereby requiring the park district to assign other landscape workers and equipment at additional costs.[2]

When the Golf workers found out they would lose their park district jobs, and the private company announced it would not guarantee their reemployment, they panicked. Most of them had obtained their jobs through patronage and had never interviewed in the private sector. I considered helping them a moral obligation; so at an executive staff meeting I requested that Human Resources conduct a résumé and interviewing program. Human Resources—for lack of qualified personnel they said—declined, so I proposed hiring a consultant to conduct a basic skills seminar, which was also denied. No one wanted any outside consultants that might question the privatization plans and send Daley into a rage. So I asked Kris, whose career was Human

Resources training, if she would do it pro bono, which she did, customizing a program of interviewing skills, résumé development, and follow-up practice interviews. All the workers who took her mini-course were hired by Kemper Sports. They thanked her profusely. Not surprisingly, no one at the park district, not even Bob Penn, said thank you, too busy worrying about their own jobs.

By the end of that summer, Bob Penn was rapidly falling out of favor with the mayor, especially after recommending a property tax increase to fund the parks. Daley reportedly was furious. Robert Penn was one step closer to the mayor's famous revolving door, which would ultimately bang into my heels as well.

A TALE OF TWO CONVENTIONS

After the November 1992 presidential election, city hall announced that Chicago would host the 1996 Democratic Convention. Daley had used his clout with the new Clinton administration to obtain the honor denied Chicago since the infamous 1968 convention, an image the younger Daley determined to change as part of his legacy.

When 1996 rolled around, I had already been gone three years from the park district and was hired as CEO of the Hammond, Indiana, Port Authority to manage one of the largest and newest marinas in the country on Chicago's south border on Lake Michigan. I had no interest in the 1996 convention until one day a know-it-all boater, Joe Puccio, came to the customer counter and shouted, "Hey Admiral, I got something for you." I recognized his voice and considered sneaking out the side door. He would always find something in the marina that "needs to be taken care of right away": a nail in the parking lot next to the front tire of his car, a tangle of fishing line floating in his slip, or a burned-out lightbulb in a power pedestal on his dock. Last month he brought in a mildewed shower curtain out of the men's washroom and gave me a lecture on how I should better manage the Hammond marina. I had known Joe, a former Chicago boater and park district electrician, for years. He worked the scoreboard in Soldier Field and maintained electrical systems in the harbors.

Joe held up a wind sock, one of those decorations often seen on houses and boats, usually with animal or fish motifs. This one was huge, six feet long, a foot in diameter with six fire-engine-red stream-ers. It looked like a giant squid. Joe laid it out on the counter reveal-ing the new park district logo, "Come out and play." The fabric was like spinnaker sail cloth with stitching reinforced to hold up in strong wind. It was handmade and very expensive.

"All week long they had me hanging these things on every light pole in Grant Park. Lots of overtime to make sure they were all in-stalled by today. Do you know what they're for?"

I thought for a moment, trying to visualize the wind socks high on the light poles, barely noticeable to people walking by.

"I'll give you a hint," he said holding the cloth cylinder up to his head and peering through it. Light through the red fabric accentuated his normal scowl and turned his white hair and scruffy beard a ridic-ulous pink. "They're color coded for different sections of the park: red from Balbo to Roosevelt, blue from Randolph to Monroe, etc. C'mon, guess."

"I haven't a clue."

Joe rolled his eyes like a contemptuous teenager. "And everybody said you were smart. Final hint. Today is the first day of the 1996 Democratic Convention."

"So R2D2 spruced up downtown for the delegates, so what?"

"R2D2" was the name given by some to Richard M. Daley when he took over as mayor. He was determined to atone for his father's great-est political embarrassment: the 1968 Democratic Convention. Called a "police riot" by the Walker Commission, it was a bloodletting for those in the antiwar movement, a chaotic farewell to the love, peace, and justice dreams of the sixties. I know because I marched in those bloody streets.

"It's not for those delegate rubes, you asshole; it's for the cops and the FBI. They color coded every area of Grant Park, so that if a riot breaks out, spotters will call out the wind-sock colors where it's going down. The cops are camped out in Soldier Field and Navy Pier wait-ing for the color-code call, so they can 'come out and play,'" he said with contempt.

"That's the most idiotic thing I've heard. There aren't going to be any mass demonstrations in Grant Park. The convention is at the United Center. Besides, Daley just held a press conference with Tom Hayden, one of the seven ringleaders tried for conspiracy to cause the riot back then. Now they're bosom buddies for God's sake."

"That's Richie playing you fucking liberal goo-goos on. Richie will do anything to avoid a 1968 repeat. You know those statues in Grant Park the kids climbed? He coated them with Teflon. He even had us set up portable stages with microphones and speaker systems for protestors to use. The loudspeakers are deliberately tiny and can't be heard beyond fifty feet. Anyway, I thought you'd like one of the 'code red wind socks' which are all around the park by the Hilton—your old stomping grounds."

"How did you know I was there?"

With a cocky smile, Joe tilted his head slightly. I had forgotten what a repository of gossip, old and new, he maintained on every public official from mayors on down.

"I know what I know, you old long-hair hippie bastard."

"They were Yippies, not hippies, and I wasn't one of them."

"Yeah, right. Why don't you come down and take a look-see tonight? Bring me a cup of coffee with LSD in it. You'll find me in the bushes behind the stages in case of electrical problems. Can you believe it? I'm working standby for the fucking protestors."

Just as in 1968, Chicagoans were warned to stay away from the Balbo and Michigan Avenue site, which, along with curiosity, motivated me to take a trip down memory lane. At about nine o'clock that morning, I parked my car in the all but empty Grant Park south garage. As I climbed the stairs to Michigan Avenue, I saw the various colored wind socks on the light poles. At Jackson sat one of the portable stages Joe talked about, a ten-by-twelve-foot platform about two feet off the ground with two small speakers. A handful of well-dressed protestors listened to a young woman speaking, not about immoral war, but about immoral wearing of animal fur. I listened politely looking for Joe who was nowhere around, then thanked a young man for the literature he handed me and walked south.

At Michigan and Balbo Drive, the epicenter of the 1968 riot, code red wind socks hung limp like bait on fishing poles. It was the intersection where in 1968 the Chicago police attacked the anti–Vietnam War protestors as they confronted delegates to the Democratic Convention staying across the street in the Conrad Hilton hotel, an epic event in American politics viewed on television around the world. I sat down on a familiar stone bench across the street from the Hilton. Almost thirty years earlier on this bench, Kris and I handed out bandages, hand towels, washcloths, and aspirin, items we hurriedly gathered from our apartment in Pullman after seeing the news coverage of demonstrators, mostly college kids, being beaten bloody and hauled off in police wagons. We rushed downtown with our bags of supplies right after the noon news. The Vaseline went first as demonstrators smeared their faces against burning tear gas. Towels and washcloths were grabbed next and soaked in a nearby fountain for additional protection from gas. Several demonstrators asked for helmets or hard hats, for protection from the fury of police nightsticks and from glass ashtrays thrown down from hotel windows by angry delegates. I remember broken bits of glass everywhere.

The burning tear gas used back then permanently singed the events into my mind. The police had already closed off Grant Park after a melee there the night before and then confined the demonstrators, several hundred, to a strip of Grant Park between Michigan Avenue and the Illinois Central tracks, which ran parallel to Michigan Avenue below grade forming a moat. Police blocked Michigan Avenue to the north so that demonstrators could not march to city hall or the federal buildings. While the hotel was completely surrounded by uniformed cops, Michigan Avenue to the south remained open, presumably so that delegates could get to the convention a few miles to the southwest in the old International Amphitheater at Forty-Second and Halsted, where several presidential conventions were historically held.

By the time Kris and I arrived, the police stood rigid three deep in full riot gear on the Conrad Hilton side of the street. Most delegates were taken in and out of the hotel through back entrances not visible to the demonstrators. But some ran out the front entrance choking and vomiting from tear gas canisters and Yippie stink bombs landing close to the air-conditioning intakes of the hotel. The wind favored the demonstrators, causing a stinking standoff. Kris stayed for an hour or so but had to leave to pick up our two children from her mother's. She begged me to come with her, afraid I would be beaten, jailed, or worse, and upset when I insisted on staying. I promised to be careful.

Instead of crossing the street, wading into the crowd, clubbing demonstrators and making arrests, police stood disciplined and unfazed by constant taunting from the demonstrators. Blocks away, sirens wailed as cops rounded up everyone with long hair and beards, whether they were demonstrators or just unlucky tourists at the wrong place and time. During this lull, there were many speeches and rants. Sometime after Norman Mailer spoke, Abbie Hoffman stood up on a hill next to an equestrian statue of General John Logan. With a squeaky bullhorn almost out of battery power, he announced, "Let's march." The crowd, bored with listening to speeches and chanting "the whole world is watching," heard these two words and moved into the street. Demonstrators taunting the police in front of the Hilton, those sitting on and around the statue, and those on the hill perched on statues and in trees, all converged onto Michigan Avenue and marched south. Without hesitation I stepped into the street and joined them.

I thought it odd that the police made no effort to stop us. We walked to Roosevelt Road, aka Twelfth Street; no police. We walked farther to Fourteenth Street, past a landmark Chicago firehouse (later a favorite restaurant of the younger Daley); still no cops. The crowd screaming "off the pigs" assumed the police were outsmarted. As they marched they focused on the convention, chanting, "dump the Hump," referring to Hubert Humphrey's imminent nomination for the presidency and his refusal to detach his support for the war. I happened to be at the front of the line with Abbie Hoffman and looked back to a sea of marchers stretching all the way to the Hilton. A flatbed truck with news cameras and crew followed along. At that time

Michigan Avenue south of Twelfth Street was slummy. The grand old Illinois Central Railroad station at Twelfth Street had been torn down for lack of use, leaving acres of abandoned railroad tracks. The loss of passengers and tourists plus a decade of white flight by city dwellers and businesses to the suburbs had left the storefronts on both sides of Michigan Avenue abandoned and boarded up, leaving angry demonstrators no windows to smash.

When we reached Fifteenth Street, I heard a crash behind us. The flatbed truck with the news cameras had stopped and cops in plain clothes were tussling with the cameramen and trying—with success— to smash their equipment. This too seemed peculiar, as I had seen no interference with the press up to that point, but then I looked back south and saw why: at Sixteenth Street an old railroad overpass spanned Michigan Avenue between abandoned storefronts on both sides, allowing only two narrow lanes for street traffic. At that time there were no lights under the overpass, making it as dark as a mountain tunnel. As we marched toward it, perhaps half a block away, I sensed something ominous. Then, in less than two or three minutes, the Sixteenth Street railroad overpass was transformed into what could only be described as a military ambush.

At ground level on the South Side of the overpass, a contingent of National Guardsmen blocked the street. Jeeps with large barbed-wire screens welded hastily onto their bumpers pulled under the viaduct and stopped. These would later be called "Daley Dozers," by Norman Mailer who was arrested taking notes on the scene.[1] Some were equipped with machine guns manned by soldiers pointing them at the marchers. Then I heard heavy rumbling. A tank, its treads digging into the street asphalt, pivoted into the southbound lane between the bridge pillars, creating a steel plug in the viaduct roadway. With engine revving, the massive thing rocked like a runner in starting blocks. In the gaps between the jeeps, two or three rows of guardsmen assumed firing positions with bayoneted rifles, bazookas, and backpack flamethrowers pointed directly at the demonstrators. On top of the overpass, more soldiers and Chicago police took crouch positions along the tracks with sniper rifles. The wall of weaponry had been carefully orchestrated.

Unknowingly, we had been herded into a U-shaped pen of boarded-up buildings and railroad embankments, surrounded by soldiers and cops bristling with weapons. Abbie Hoffman held up his arms signaling the marchers to stop. While those of us in the front line halted immediately, those in the rear did not. Whether they couldn't see the massive force ahead in the darkness or simply wanted a confrontation was unclear. Struggling to stand still against the surge of flesh from behind, we were pushed closer and closer to those bayonets now lowered to gut level. I squeezed myself into a partially boarded-up doorway not ten feet from one of the jeeps. The gunner in the rear of the jeep saw me and slowly pivoted his machine gun aiming at my chest. My heart raced. I could see discipline in his eyes, trained and focused, waiting for the order to fire. My eyes bulged with fear. Was the machine gun loaded with blanks or real ammunition? Was the backpack flamethrower full of napalm? Would the tank charge, elephant-like, into the crowd?

Abbie realized what was about to happen. He turned to face the crowd and shouted frantically, "Go back, go back to the park." Those of us in the front line repeated his order. But militants in the crowd kept inching forward. Some stripped boards off the buildings to use as clubs. Screaming for a charge, they refused any argument for retreat. I prayed none of them had guns. A shot from the demonstrators would surely have set off the unthinkable.

Thank God, there was no shot.

As the militants got close enough to see the force majeure they were up against, they paused for what seemed like hours, but were only minutes. Their courage had ebbed. They listened to Abbie's pleas and turned around. Being closest to the soldiers, I was one of the last to follow. Instinct made me walk backward, my face to the soldiers in case they fired or charged. A slaughter at Sixteenth Street, unlike the one two years later at Kent State University, did not happen. Walking backward all the way to Grant Park, I realized I was also backing out of "the movement," out of the life of the church, and out of the sixties.

The 1968 convention marked the unraveling of the movement. The Left splintered into factions: Yippies, hippies, Black Panthers, and Weathermen bombers to name a few. For the years 1965 through 1967, before the unraveling, I was proud to be a fellow traveler, a chaplain managing a coffeehouse ministry at Cornell University called The Commons. The coffeehouse became the center for counseling young men of conscience, radical students, and visiting organizers: A. J. Muste, an octogenarian who fought for peace in World War I and who would be waiting for me to open up in the morning, said eloquently, "The heart of the body politic, like the human heart, is always on the left." Allen Ginsberg, before reading his antiwar poetry at Bailey Hall, ate the flower centerpiece in the faculty club rather than sup with conservative faculty supporters of the war at the table. Saul Alinsky, the so-called radical community organizer, spoke at The Commons. When asked how much of Lyndon Johnson's War on Poverty money actually reached the poor, he said it was like a man urinating, which starts with a heavy stream and ends in a trickle. The part the poor received was the few drops shaken off at the end. I worked for Saul Alinsky's FIGHT (Freedom, Integration, God, Honor, Today) organization in the summer of 1966 in Rochester, New York, after the riots there.

Counseling students on resisting the war led to my own crisis of conscience: When mysteriously reclassified 1-A, I became more than a fellow traveler. I metamorphosed from counselor to resister, one of the five organizers, including Bruce Dancis, one graduate student, and three undergraduates, of the "We Won't Go" movement, which resulted in the first mass draft card burning in New York's Central Park on April 15, 1967. My responsibility was to contact those who pledged to burn their draft cards and explain the legal consequences: up to five years in prison and $10,000 in fines, as specified in the congressional bill of 1965 for "knowingly destroying" or "knowingly mutilating" a draft card. At least two hundred (we deliberately kept no lists) young people and one active Green Beret, Gary Rader, and myself thrust our draft cards into a can of Sterno held by Bruce and burned them down to our fingers. We were surrounded by FBI agents with cameras and tiny dustpans, which they used to scoop up the burned draft cards and file them in small manila envelopes.[2]

I was promptly fired by Cornell. Ironically, Bill Hamilton was forced to resign from Colgate Rochester at the same time. Bruce Dancis was subsequently arrested and imprisoned for nineteen months (for tearing up his draft card at Cornell in 1966 and sending it back along with a statement to his draft board). Dr. Benjamin Spock, the world famous pediatrician, and Rev. William Sloan Coffin, chaplain at Yale, were indicted and later convicted of "conspiracy to aid, abet, counsel draft registrants to violate the Selective Service Act." Kris and I fled to Scotland just ahead of a federal grand jury subpoena, which fortunately never left the United States. We landed in Edinburgh with our two-year-old daughter and a baby on the way. For a year I tried to write a book, until both inspiration and savings ran out and life with a newborn crawled in. It was time to come home to our birthplace, to the heartland of America, where our hearts longed to be—Chicago.

Like Zacchaeus I had climbed a tree to witness a great movement, but never answered its burning call to revolution. Change based on a sense of the common, yes; but revolution with no basis in common sense, no way. By 1968 my radicalism drifted to the periphery, and then I drifted into middle-class life. Whatever the future of the movement, it was not my future.

When we came back, I had no job. My father-in-law gave me a summer job in his brick factory. The foreman in charge put me on the "boxcar gang," four black guys who cleaned raw asbestos out of railroad cars. The heat and dust (no masks in those days) were unbearable, and every morning at break time the gang and the "white boy" would pile into an old car and head for the nearest liquor store for a six pack and pint of whiskey, which we gulped down on the way back to the job. By ten in the morning, I was drunk as a skunk while the black guys laughed and laughed while picking up my slack.

I too laughed briefly at the absurdity of someone with my background suffocating in boxcars full of asbestos. I had to get a permanent job working inside the hated "system," not on the streets. Why not be a "Publican" like Zacchaeus and work for the very governmental authority I had challenged? If I really believed in social change, shouldn't I work from the inside where change ultimately happens? I applied for two entry-level government jobs in Chicago: special education counselor at the board of education and case worker at the Cook County Department of Welfare. At the board of education, the interviewer explained that my degrees in English and theology were of no value. I had to be a certified teacher before I could qualify. As he talked, I couldn't help but notice the bulletin board behind his desk covered with FBI wanted posters and a flier advertising an American Legion "Law and Order Dinner." I couldn't get out of that interview fast enough. Next I made my way to the Cook County offices next to city hall. The county was hiring a ton of case workers with new federal money from War on Poverty programs. I aced the test and was interviewed and verbally assured of being hired pending a "routine check" of my references. I was so pleased. My potential for public service was recognized and about to begin. I relished the idea of becoming an entry-level clerk, the root word for which is "cleric," from the Middle Ages when the church was the government and clergy ran the bureaucracies.

When a month passed without hearing anything, I trekked down to the county building and inquired about my status. The interviewer no longer worked there. Another clerk coldly said there was no record of my application or interview and besides all case worker positions had been filled. What happened? Did they check my FBI file or the file of Chicago's infamous counterpart, the Red Squad? Did I show up in police photos from the Sixteenth Street overpass? Or was my lost application just Chicago politics— "We don't want nobody nobody sent."

Rebuffed but never without my eye on public service, I waited. Didn't Tom Hayden become an elected official in California? Julian Bond, mayor of Atlanta and an ambassador to the United Nations? And that icon from Bloody Sunday at the Petus Bridge, John Lewis, congressman extraordinaire from Georgia? So many transitioned from outside to inside government, and I wanted to be one of them. It would be twenty years before I applied for a city job again. There was no way I could morally work for a machine-style government with

Richard J. Daley or his carbon copy successors, Bilandic and Byrne, in charge. I had to wait for someone I could work for, and that turned out to be Harold Washington.

It was late by the time I returned from the stone bench at Balbo to the portable speakers' platform at Jackson. The little stage was empty. The fur people had gone home leaving a neat stack of fliers with a rock on top, not for throwing through storefront windows, but to keep propaganda from blowing away. I climbed up and tapped on the microphone, which was still live, even though Joe Puccio was nowhere around. From the platform I could see the outline of the Sixteenth Street overpass over a mile to the south, now brightly lit. In the last twenty-eight years, the whole area from State Street to the Illinois Central tracks had become a glittering gentrified gateway to the South Side. The boarded-up storefronts had reopened as upscale shops and cafes. Abandoned railyards sprouted luxury high-rise condos and million-dollar town houses behind wrought iron fences. Mayor Richard M. Daley moved out of his father's Bridgeport neighborhood into one of them.

I tapped on the microphone one more time, tempted to tell my story to the few people walking down Michigan Avenue. Would I start with the scene in the movie *Rosemary's Baby* (born of the Devil) with a copy of Bill Hamilton's book *God Is Dead* on a coffee table and trace that theological movement to ethics in government? How ridiculous. No one would listen, so I said nothing.

Although very late, it was such a beautiful summer night that I detoured over to Monroe Harbor for a nostalgic look. A boater was rowing out to his mooring in a dinghy with a combination flashlight and running light clamped onto the bow. He rowed skillfully out to his sailboat near the harbor entrance very near the mooring where my sailboat had been moved and broke loose. Occasionally, he turned his head to check direction. Rowing a dinghy is not as easy as it looks. You have to face backward in order to row forward, but you don't need to see where you're going as long as you pick out something imposing and unique on shore and row in a straight line from there.

FROM MALCOLM X
TO MUHAMMAD ALI

I was reading one of Steve Neal's commentaries in the *Sun-Times*, slamming Bob Penn's administration and Mayor Daley for not replacing him, when a package was delivered—no dead flowers this time. Inside was a transcription of Malcolm X's last recorded public speech, in February of 1965, before his assassination. The lecture, delivered at Colgate Rochester Divinity School, was taped and then lost until it reappeared in a storage cabinet in the previous year. Audio enhanced, it was given to William Hamilton for editing. Hamilton, along with Rev. Franklin Florence, a close friend of Malcolm's, had invited him to speak to the school. Bill sent me a copy of the speech, which we had talked about many times. He thought it might take my mind off petty Chicago politics and bring it back to the moral underground of the sixties whose imperatives Malcolm's life and death personified.

I vividly remembered Malcolm X standing tall, his large, perfectly formed hands, the hands of a sculptor's model, gripping the podium then extending out as if to shake hands with anyone who would share his newfound vision. His pilgrimage the year before to Mecca, where Muslims of every race and color from across the world gather in simple white garments, changed his worldview: "It's impossible to tell whether one is a king or whether one is a beggar," he famously said.[1] That experience of racial and class equality transformed his thinking from the fiery separatism of the Nation of Islam to inclusion and diversity. He established the "Organization of Afro-American Unity," a movement that split the Nation of Islam down the middle. Its militant wing saw Malcolm as a charismatic threat that had to be eliminated.

Obviously tired, he cut his speech short and answered questions instead. A Pakistani asked sarcastically if there were any non-Muslims at the pilgrimage in Mecca. Malcolm admitted they were not allowed. Another student asked how he could extol Islamic brotherhood when in Pakistan fifteen years previously, the Muslim government stripped its Hindu citizens of all their property. Malcolm did not argue; he admitted that Islam, like Christianity, was not perfect.

Next, a Palestinian reminded Malcolm that most of the slave traders in Africa were Arab Muslims and that in Arabic the words for "Negro" and "slave" are the same. Malcolm tried to make a fine distinction between "Arab" and "Muslim," but it didn't wash. Whether fatigued from battling his critics or worried about lethal enemies, Malcolm showed no fire in his belly; rather he exuded the calm resignation of a prisoner on death row.

After the questions I walked up intending to shake Malcolm X's hand, but he was running late. He was scheduled to give another private speech at a black church in the heart of Rochester's third-ward ghetto, one of two wards that had nearly burned to the ground in the riot the year before. Ironically, I was in the middle of that riot as well. I worked part-time for Hertz, and when well-known CBS correspondent Hughes Rudd called for a car, I offered to drive and be his guide. My real intention was to use the connection to get a job in television. Hughes Rudd had been a decorated WWII veteran who became a reporter and was fearless. He ordered me to drive to an intersection that was on fire and where cops and rioters were shooting at each other. When the camera lights were turned on, the bullets zeroed in. While I dropped to the ground motionless in fear for my life, Hughes Rudd stood in the gunfire calmly describing the scene. Seeing my distress, he smiled and suggested I go to the car and get a hard hat. I crawled to the Hertz station wagon, which had several bullet holes and a cracked windshield. While that riot experience did not lead to a job with CBS, it gave me some semblance of what war was like.

Reverend Florence invited me and a few others involved in civil rights demonstrations in Rochester to Malcolm's second speech. At the black church, before Malcolm spoke, I, along with everyone else, was patted down by Malcolm's Fruit of Islam armed guards dressed formally in black suits, white shirts, and black bow ties. They stood at attention at every door, every aisle, and every point of access to the pulpit while Malcolm spoke passionately, extending those hands out over the congregation as he did at the school. Concentrating his remarks on reform in inner-city schools, he compared the changing status of blacks to that of white immigrants a century earlier, their flight from European poverty and prejudice and their move from indentured servitude and discrimination to mainstream American life through education. He cited old-style Catholic education with its strict discipline and corporal punishment as the best model for instilling the value of education in poor black children. You could hear a pin drop in the church that night. Unfortunately, that speech was not recorded.

Five days later Malcolm X was murdered in Harlem, followed by Martin Luther King Jr. three years later. Both only reached the age of thirty-nine; both illustrated with their lives Jesus's remark that "no prophet is acceptable in his own country." On parallel rails they moved the American psyche closer to belief in equal access for all. Steve Biko, the black South African contemporary of Nelson Mandela, who was tortured and murdered in his cell by apartheid police, said it best: "It is better to die for an idea that will live than to live for an idea that will die."

Reading Malcolm X's speech, I wondered what would have happened to Malcolm, Martin, and Bonhoeffer had they not been martyred. Surely, they would have found their place in the establishment, in government, university, church, or in some not-for-profit organization. Radicals either die as martyrs or find regular jobs. The thought put my uncertain employment in perspective. Thinking it might do the same for others, I gave a copy to Colette Holt, who politely set it aside. She had other things on her mind, like her threatened sexual harassment suit against Bob Penn. I never asked for details, but it was common knowledge that if a settlement was reached, she would quietly take her leave from the district.

For the second time in my brief tenure in city government, a black administration was coming apart. Blistering attacks by the press, Bob Penn's very weak responses, the threatened sexual harassment suit by Colette, and—most damaging of all in the public's mind—Penn spending some $40,000 remodeling his office, all sucked the energy for reform out of the place. Rumors abounded that Penn would be replaced very soon.

Steve Neal fired volley after volley: at Penn's chauffeur; his proposed property tax increase; lack of programming.[2] Like Jesse before him, Penn wrote a tepid defense challenging Neal's attacks, which the *Sun-Times* published—a sure sign that the end was near. Instead of the traditional wood shed, Daley held a news conference publicly blasting Penn's tax proposal and then also ripped into the parks for lack of programming. Alderman Mary Ann Smith, chairman of the city council's Committee on Parks and Recreation and mayoral mouthpiece, attacked the park administration saying there was a "profound lack of vision" at the district. She questioned my management of the harbors as well. The press was all over Penn's management style and the lack of progress in capital improvements. Calls for his ouster snowballed; his threatened firing of Colette Holt over a bungled Kellogg Foundation grant further highlighted his problems. "Chief's Ouster Seen as Imminent" was the *Tribune's* headline.[3] Penn, who just as Jesse had done, boldly asked for his contract to be renewed. At the same time, he did not help his cause by refusing to promote an already overpaid Daley cousin to a job in Recreation.

Good people from the halcyon days of Harold Washington began jumping ship. Nancy Kaszak, my close advisor and friend, was elected to the Illinois House of Representatives (I admit I did attend one of her fund-raisers and made a small donation). Holdover department heads, of which I was one of the last, waited for more shoes to drop. In the cafeteria, bets were made as to when Daley would replace Penn. I worried over adapting to a whole new administration. It took all of Penn's two-year tenure for me to fit in; the thought of going through that again gave me heartburn. The main hall leading past my office to Penn's, normally a river of people, turned into a dried-up creek. No snagging of VIPs. Whenever I had the chance, I got the hell out of the building.

So when a film production company requested permission to shoot a public service announcement at the South Shore Cultural Center featuring Muhammad Ali, I gave it gladly and made sure to be there, not only to get away from my office, but to meet one of my great American heroes. In 1966, when the Selective Service System reclassified Ali 1-A for the Vietnam War draft, he announced he was a conscientious objector and would not serve: "Why should they ask me to put on a uniform and go ten thousand miles from home and drop bombs and bullets on brown people in Vietnam while so-called Negro people in Louisville are treated like dogs and denied simple human rights?" Later he famously added, "I ain't got no quarrel with the Vietcong. No Vietcong ever called me 'nigger.'" The greatest heavyweight fighter in the world refused to fight in Vietnam. We activists were inspired.

Conservatives labeled him a traitor, a brainwashed Communist pawn, and a disgrace to his race. He dutifully reported for his army physical, but when asked to step forward for induction into the armed forces, he declined. Three times he was warned of the consequences, and three times he refused to step forward. He was arrested and charged with violation of the Selective Service Act, punishable by up to five years in prison. At that time draft resisters were routinely sentenced for two to five years.

On June 20, 1967, his trial began. Like so many conscientious objectors, who either by faith or intellectual search came to oppose the war, his claim was denied. Nor did the jury believe his Islamist religious convictions, deliberating less than twenty-two minutes to convict him. While his appeal took four years to reach the Supreme Court, he was immediately stripped of his heavyweight title and banned from boxing. Like so many who opposed the draft, his career was ruined. Then on June 28, 1971, the Supreme Court in *Clay vs. United States* (Cassius Clay being Ali's former name, which he considered to be his slave name) overturned his conviction, and he fought his way back.

I also was reclassified 1-A in 1966, even though I was a chaplain. Most likely I was reclassified because I not only counseled young men torn between conscience and an unjust war but appeared at draft board hearings on behalf of students requesting conscientious objector status. They could have asked family doctors to write phony medical excuses or used daddy's political influence to gain an exemption or lost themselves in the counterculture of "tune in, turn on, and drop out," as LSD guru Timothy Leary famously urged. But those I testified for took the moral route. Like Muhammad Ali they believed in the American system and respectfully requested conscientious objector status, intellectually joining those with deep beliefs like Quakers and other pacifist religious groups that historically refused to take part in any wars. One student who arrived at pacifism was called "a liar of convenience who used libraries to concoct his testimonial." He was denied conscientious objector status.

But that was "back in the day." As lights were adjusted and cameras rolled into place, Muhammad Ali sat patiently on a gold-and-white armchair at the park district's elegantly restored lakefront gem, formerly the all-white South Shore Country Club. In 1966, the declining club membership debated whether to allow blacks as members. The vote to integrate was soundly defeated, and the club withered on the Chicago segregation vine. The South Shore neighborhood changed quickly; white flight accelerated full throttle from stately homes and luxury lakefront high-rises and club membership rolls.

In 1973, the club went bankrupt and voted to liquidate assets. In 1975, the park district bought the property and spent millions restoring its golf course, riding stables, ballrooms, and dining facilities for public use. Along with jazz festivals and political meetings of all kinds, catering of parties and receptions became a central activity, especially for African Americans now living in the area. A young black lawyer and community organizer named Barack Obama and his fiancée, Michelle Robinson, would hold their wedding reception there. I often wonder if those whites who fled the changing neighborhood in the fifties and sixties would have stayed if they had known that the only black female US Senator, Carol Mosely Braun, would reside there, along with two male African American residents, Jesse Jackson and Barack Obama, who would run for president of the United States, one of whom would win two terms. Having lived in South Shore for over thirty years, I so enjoy those ironies.

Ali sat expressionless as the makeup artist fussed with his forehead and cheeks. The director showed him the cue cards and Ali nodded, barely moving his head. The effects of advancing Parkinson's disease were apparent. His head drooped, and he spoke very little: no public boasting, no taunting of opponents—boxers or governments—and yet for millions of followers around the world he is still "The Greatest." In my mind he will always "float like a butterfly and sting like a bee" in America's small but beautiful moral garden.

After a few takes the director called for a break, and I asked if I could speak a few words to Ali. Certainly! I walked quietly over to the man in the armchair. I had no intention of asking for his autograph; that would be demeaning. With no prepared words, I simply introduced myself, explained my position in the park district, and without boring him with my own antiwar stories, thanked him for his courage and example. He raised his head, smiled thinly, and with slurred speech whispered, "You're very welcome."

Ordinary words undoubtedly uttered to well-wishers thousands of times, but at that moment they were unique to me. We were reunited antiwar combat buddies a generation after the war. He lifted his trembling right hand for me to shake, the same hand he refused to raise at induction. We shook hands as if members of a secret fraternity.

SO SAD, TOO BAD

September 1, 1993.

A new wave hit the park district. Daley appointed Forrest Clay-pool, his former chief of staff, as general superintendent. The transition from the Penn administration moved along quietly if not secretly. I was working on another sailing motivation speech for an all-black high school on the South Side when Joe Fratto, superintendent of Financial Services, the counterpart to Special Services, called me to his office and handed me a plain envelope with my name on it. I assumed it contained another lawsuit, a special request for a slip from some political heavy Joe regularly tried to intercede for, or some other sensitive matter. I had no clue it was my termination letter. As I sat down and read over the two brief paragraphs, Joe squirmed in his chair which squeaked annoyingly.

"I want you to know I had nothing to do with this," he said, and rambled on about his peripheral involvement with the new administration. Of course Joe was not fired. Even though he was a Jane Byrne appointee, the Fratto family's generations of influence in the Democratic organization of Chicago was too powerful. Instead of staying, Joe maneuvered himself into one of the cushiest jobs in the city: executive director of the park district pension fund.

"Joe, I don't blame you," I replied, putting him somewhat at ease. We worked closely together for over six years and developed a warm working relationship. The fact that he was designated delivery boy of bad news obviously bothered him. The letter was businesslike. Today was my last at the Chicago Park District. I would be paid six weeks' severance plus vacation time. The final sentence read, "During the six-week transition period, you will not be expected to report to the office on a daily basis. Rather, you should be available to provide assistance as requested."

I folded the letter and slid it back in the envelope. A feeling of relief washed over me. No reinventing myself with a third new administration, trying to figure out its management style, no winning over a new inner circle of chosen ones, no stoppage of projects underway from the old until given permission to proceed in the new.

While I inhaled a strangely satisfying breath, the phone rang. Joe excused himself, telling me to take all the time I needed and closed the door behind him. I sat back and recalled previous terminations: from the conservative church in Rochester for participating in that police brutality sit-in; from Cornell after two peace activist years.

What was the final straw that got me fired? The Christmas tree demonstration on the main quad decorated with war toys set on fire with napalm made by students using army manuals from the library? Or was it the march across the Peace Bridge from Buffalo to Canada to deliver medical supplies to the North Vietnamese Red Cross, where we were informed mid-bridge by federal agents that we risked federal charges of aiding and abetting the enemy? We pushed past them anyway. Whatever it was, I was called in to the head chaplain's office and let go with the oldest bureaucratic excuse—that unfortunately the budget had to be cut and my job eliminated. When I suggested combining my coffeehouse job with the director of volunteer services position, which had become vacant, I was told that would not be possible.

However after I left, Cornell combined the two jobs as I had suggested and, in another stroke of irony, hired the radical priest and my friend, Father Daniel Berrigan, for the position. I felt like John the Baptist.

After six months at the brick factory, I was hired at the University of Chicago in 1968, initially as a draft counselor, until the legal department nixed the idea; instead I was given the title "assistant director of student activities," where I could counsel students on the war unofficially. When radical students took over the administration building, I was the only administrator allowed in. Even though I opposed their actions, they trusted my integrity based on my past. My boss, the dean of students, called me late that night and asked if it was true I had been in the building. I explained that I entered to make sure the students didn't destroy or copy sensitive files, particularly in his office. The dean didn't care about my efforts. He demanded a list of every student involved on his desk the following morning in order to expel them.

"Who is going to expel the students?" I asked.

"The Faculty Disciplinary Committee."

"Then let the faculty members give you their names," I responded without hesitation. "You will not get a list from me."

He fired me for insubordination, and then rescinded the action the following day. I don't know why; perhaps he feared further demonstrations from the students. I was marginalized and never again invited to important meetings regarding student issues. When an opening occurred to manage the university's theater operations, I grabbed it. After three years of managing Court Theatre, I decided theater life was not for me, resigned, and moved on to a simpler world free of entrenched bureaucracies: peddling sailboats in Chicago harbors.

My father, who worked at Illinois Bell all his life, could not understand being fired from an Ivy League university and blamed me. How could I let that happen? When I explained the firings were political and out of my hands, he refused to buy it. "People get themselves fired," he said. We argued for a long time, but thinking back, he was absolutely right: people who follow the spirit instead of unjust laws get themselves fired.

When Joe Fratto returned, we calmly discussed transition matters including who would take my place. Joe cleared his throat a couple of times. He already knew. "You need to tell Joe O'Malley he will be in charge temporarily," he said, averting his eyes.

With nothing left to say, I walked back to my office. The first person I met in the hall was Bob Wulkowicz, who was totally unaware of the bloodbath taking place throughout the building. Twelve other Shakman-exempt executives were handed their letters; some escorted out of the building by security. Wulky greeted me sarcastically. "If it isn't Admiral Dim Bulb, VIP—Vaguely Important Person," he said and for a moment I realized how "dim bulbed" I had been since Claypool was sent over by Mayor Daley. Claypool's constant media message about bringing his "businesslike management" to the district made me overconfident. After all, I came from the private sector and implemented numerous efficient business practices over my six and a half years. At that first meeting of senior staff in June, Claypool singled me out. "So you're Bob Nelson. I've heard so much about you. You're doing a great job." I was flattered, naturally, and foolishly believed him. And a month later, when he replaced the new tagline, "Pride in Our Parks" with the old, "The Only Reason You and I Are Here Is to Serve the People of Chicago," I thought we might even become soul mates.

And then, a week after Daley appointed him president of the board, John Rogers, whom I never met or knew anything about, called me personally, repeated Claypool's praise, and asked for a guided tour of the lakefront. We spent three delightful hours driving around the harbors and lakefront parks. At the end, he complimented my work and future vision for the harbors. Commissioner Michael Scott and others told me I had nothing to worry about.

Of course, Steve Neal bashed Claypool as a "veteran political operative" in a July column titled "Daley Chooses Amateur to Run Parks," but I took that with a grain of salt. Steve Neal bashed everyone except his friend, the ousted general superintendent, Ed Kelly.[1]

I should have suspected something was up when I sent formal invitations for our annual Junior Golf Banquet to all of Claypool's new staff. A grand affair attended by over three hundred kids and parents from park golf programs around the city, the emcee was Oprah Winfrey's significant other, Stedman Graham. Yet not one of Claypool's new staff attended or even responded. Then in July I should have been suspicions when at the Grant Park Symphony gala concert, I decided to sit with these same staff members, who barely said a word to me and never asked a question about the wildly successful symphony program.

Two days before my termination, I should have known a change for the worse was coming when my plan to transform the old South Shore Gun Club into the South Shore Golf Course's starter building and a lakefront café was turned down at a special meeting chaired by one of Claypool's confidants, who knew absolutely nothing about the needs of the South Side lakefront. I was oblivious to her purpose.

Bob Wulkowicz sensed something was wrong as I handed him the letter. While he read it, I suggested deadpan that he hide under Soldier Field and under no circumstances accept any hand-delivered envelopes. Bob was shocked and apologized for calling me a "dim bulb."

People stared at me like gapers passing an accident on an expressway, so I excused myself and closed my office door and called Kris on the green phone. She answered cheerfully, "I was just going to call you. I landed the human resource director job at the insurance services agency!" A year ago Kris had been downsized from Talman Bank, a venerable Chicago neighborhood savings and loan, where she had worked seventeen years. She was at the top of her game when the S&L was swallowed up by LaSalle Bank. Kris had been looking for work for almost a year.

"Well, that's great, because I just lost my job." After exchanging gallows humor to relieve the pain of loss, Kris told me she was actually glad I would not be working at the district anymore.

"The lines on your forehead were getting deeper and deeper," she said. "Now I won't have to worry about you having a heart attack—and neither will you," she added. As we made a dinner date for that night to celebrate her new job, someone pounded on my door. I didn't want to hang up, but she advised we talk more at dinner and then, ever so softly, whispered, "Remember what you told me when I was let go: 'It's their loss, not yours.'"

Rich Tinker charged into my office as if chased by a mugger.

"Tell me it's not true." I handed him the letter.

"Today? Today is your last day?" Rich was incensed. He wanted to immediately march into Claypool's office. I calmed him down as other Marine staff came in. Reactions were touching. Katie, the hardest government clerk I had ever met, and Deb, the first black woman in Marine, both became teary eyed and speechless. Marty came up from his office on the first floor, bragging as usual about his clout, George Dunne, keeping him off the hit list.

"And you thought you could work with Claypool. I warned you," he said, restating the old political adage, "Payback is a motherfucker." Marty did not care what he said or who heard. He knew Auto Parking was scheduled to be privatized by the end of the year anyway, and he looked forward to retirement on a fat pension. Joe O'Malley, who was too young to retire, wanted to know if he too was going to be fired. I responded that I didn't think so, that until further notice, according to Fratto, he was in charge of Marine. Joe was as dumbfounded as I was when Tom Elzey gave me similar news on my being superintendent of special services over five years ago.

"You can move into my office tomorrow, Joe," I said professionally. But he was so nervous he didn't respond and quickly disappeared into his office.

Jimmy Duggan called from the stadium and repeated "This is not right" several times. Then he told me Bobby Mazziola, head of Central Services, his closest friend, and Al Nieman, had also been fired. Al was escorted out of the building by security guards. Al Nieman? Bobby? After all the years they served unconditionally twenty-four hours a day? Their terminations were more shocking than mine.

"Thanks, Jimmy. At least I know I am in good company."

The staff gathering did not last more than a few minutes. What was there to say? Rich was the last one out just as a cartload of new "recycling station boxes" with staff names, including mine, stenciled on each was delivered by two custodians. Attached to each box were recycling and sorting instructions signed by Claypool.

After soccer-kicking his box across the office, Rich said with a smirk, "It's paper recycling day, and we all know how important that is." He put on his sport coat and stormed out of the building.

Rich's remark gave me an idea. I read the termination letter again. It stated my employment as "superintendent of special services is hereby terminated" but failed to mention my other official position as director of harbors. How odd that a supposedly bright lawyer like Claypool didn't include both positions. Maybe someone else wrote the letter and assumed the Harbor position to be part of the Special Services position, but according to the budget and park board official actions, they were separate executive positions and I held both.

My idea, a long shot for sure, was to suggest an option to Claypool: recycle me back into the harbor position and leave the stadium, parking, golf, concession operations, symphony, and South Shore Cultural Center to others. If I could convince him that such a move was in his best interest, he might reinstate me as a demotion. I immediately called Claypool's office for an appointment the next day.

I realized that Cathy Cahill, who had been at her office in the Petrillo Band Shell all day, probably did not know what had happened, so I drove over to Grant Park to tell her personally. Cathy and I had become good friends as well as colleagues ever since Bob Penn and I, after a national search, agreed she was the best person for the job. Hearing the news, she became sullen and angry, not only with Claypool, but with me for spending five years trying to convince her that public service was worthwhile and needed highly talented people like her. She shook her finger, reminding me of those discussions.

"You are so full of crap," she muttered and started to cry. I bit my lip and gave her a hug. This was the first time I had seen her composure wobble. For a few moments, we sat silently in the below-ground practice rooms, instruments lying everywhere waiting to be put away. She would be the only one of my managers Claypool would attempt to keep, wining and dining her at jazz clubs with his "wunderkind" advisors, even arranging a private meeting with Mayor Daley to convince her to stay on as director of the Grant Park Music Festival. Cathy had transformed the sleepy summer orchestra program into one of the finest in the land, attracting first-rate talent, implementing classical music outreach to minority neighborhoods, and receiving kudos and consistent raves in the press, a sparkling jewel for any superintendent or mayor to wear. But she refused Claypool's efforts, saying privately she couldn't possibly work for a man who fired me. Instead, after a few months, she landed a top job with the New York Philharmonic.

The next day I was politely ushered into Claypool's office, formerly Bob Penn's and Jesse's, where I sat in on countless meetings. I adjusted the blue tie that Kris picked out for me to wear while warning not to be "too disappointed." The new general superintendent and I sat opposite in leather chairs. His face displayed the stone-cold look of a Labrador cod on ice.

"First of all, thank you for seeing me," I said sincerely. "I am not here to question your decision to fire me. As a Shakman-exempt employee, I know I can be fired at any time for any reason; if you don't like the color of this tie, that's enough reason." It was a dumb thing to say, and I could tell Claypool looked puzzled, so I moved to my notion of recycling jobs.

"I want to suggest an idea for you to consider. Naturally you want your own team in the top policy-making positions like superintendent of special services. That's fine, but you may not be aware that I was originally hired for the harbor director position and then additionally promoted to special services superintendent the following year. I have held both positions for the last five years and—"

Apparently not interested in fine points, he interrupted me in mid-sentence. "I want you to know that my decision was nothing personal." I paused for a moment wondering why people in positions of power always say "It's nothing personal" when they really mean it is nothing personal to them. I cleared my throat and continued.

"What I am suggesting is that you put me back into the Harbor position. Recycle me, so to speak. Call it a demotion; I don't care. I will work as hard for you as I did for Bob Penn and Jesse Madison. My commitment is to city of Chicago and the lakefront—"

He interrupted again, this time definitely irritated. "This is a man-

agement decision that was carefully thought out before being made."
I would argue the opposite, but obviously this was not the time.

"Right, it's about management, and that's what I'm talking about.
Everything I have accomplished in the harbors, the new projects in
the pipeline, the awards and good press, will make you look good and
make Mayor Daley look good. The boaters are happy for the first time
in twenty years—"

Again he interrupted, with what would become his trademark
smirk. "I know you have your fans out there."

Fans? What was he talking about? Did he think I wanted to run for
office? This was not going well.

"Simply put you are not part of the plan," he said, looking away as
if avoiding eye contact with a panhandler outside city hall.

"Is the plan to privatize the harbors?" I asked, knowing as soon as
the words escaped that they were the wrong words. Employees on the
way out are not told such things.

"That is not something I will discuss," he said frowning and added
coldly, "Is there anything else?" I thought for a moment, looked
around his plush office, and took a deep breath.

"Yes, there is one other thing: Is the six weeks of severance pay negotiable?"

Standing up immediately he answered, "Absolutely not!" I smiled
to myself thinking back to the morning six and a half years ago when
I was ushered into this same office—sitting down while park district
lawyers and Jesse were on the speakerphone with Pfeiffer's lawyers
negotiated a far more generous severance—a golden parachute compared to mine. Pfeiffer was fifty-four years old on that day; I would
turn fifty-four in three months. How ironic that I was the first Harbor
Boss in thirty years *not* sent to federal prison, and yet there was to be
no discussion of my severance pay. With privatization there would be
no more park district Harbor Bosses. I was the last one.

Without another word, Claypool walked briskly to his office door
and held it open. As I took the hint, stood up, and walked toward it, I
once again felt relief. My feeble attempt at being recycled failed. It was

over. I grinned ever so slightly and recalled various ironies, from the political killing of Jesus to political firings without cause. God, how I loved working on Chicago's sacred lakefront, but when the arrogance of love confronts the arrogance of power, power always prevails and love always fails.

Didn't Zacchaeus teach that love always fails?

Yet even in failure love endures, bears all things, believes all things, and hopes all things. Even though the city betrayed one of its most ardent lovers, coldly with a form letter that seemed to blink "Next" like a neon sign, my love for Chicago and the common good endured. As I reached the door, Claypool turned away. I took a last look and glimpsed out of the corner of my eye the new general superintendent walking deliberately across the room to his private bathroom—I assumed to wash his hands.

GLATT

Two days after being fired, licking my wounds over morning coffee, I unfolded a story in the *Sun-Times* on page two under the headline "Boater Sues":

> Frank H. Glatt, assigned a "different unsafe and less desirable mooring" in Diversey Harbor, filed a $60,000 lawsuit in federal court against the Chicago Park District, alleging that Robert Nelson made the switch after he had improved his previous slip. Glatt said he complained "because of the internal corruption at the Park District and the bribes and payoffs" and because "money changes hands under the table."[1]

I couldn't believe the growing list of corruption charges. First, Batman's accusations, then, Gibson's McCartney tickets article; now, this: a lawsuit implying corruption on my part two days after being fired? The public couldn't help but connect my firing with corruption. And later in 1995 yet another corruption charge was leveled against me by John Grant, director of property, in a lawsuit alleging discrimination while I was director of harbors.[2] The Glatt lawsuit claimed I violated his constitutional right of free speech. In fact, last May I moved his boat with his permission, in order to satisfy another boater's request for a larger slip for his newly purchased boat that wouldn't fit in his existing slip. Switching boat slips for such reasons was a normal component of harbor management. Glatt did not like the first slip we moved him to, so a second slip was found and he was not only satisfied but thanked the Diversey harbor master for enabling the change.

Near the end of May, Glatt did come to see me. He seemed unbalanced, ranting and raving about corruption at Diversey and insisting that the boater assigned to his former slip received it by paying bribes. I assured Glatt that was not the case. He then explained he had hired Kurt Kleist, a lifeguard and certified scuba diver whom I knew well, to examine his slip and reported it was dangerous and infested with zebra mussels. (Kurt later told me he said no such thing, and in fact Glatt's slip had no zebra mussels or anything else that might endanger his boat.) In June, Mayor Daley's deputy chief of staff, Cheryl Thomas, called and said Glatt had met with her complaining about corruption in the harbors. After I explained the situation, she said no further action was required on my part.

Glatt would not give up and in July filed a complaint with the new Claypool administration. An internal investigation was immediately launched. Weekly meetings with lawyers and investigators and court reporters taking statements from myself and the Diversey harbor master, dragged on until the middle of August. A final report found no corruption but reprimanded me for not having a written procedure for boaters to sign off on slip changes—the golf locks and long-stem roses episodes all over again.

After reading the report, Glatt became more incensed, calling my office repeatedly and screaming at whomever answered. His paranoid behavior, identical to Batman's three years earlier, scared me. I begged the Investigations and Inspections Department to do a background check on Glatt, but the cautious new administration would not allow it, even when I showed evidence of death threats from Glatt, not only toward me but to other boaters in Diversey. Glatt hired a lawyer and filed his federal lawsuit in September, the day after my termination.

I immediately drove to the park district to see the new general attorney, Randy Mehrberg. A close friend of Forrest Claypool, he left a prestigious downtown law firm to work at the district. The contrast between the two men was striking; whereas Claypool was cold and aloof, Randy was warm and gregarious. In July when I first met him, our conversation drifted to a parking problem he was having. His Lincoln Park condominium garage was closed for repairs, and he had to park on the street, which in Lincoln Park after working hours was virtually impossible. I helped him out by obtaining a temporary permit from the science museum on park district land a couple of blocks from his condo. Randy was so grateful that I would help a member of the new administration that he began calling me for advice on a variety of lakefront issues—that is until I was let go.

Randy graciously changed his schedule to see me. He had both the *Sun-Times* article and the lawsuit on his desk and had already indicated to Glatt's lawyer that the park district wanted to settle out of court.

"Settle?" I said dropping my jaw.

"Yes, but not for money. We will give him another slip of his choice," he answered, proud to have negotiated the complaint without spending public funds on a protracted lawsuit.

"Randy, you don't want to settle this case. If you do, you will have a line of boaters and their lawyers stretching around this building." He leaned back in his chair and gave me a befuddled look.

"This has happened before," I continued, citing examples of boaters who claimed they were denied slips because they refused to pay money under the table. In each case after thorough investigation, there was not one shred of evidence to substantiate their claims. Still, their lawyers dangled the prospect of protracted lawsuits and damaging articles in the press. A few got their way until I convinced Nancy Kaszak to call their bluffs.

Randy tapped his fingers on his desk. I could tell he was thinking of unintended consequences should the district settle with Glatt, so I gave him more insight.

"Frank Glatt has been a problem for years. Look in his file."

"You kept files on boaters?" Randy asked innocently.

"Yes, and you will be amazed what you find there," I responded, handing him the Glatt file, which I had picked up at the Marine office from a somber but willing to help Rich Tinker a few minutes earlier. In addition to written demands from other Diversey boaters to expel Glatt, there was the assault charge he filed against a harbor worker, who ironically was cleaning Glatt's slip with a weed harvester. Glatt alleged the harbor worker hit him. The worker hired his own lawyer and countersued. The case was dismissed for lack of evidence.

"This guy has written his alderman, the police commissioner, the mayor, not to mention the park district Internal Investigations Department. In one of those letters, he boasted that he won $70,000 in damages from a boat manufacturer because the bottom of his boat wasn't smooth enough and affected the boat's speed! Mr. Glatt is loaded with money and apparently loves to spend it on lawsuits."

Randy carefully leafed through the file while I continued pleading.

"Randy, I moved hundreds of boats into different slips every year for all kinds of reasons, mostly because they didn't fit. Most of Chicago's boat slips were built when boats were wood with narrow beams. Now, they're fiberglass with wider and wider beams. Assigning boat slips is a real jigsaw puzzle."

He scratched the back of his head and closed Glatt's file. "So you are convinced we should fight this lawsuit?"

"Absolutely! I know this sounds like it's about my reputation, and in one sense it is. But the underlying issue is the integrity of the management system that I and the park district put in place after the indictments of my predecessor and his staff. Right after Pfeiffer was indicted several lawsuits similar to Glatt's were filed; since then there have been none—until now. The system works well, but if you let a guy like Glatt win for the wrong reasons, the Law Department will be running the harbors."

Just when I thought he was going to say that my information was all very interesting and then reject my plea, he reached over to shake my hand. "I'm convinced. You have my word," he said adding, "We will fight this case." And then his smile changed to puzzlement. He apologized in advance for getting personal.

"May I ask why you were fired?"

You would think he and Claypool would talk about such things. Obviously Randy was not consulted. The decision came down from Mayor Daley.

"I have no idea, but I think you are asking the wrong guy," I responded, trying to dampen my sarcasm. Randy asked nothing further.

His word was good, and the new administration fought Glatt. The case took three and a half years to wind through the courts. I was deposed several times by different lawyers for Glatt. (He changed lawyers like boat slips.). There were numerous investigations, reports, affidavits, and FOIA requests for documents. Over the years, five different park district lawyers worked on the case. Finally, on June 17, 1996, in the US Court of Appeals for the Seventh Circuit, Chief Judge Richard Posner dismissed the case and wrote:

> The Constitution is trivialized, the majesty of constitutional law degraded, when the concept of property is allowed to expand to a point at which irascible rich men can use it to lever petty disputes with local officials into federal cases.[3]

My faith in justice, shattered in the Batman case, was restored. I called the city editor of the *Sun-Times* and asked that the decision be reported in the metro section. Even after reading Judge Posner's decision over the phone and suggesting it be printed as a wonderful example of frivolous lawsuits that tie governments and courts into time-consuming knots, the editor curtly refused, saying that a three-year-old case was no longer newsworthy, that if I felt that strongly, I should write a letter to the editor. Even though I had written numerous such letters, I decided not to this time. He was right. It was old news and so was Chicago's last Harbor Boss.

As for Frank Glatt, he would neither see Judge Posner's ruling nor appeal it to the US Supreme Court, which he vowed to do after losing earlier court appeals. A month before the decision was handed down, the wealthy forty-eight-year-old misfit, owner of a high-speed powerboat called *Shotgun*, committed suicide.

AFTERGLOW

The windowless auditorium smelled like a well-used gym, reminding the commissioners who met there every other week of their recreational mission in Chicago's parks. The 300 theater-style seats were upholstered in the original dark green from the 1930s and desperately needed deep cleaning if not replacement. The seats smelled from thousands of sweaty, squirming citizens who over the decades took the time to come to board of commissioners' meetings to speak passionately about their neighborhood's parks. Now I joined them and waited my turn at the back of the hall. The people's podium at stage left faced the black-skirted dais behind which sat the five commissioners, the general superintendent, general attorney, and recording secretary.

The meeting was running late and finally moved to the public comment section known as "People in the Parks." The first speaker, to my great surprise, was Ron March, chairman of the Diversey Harbor Advisory Council, who moved resolutely to the podium when his name was called. Ron was the most vocal critic of the harbors until I established the councils, which held standing-room-only meetings in this very room. Ron's voice was strong and angry:

"For the first time in anybody's memory, the harbors are being run right, and now this! I have three questions: What is the future of the harbors? What is going to happen to our harbor councils? And why in the world was Mr. Nelson terminated?" My face flushed.

Superintendent Claypool pulled his microphone close. "The assistant director is now in charge of Marine operations. Secondly, this administration has no plans to change any advisory bodies now in place. As to Mr. Nelson, it has always been the policy of the park district not to discuss personnel matters publicly." He pushed his microphone away hard, a gesture to indicate he would say nothing more. Ron March sat down. Two more boaters gave long statements, praising my accomplishments, causing me to slouch in my seat. I had no idea such boaters would be there and was deeply touched.

Like generations of speakers before me, I started to sweat, wondering if addressing the board of commissioners was such a good idea. I was not there as a "former disgruntled employee" to embarrass Claypool, nor to make a slobbery request for my job back. I was responding to a compulsion, to a fuzzy afterglow bubbling up from my spiritual subconscious, which was formed in the sixties, to say thanks for the privilege of serving the people of Chicago.

The new president of the board, John Rogers, looked at his watch and asked the secretary how many more speakers had signed up. As she answered "three," I realized I had not signed up to speak. For six and a half years in this auditorium, I had addressed the board as a senior staff member numerous times, but today I forgot that private citizens must formally sign up before each meeting begins. I quickly rose to my feet, walked to the stage, and whispered my apology to the secretary, who fortunately knew me quite well and, though technically against the rules, added my name to the list. Mr. Claypool saw me and in turn whispered something to Randy Mehrberg as I joined the speaker line against the wall closest to the podium. Within minutes, two security guards entered the auditorium and stood in the back watching me. Did Claypool think I was going to do something violent? President Rogers leaned into his microphone and made an announcement.

"I'm sorry, but I have to ask the speakers to limit their remarks to one minute. The Field Museum Centennial Celebration dinner is about to start and all the commissioners here will attend. Please make your remarks brief."

Two more boaters criticized Claypool for letting me go. He listened deadpan and without comment. The last speaker before me, Nancy Hayes, a celebrated Hyde Park environmentalist in her seventies, who once chained herself to trees in Jackson Park scheduled to be cut down for a new cross-town expressway (never built, thankfully), made her way slowly to the podium. She used a cane now and handed it to me with a smile. I had held her cane before and driven her home from many board meetings. She complained about park workers driving heavy trucks over tree roots in Jackson Park in careless disregard for her beloved trees. When she spoke over the one-minute limit by two or three, two commissioners excused themselves and departed for the museum gala. Then it was my turn.

"I am not here today to complain or criticize, but to give thanks to the Chicago Park District for affording me the opportunity of public service for six and a half years. I have always considered and will always believe that public service is a high privilege for any citizen, especially for one who comes from the so-called private sector. To leave this place is a deep disappointment but, as a great influence on my life and on all American lives, Martin Luther King Jr. wrote from a Birmingham jail, 'there can be no deep disappointment where there is not deep love.'

"I want to thank those I worked with, especially the old-timers, the 'lifers,' who year in and year out take great pride in this place. Thanks to those who get involved: the community groups, the committees, and especially the harbor councils. Thanks to the 'blue space' users, the boaters, fishermen, disabled sailors, charter operators, and scuba divers, all of whom care about the waterfront of our great city.

"It is unfortunate that those who criticize the park district for the amount of acreage, compared to population, never include the thousands of acres of Lake Michigan under park jurisdiction—the blue space. Each year over a million sailors and their guests use the blue space rather than green space for their recreation. Another million fishermen, in summer and in winter through harbor ice, catch bass, trout, salmon, perch, smelt, and even an occasional northern pike, making Chicago if not the finest, then one of the finest urban fisheries in the world. Over forty dive groups search beneath the water to uncover shipwrecks from Chicago's heritage as a tall-ship maritime port. A large part of Chicago's quality of life is related to its blue space. While it is a myth that all boaters are wealthy, it is true they are all successful; it does not matter what size boats they own. Do we not want the success models they embody in our parks? While a factory or business will move out of the city when the business climate changes, the harbors will not move. Blue space users will always be here, racing across the waves or watching the moon dance on the water on a summer night or finding respite a mile out as the sun sets behind the skyline wonder that is Chicago.

"But I digress. I want to thank the board of commissioners who appointed me to reform a corrupt Marine Department, whose last four directors were sentenced to federal prison. It is mystifying—when we have public service examples like Martin Luther King Jr. and Nelson Mandela and countless others imprisoned for morally urgent, just, and right reasons—how anyone in public life could waste valuable time going to prison for the wrong reasons.

"Finally, I do not feel terminated—just moved up on the organization chart from third-level box to first-level box, the one to which you commissioners report, the one at the top of the chart labeled 'The People of Chicago.' Whereas I used to work for you, now you work for me and my fellow citizens. Incidentally that box to which you report is not labeled 'The Taxpayers of Chicago.' We citizens should neither call ourselves nor allow ourselves to be called 'taxpayers.' It is politically incorrect. Referring to a citizen as a 'taxpayer' is like referring to a woman by one of her body parts. In this era of politically correct speech, we should not allow politicians, commentators, and critics of public servants to get away with it. Taxpaying is only one body part of a citizen, the least important part when you think of the others: voter, juror, soldier, and protestor.

"Perhaps it is time to change that heading, 'The People of Chicago,' to something else. I have an old fashioned suggestion: 'We the people.' I thank you for your attention."

Like a monk at vespers, I whispered amen. Unexpectedly, people stood up and started clapping, first the people in the worn-out seats, then the commissioners. Even Forrest Claypool stood and applauded. I would like to think they clapped for my pneumacratic spirit, no longer embodied in their world, alas, but released involuntarily to fly into the wind.

I tried to leave quickly but was stopped by several employees and boaters wishing me well. Kris was there—she is always there—and we walked out together, arm in arm upstairs to my former office to pick up some personal items. The office door was locked, but I still had the key. I could see by my spotless desk that Joe O'Malley had moved in. My stuff was piled neatly in boxes in one corner. My enlarged photographs were still on the walls.

Kris and I did not feel like carrying boxes; I would come back on Sunday morning for them when no one was around. We took only the pictures. She removed the two smaller iceberg photos while I lifted the larger mid-Atlantic scene showing a massive cumulonimbus storm cloud fifty thousand feet in the air imploding onto the horizon. Such beautiful clouds disappeared into themselves so quickly that it had been difficult to focus my camera in time, but I had managed to capture that one perfectly. Beneath the disintegrating mushroom cloud, a black-hulled freighter crawled like a determined caterpillar along the horizon. It is one of my favorite sailing photos, and I labeled it "Dead Calm."

FILAN REPORT

A month after my termination, Bob Wulkowicz called me at home with news from the district. "You know that payback is a mother-fucker? Well, the new administration is cutting you up like a dead carp." Wulky had somehow obtained a copy of "Report to the Super-intendent, Preliminary Findings for Certain Departments."[1] He told me the report was put together by a politically connected accounting firm owned by John Filan.[2] It devoted over thirty pages to stinging criticism of Special Services management under my watch. Curious, I asked Wulky to give it to Rich Tinker who could drop it off at my house on one of his inspections in the south harbors.

The next afternoon, Rich showed up with the bound 110-page re-port. We sat on my screened-in front porch, where he fidgeted, angry after peeking at the section on Harbors. "Only a couple of weeks after your speech to the Board and they go out of their way to make you look bad," he said. "It's not right. You're the best thing that ever hap-pened to the Marine Division."

"Rich, stop it. You're embarrassing me. It's over. I'm history."

Rich knew the clichés, knew he had to move on. Along with a strong sense of civil righteousness, positive thinking was at the core of his belief system. I knew he would do fine once he got over his im-mediate feelings.

"Our roles have changed. We're not boss and employee anymore," I said.

He sighed as he related how some Marine Department employees were already bad-mouthing me. I put my finger to my lips and told him to stop. "Employees naturally go into survival mode when an administration changes. It is best not to talk about them." He nodded in reluctant agreement.

"We're friends now, and that's more important than what goes on at the park district. Let me tell you what I told Jesse Madison at his farewell party: 'A friend is somebody you can't get rid of no matter how much you might want to, and no matter how hard you try.'"

Rich looked at me for a moment, digested the thought, and then squeezed out a smile. We talked about some of the good times for a half hour before he looked at his watch. It was time for him to inspect sanitation devices on some boats in Jackson Inner Harbor. We shook hands and discussed getting together for lunch on a regular basis.

As soon as he left, I read the report, fuming over factual errors, misinformation, and self-serving conclusions. Every Special Services division was slammed except Golf; while Golf was listed in the report's introduction as one to be reviewed, it was noticeably absent. (Could it be because the private management company chosen to operate Golf had political ties to Mayor Daley?) In the Harbors section, the report played games with numbers.

Another section attacked the yacht clubs, referring to them as "concessionaires" instead of not-for-profit organizations, accusing them of having monopolies on fuel sales. Yet it ignored the new fuel facility built at Jackson, which replaced three yacht club fueling stations and was managed by an independent concessionaire who had nothing to do with yacht clubs.

In a scathing section on mismanagement of all park district capital improvement funds, the Harbor Improvement Fund was conspicuously not mentioned. Could that be because it had been properly managed, with all projects fairly bid, at or under budget, and completed on time? Such success was not what the Filan report was instructed to find.

What upset me was that so much was left out. Last July when Filan's staff interviewed me, I provided lists of successful new revenue

initiatives and plans in the pipeline—the Turning Basin marina with
in-water winter storage, the profitable Monroe water taxi service, the
Montrose Harbor total rebuild, the proposed new thousand-slip marina at Thirty-First Street, replacing parking meters with attended
parking facilities up and down the lakefront, eliminating no-bid concessionaire contracts at the South Shore Cultural Center and substituting caterer lists from which clients could choose—none of which
were mentioned in the report.

I had enthusiastically explained my idea to reserve a section of
Soldier Field's south parking lot for motor homes. Bears fans would
be delighted to pay a lot of money for a season pass to park their RVs
for tailgating. In the summer off-season, the lot would be utilized for
campers with RVs visiting the city. Currently there was no designated
place anywhere in the city for vacationing families with RVs allowing
camping access to Chicago's lakefront. Soldier Field's south lot was
within walking distance of beaches, museums, and downtown, and
stadium staff could easily handle the summer campers. My income
estimate was $150,000 to $200,000 net per year. This idea, which
had already gained traction in the Planning Department, was nowhere
mentioned.

The interviewer also left out my caution on privatizing harbors,
that they were neighborhoods not parking garages for boats. I explained that private companies managing public marinas immediately
cut unprofitable services to public areas of the harbors and eliminated
such things as public washrooms and picnic facilities.

The report claimed to have compared Chicago harbor fees to others
within a "90-minute drive," but left out Michigan City, Indiana, only
forty-five to sixty minutes away (thirty-five miles by water). That
public marina had lower fees and more amenities than Chicago harbors, and 90 percent of the boats there were owned by Chicagoans.
Furthermore, Michigan City most closely resembles Chicago's system;
it lies within a public park system with public beaches, historic buildings, and like Diversey Harbor, even has a zoo; and it is managed very
well by the municipal government. At almost every Chicago harbor

council meeting, Michigan City's marina was brought up as the example for how Chicago should manage its harbors—and yet it was deliberately left out of Filan's report. No boaters were interviewed for the report. Perhaps because in every survey I have read, boaters prefer municipal management over privatization.

For several days I obsessed over the "confidential" report, writing in the margins, and composing a ten-page reply following a basic rule of politics: "Never let a personal attack go unanswered. Any charge not answered is a charge believed." I knew it was like writing in sand, but I didn't care. I sent it to Superintendent Claypool, board president John Rogers, all commissioners, and John Filan. While I would never receive a reply, that didn't matter; truth mattered. If they stereotyped me with the lunatic fringe of loose cannons, whistle-blowers, and disgruntled former employees, I didn't care. At least they couldn't spin their ridiculous report to the press, supporting Daley's agenda for privatization of the harbors without my certified mail rebuttal.

BASEMENT DREAMS

Unemployed for two months, I tried networking. Most of my politically connected colleagues who were fired found other government jobs within a month or two. The board of education was going through a huge reform; I could fit in there. I made an inquiry to Paul Vallas, rumored to become the new CEO, whom I worked with when he was city budget director. My calls and a letter went unanswered. Larry Bloom was empathetic but knew of no opportunities in city government.

I thought that at least one of the many reporters I knew would write some kind of follow-up to Claypool's purge—the good flushed out with the bad sort of thing—that might lead to a job offer. But, in spite of a bunch of letters in both papers criticizing my firing, no story materialized. In public service when you're out, you're out. The press moves on to your replacement.

At the unemployment office, I received another slap in the face: Claypool's administration, loaded with lawyers, challenged my eligibility for unemployment compensation based on my status as a Shakman-exempt employee. After a long delay, an internal hearing determined I was eligible. I should have felt the joy of victory, but the process only saddened me. Then a second hit: as part of his reform, Claypool stopped all payments to independent contractors until their claims for services were reviewed, standard procedure for all new administrations. I had no problem with it, being well versed on the pluses and minuses of the practice. But he refused a final payment (around $300) to the only independent contractor in Special Services, a college student summer intern doing research on harbor history and the role of the yacht clubs (which I planned to publish as part of an in-depth "Chicago Harbor Guide").

The idea for the guide came from my regular appearances on Bill Cullerton's *Great Outdoors* show on WGN radio, which boasted a following of over a million listeners, many of whom called in with questions about Chicago's harbors. For generations there was virtually no information, not even telephone numbers to call. They were a filled-to-capacity monopoly, and the district saw no point in advertising. On Bill's show, when I explained some of the history and features of the harbors, the phones lit up with questions and interest. A local publisher showed interest in publishing the guide, convinced it would be popular with nonboaters as well.

When the intern first called me in mid-September about her check, I assured her it was a common oversight when administrations change and that I would follow up. I sent Claypool and Joe Fratto a letter of explanation including copies of her time sheets and a synopsis of her research, only to be told a month later by Joe that her payment was denied. Denied? She did the work assigned. The most depressing part was not the fight over a $300 check; it was my inability to convince the student, who became fascinated studying the harbor system, to consider a career in public service.

Like Cathy Cahill, this bright young student turned her back on government after not being paid. Finally, her upset father, a former yacht club commodore, told me he would take care of it. He called a law firm with strong mayoral connections, and the intern was paid in a couple of days. Being cloutless to redress a simple legitimate claim for payment, something I was previously praised for in the contractor community, was extremely depressing.

I took solace in listening to my collection of black gospel records: the Dixie Hummingbirds, the Hawkins family, and my favorite,

Brother James Cleveland, and attended the black Apostolic Church of Christ mega-church on Sixty-Fourth and Dorchester—for the music not the theology.

To be suddenly unemployed was like being becalmed mid-ocean. Like a good sailor who proves his worth in heavy weather, a pneuma-crat proves his worth in bureaucratic storms. But in the dead calm of my unemployment, there were no battles between political armadas, no chasing of corrupt pirates, no navigating through dangerous bu-reaucratic reefs. On tall ships, being becalmed allowed time to learn knot tying, sing sea shanties, or carve scrimshaw on the bones of whales; if a seaman could not sing or carve, he scraped away rust and revarnished bright work. Sailors used their hands to break up the boredom, and that, I decided, was what I should do.

There was plenty of work to be done in the basement, where my workshop doubled as an office, including sorting through my files from the park district (enough to fill up two four-drawer filing cab-inets). My "Chicago Harbor Guide" *still* lurks somewhere in there. Fourteen creaky steps lead down to my basement, which is like the hold of an old ship. While creepy to my grandchildren, who imagine monsters live there, the hundred-year-old basement appeals to my psyche: warm in the winter from radiator pipes crisscrossing below eight-foot ceilings, yet cool in the summer, being below grade.

Old basements smell like tombs, and like ancient Egyptian tombs, mine was filled with artifacts from my 1960s antiwar collection: a serigraph by Sister Mary Corita with one of Father Dan Berrigan's best quotes ("No one walks waters. Isn't that Jesus though? The only God love we know is human love."); a 1967 silk-screen portrait of Allen Ginsberg with his hand-drawn Buddhist peace symbol; a 1968 poster of Nixon growling, with the caption "Would you Buy a Used War from This Man?"; a 1970 woodcut from the International Work-ers of the World office in Chicago, signed by its secretary, Don Moir, that reads, "Draftees of the World Unite! You Have Nothing to Lose but Your Generals." (Moir sold it to me the night Jane Fonda spoke there.) But my favorite poster is an elaborate McGovern for President silk screen from 1972 with nine colored squares highlighting various causes of the time—peace, environment, gender equality, justice, and most prominent, "Service Above and Beyond Ambition." There is also Kurt Vonnegut Jr.'s classic antiwar novel, *Slaughterhouse-Five*, with the inscription "Peace and Plenty to My Pal Bob Nelson," sent to me in response to my long letter.

Many of the picture posters had mold on the glass and frames. Like rust on becalmed ships. I carefully cleaned them all. Next to the red wind sock from the 1996 Democratic Convention hung a very moldy American flag between two windows. I found it discarded on the muddy ground of Grant Park during the Democratic Convention riot of 1968. It was not bloody or torn, just filthy and full of mildew. I took it down and carefully hand-washed it with Woolite in cold water as if it was the Shroud of Turin. But it was only an inexpensive flag, and when I hung it reverently from a clothesline, I noticed the white stripes turned pink like the movement for which it was carried.

With great care I rehung the artworks, apologizing to each one for my neglect. I could almost hear them talking to each other like honored guests at a ceremony consecrating a new memorial, perhaps, in my imagination, a future tomb of the unknown antiwar soldier.

On the final day of cleaning, I bought a dehumidifier and set it up to drain into an automatic sump pump next to the hot water heater and furnace. There I collapsed into a 1950s deck chair from Grebes. When the sump pump switched on, I heard that familiar voice.

"Zacchaeus?" Where have you been? I could have used some help."

"I don't clean pictures."

"Not the pictures. Losing my job."

The flag furled slightly as Zacchaeus said, "I have never been in a basement before. I didn't know you were allowed to fly the American flag underground."

"Forget the flag. Where were you when I was fired? I felt so abandoned."

"Well, of course you were abandoned. That's what happens when you try to repair the world: you fail. How many times do I have to tell you? But be aware that the instant you were handed that letter, your failure celebration began. What a beautiful ceremony. The clouds lit up with an aurora borealis waterfall of color while heavenly hosts sang.'"

"You celebrated my termination?"

"Of course! We have failure festivals all the time. The Corporal Knobloch party lasted several months, and the Bonhoeffer party has been going on for over fifty years. I suspect it will last at least another hundred. Martin Luther King Jr.'s is just getting started and will last as long as your country lasts. Oh, in case you're wondering, your party lasted two months. Being fired for no cause is not very high on the pneumacrat celebration scale. Now if you had gone to prison, the celebration would last much longer."

"Now I am truly depressed. I'm not sure I can take another failure."

"Of course you can. Failure is the moral way of life in the world. Shedding the snake skin of success regularly is a natural thing for pneumacrats. That's what it's all about."

"Why are you here?"

"To say good-bye, of course. Did you think you are the only church dropout?"

"I am not a dropout; I am a drop-in."

"True, but you're not alone. You people multiply like fireflies and Tikkun Olam counseling resources are repeatedly cut out of the eternal budget. Still, to light up the world we must help all of you out of your little jars. They want me to recruit more pneumacrats for government jobs. I really must go."

That night I had a dream, another voyage, sailing out of Chicago, through the Great Lakes, across the Atlantic, pausing at the deepest point in dead calm, and diving once again as deep as I could into the enormity of it all before resurfacing on a blue and green beam and waking up. It was just before sunrise. I dressed and drove along Lake Shore Drive. At Jackson, timers turned off the spotlight on the flags at the Jackson Park Harbor Station. At Fifty-Seventh Street Beach, two people sat in lotus position and chanted mantras. At Burnham,

Figure 13. Removal of old seaplane ramp that caused so much damage to boats in Monroe Harbor over several decades, 1992. (Photo by R. J. Nelson.)

fishermen cast their lures between boat slips. At the south end of Monroe, I drove down the service road to the water's edge by the Shedd Aquarium, dodged early morning joggers, then paused at the site of the old seaplane ramp built in the 1920s when seaplanes were considered the future of commercial aviation.

For decades the largely submerged concrete-and-steel ramp posed a navigation hazard for Monroe boaters who frequently smashed into it—even though it was well marked. In northeast storms, boats that broke loose drifted into it and smashed into pieces. When I was able to finally remove it two years ago, over a hundred anchors were found underneath the massive structure.

I drove past Queen's Landing, past the Chicago Yacht Club, and out the extended park landfill to Columbia Yacht Club at Randolph. In the late 1970s, the city reconfigured Lake Shore Drive to straighten out two right-angle turns that over the years caused numerous accidents and traffic jams. The straightening was accomplished with landfill that extended park land much farther into Monroe Harbor and the adjacent Turning Basin to the north. This allowed Lake Shore Drive to make a sweeping curve out over what used to be harbor.

As the park was extended using thousands of truckloads of demolished bricks, crushed sidewalks, sand, and clay, the Columbia Yacht Club ship had to be moved a half mile east with a temporary dirt road installed for member access. I was a member. Even though "No Dumping" signs were posted everywhere, I confess to illegal dumping. In 1981, I broke up a crumbling flagstone patio in my backyard and hauled several station wagon loads to the site after dark and dumped them. I justified dumping the broken flagstones because they were better-quality fill material than that used by the city. Long before working at the district, I practiced pneumacracy.

I stopped at the corner of the unused Turning Basin waiting to become a marina for four hundred boats. What a struggle the project became. Four other governmental entities shared jurisdiction: the Metropolitan Sanitary District for the south wall sluice gates, the state of Illinois for the east break wall (keeping Lake Michigan out of the river system except for the regulated lock diversions), the park district for the new park land and west wall, the federal government for legal jurisdiction of commercial traffic, and the adjacent Army Corps of Engineers Chicago Lock from Lake Michigan into the river. As the state's stone and concrete break wall was falling apart, allowing substantial leakage into the river system, it was willing to join the project for a new wall. The Metropolitan Water Reclamation District was also ready to have someone pay to rebuild its leaking sluice gates; the park district desperately needed more boat slips. But the federal government held the key: the water and bottom rights. The US Congress would have to pass a bill "de-authorizing" the basin for park district control, basically a transfer of title.

After Harza, the prestigious engineering firm hired to design the marina, pointed this out, I went to Jesse, anticipating a long federal delay in the project. But when I explained the problem, he immediately called Rep. Gus Savage, Chicago's maverick Second District congressman, and an old friend of Harold and Jesse. I couldn't believe my

Figure I4. Turning Basin before becoming DuSable Harbor, showing parkland extension into Monroe Harbor to straighten out Lake Shore Drive. (Photo by R. J. Nelson.)

ears when Jesse cupped his hand over the mouthpiece and asked if I could meet with Congressman Savage that night. Of course.

Around ten o'clock, I met with Gus Savage in a hotel bar in Hyde Park. He was well lubricated as he conducted political business with various favor seekers. When it was my turn, he said nice things about Jesse and Harold and asked what I needed. Obviously uninterested as I explained the marina project and the need for a "de-authorizing" bill from Congress, he asked for my notes, handed them to the aide who supplied his drinks and said, "I'll take care of it."

I reported back to Jesse the next day expressing my doubts anything would happen. Jesse laughed and told me to keep the faith. Sure enough, a few months later the de-authorization, attached to some other bill regarding rivers, passed unanimously. The project was back on course; unfortunately it would not be completed until several years after my termination.

I kept driving north. At Belmont, the yacht club was serving breakfast to participants in a youth regatta, and the smell of bacon tempted

Figure 15. Wilson Avenue toilet building before restoration and concession expansion, 1994. (Photo by R. J. Nelson.)

me to join in. But I was in no mood to socialize. Instead I drove down the dirt maintenance road to Montrose and paused as the harbor's solar-powered entrance lights stopped flashing as the sun rose.

A cop driving the other way rolled down his window and asked what I was doing there. "Inspecting the harbors," I answered and showed him the "All Lakefront Areas" official park pass on my dashboard, which was valid until the end of the year. When I turned in my office keys and pager, the pass was not requested, so I kept it. The cop looked at it for a minute and then without a word drove off. I moved on, past the Wilson Avenue launch ramp and the toilet building with its roof caved in. I wondered if that restoration project, my last public washroom project funded by state of Illinois water access grants, would be cancelled like all the others. It was not. When the new building finally opened two years later, I toyed with petitioning the park board to name it after me. Then, circling the parking lot where the golf dome should have been, I headed back south.

At the Lake Shore Drive Bridge over the Chicago River, the gates

Figure 16. Wilson Avenue toilet building after restoration, 1995. (Photo by R. J. Nelson.)

lowered, halting traffic as the massive double-decked bascule bridge
lifted. A flotilla of sailboats passed up river, marking the melancholy
end of the sailing season. Their masts and booms stripped naked of
sailcloth, forced to use auxiliary power, they looked embarrassed. The
steel arches of the open bridge looked like prison guards, keeping an
eye below on the forced march toward the boatyards along the river
for solitary winter confinement.

Most drivers honked, angry for losing the half hour or so required
for the boats to pass; every year they called the mayor demanding he
do something. Daley pressured the coast guard to close the downtown bridges permanently, but even he held no sway over access to
federal waterways that belong to the people and are free of charge.
A few motorists stepped out of their cars and strolled to the river to
watch. Some relished the experience of walking on Lake Shore Drive
to gaze close-up at the giant bascule bridge decks pointing skyward. I
mentioned to one tourist that Chicago had more opening bridges than
any other city in the world, but because commercial ship traffic had
all but disappeared except for barges, now equipped with hydraulic

wheelhouses, that float underneath, Chicago's bridges only opened for sailboats in spring and fall.

"Isn't that awesome? A great city like Chicago forcing busy citizens to a halt for a few sailboats passing by, their masts poking fun at frenzied lives," I said, but he did not answer as the rumbling bridge decks lowered slowly to a close.

AFTERWORD

Privatization of the harbors was implemented in December of 1995. Westrec Marine of California was awarded the management contract. Prior to the award, Westrec hired me as a consultant to assist them with information and suggestions, which I provided. But after a short time, as I found out more about the company and the political way it operated, I severed my association.

The initial contract allowed for a low annual management fee plus an "incentive component," a very high percentage of gross revenues that increased with fee increases or new revenues. Subsequent contracts included the most lucrative provision for "project management fees," a sliding scale (as high as 11 percent) on any and all harbor improvements. These provisions accounted for millions paid to Westrec each year for completing what I had already planned or already had in the pipeline awaiting approval of the park board. The contract also required the park district to pay all operational expenses, including insurance, legal, accounting, auditing fees, and outside bank service fees, formerly part of normal park district operations at much lower costs. To verify the private operator's every move, the contract required a park district appointed "agreement administrator," whose contract-specific duties created a new bureaucracy inside the district.

In 1996, in describing Westrec's capital improvement plans, all of which were previously planned, Forrest Claypool announced, "Chicago's harbors haven't had significant renovation and upgrading in 60 years."[1] Really. As docks are the most important component of harbor design, below is a comparison of Westrec's new dock systems with those designed by Fred Hunt, a world famous engineer of floating docks, and installed on my watch.

FRED HUNT DOCKS	WESTREC DOCKS
Steel frame and cage to hold floats against ice damage	No steel cage for floats
Additional heavy-duty floats	Minimal number of floats
High level of stability under heavy loads	Unstable under normal loads
Padded uprights for easy docking	No uprights
Parallel decking to reduce tripping	Traditional decking
Horn cleats for strength	"S" cleats that fail in comparison tests
Rub rail screwed into wood rails	Rub rail stapled into wood rails
Low maintenance.	High maintenance

The Fred Hunt docks are specifically designed for Chicago's harsh conditions. Westrec docks are generic and have experienced several design failures (not including ice-related failures) over the years.

Daley changed my paradigm of harbors as neighborhoods to harbors as parking lots to be primarily used as revenue producers; and because they were a monopoly, harbor fees could be raised to whatever the market would bear, thus enriching Westrec's percentage revenues.

Always looking for new revenue sources to increase its incentive payments, Westrec convinced the district to get into the winter storage business for large boats. At Montrose, a parking lot was fenced and improved for three hundred boats, and a travel lift extending into Montrose Harbor was installed. This project, not required to be brought before the Chicago Plan Commission for approval like the golf dome, was constructed ironically in the adjacent parking lot to the dome. The cost was $1.87 million. More ambitious was a heated building for indoor boat parking at Thirty-First Street Harbor for eighty to one hundred large boats, wrapped into the $110 million total cost of the harbor.

The harbor management firm, knowing that large boats pay higher fees, designed Thirty-First Street Harbor for them, with slips from thirty-five to seventy feet (all other public marinas I am aware of are designed to include thirty- and even twenty-five-foot slips for middle-class boat owners). Additionally, as the Great Recession decimated small boat ownership, Westrec removed more than five hundred less expensive mooring buoys from Monroe Harbor, effectively pushing small boat owners into more expensive slips. My plan for Thirty-First Street included not only small slips, but would have moved both the sailing programs out of congested Burnham and the Marine Department offices to the lakefront, making them easily accessible to visiting boaters and prospective slip holders in all seasons. Westrec preferred to rent offices at park district headquarters, which had been moved to rented floors in a North Side office tower. (The old building on McFetridge Drive was torn down as part of the Soldier Field renovation.)

Public records show that over the years Westrec has made several thousand dollars in political contributions to elected officials: Gary Chico, when he ran for mayor; Governor Pat Quinn; and Forrest Claypool, after he left the district to run successfully for Cook County commissioner and unsuccessfully for both chairman of its board and later for Cook County assessor.[2]

In 2006 when Westrec's contract was up for renewal, a group of black boaters and investors asked me to consult on their bid to manage the harbors. I did so, without compensation or any interest in being their CEO if they succeeded. They did not succeed, although several of my proposals in the bid were implemented by the district and Westrec.

The partnership for profit between park district and Westrec was best expressed by Scott Stevenson, Westrec's senior manager in charge. In a 2013 story on the new harbor at Thirty-First Street, he said,

"These harbors make the Park District a lot of money, and now it's going to be a cash cow for 100 years."[3]

Whether Zacchaeus pulled some strings or not, I bounced from Chicago's harbors to the Hammond (Indiana) Port Authority, which borders Chicago on Lake Michigan. After a thorough investigation of corruption charges against me, I was hired as its CEO. At first the port authority board and the mayor of Hammond resented the know-it-all from the big city. But after a difficult year, things improved, and like exiled Kent in King Lear, I shaped my old course in a country new, including establishing a disabled sailing program. Gerry Dahl, who was fired by Westrec for insubordination, at my request headed up the Hammond program.

Hammond mayor Duane Dedelow gave me carte blanche to restore that marina from near bankruptcy to its 1,300 slip capacity with waiting lists of Chicago boaters. By 1997 they accounted for 87 percent of the slip holders. In the spring of 2000, the Hammond marina was featured at an annual International Conference of Great Lakes Mayors in Gary, Indiana, as an example of excellence in waterfront development. Ironically, Mayor Daley was the main speaker. I buttonholed him, not to spit in his face, but to discuss my idea for locating a Chicago Maritime Museum in an abandoned factory building at the mouth of the Calumet River. He seemed interested, took my pictures of the site and my phone number, and promised one of his people would call.

I'm still waiting.

For nearly a year after leaving the park district, I kept receiving emergency calls at all hours on various fronts. I finally wrote Superintendent Claypool asking him to please remove my name from the emergency call list. When he didn't respond, and the calls kept coming, I sent a copy of my letter to Michael Sneed's column in the *Sun-Times*, the only time I ever leaked anything to the press. It worked: no more emergency calls. But there were plenty of requests from the park district Law Department asking for my testimony in cases that happened on my watch, including a particularly sticky case involving an employee who had appealed his termination to multiple government agencies for seven years. Based on my testimony, he lost.

While revising this book for publication, some editors and outside readers repeatedly asked what clout I must have utilized to obtain the highly political director of harbors job, even though I repeatedly pointed out in the manuscript that I had none. So I called my only contacts prior to my hiring, Larry Bloom and George Galland, acting general attorney for the park district at the time, and asked if there was any clout involved in my hiring. Unfortunately, both Walter Netsch and Jesse had passed away. I did talk to Jesse's widow, Francis, who said that he often talked about me and the harbors and that he was so pleased at how "professionally" they were run. Larry, my alderman and lawyer when we sold our first house in Hyde Park, and by coincidence the seller's lawyer for the house we bought in South Shore the same year, told me, "Bob, there was no clout on my part. I barely knew Jesse Madison. We had no special relationship. He never called me about you nor did anyone at city hall. Based on your request to me, I asked him to interview you and that was it."

George Galland was picked by his law partner, Judd Miner, corporate counsel for the city under Harold at the time, to go over for a few months and straighten out the park district during the transition when Harold gained control of the park district board. George explained, "Nobody wanted to go, including me. The park district was a cesspool and the new board members that Harold sent over were particularly naive and disorganized about everything. Walter Netsch thought he had the power to hire and fire and started hiring all sorts of people. I had to officially write him a memo saying he had no such power as president of the board. Jesse and I never discussed your being hired. Honestly I think you simply surfaced at the right time, and Jesse just liked you. I'm quite sure nobody politically connected wanted anything to do with the harbors, especially with the federal investigation unfolding. If Jesse did call city hall for approval, which I don't think he did, they probably said hire anybody you want." There never was a national search for a harbor director. Those are the facts.

Sailing was my clout and often showered me with favors. One summer I was privileged to take the helm of *Amistad*, the replica slave ship, and sail her from Navy Pier to Hammond, thanks to Bill Pink-

ney, the *Amistad* Foundation president, and the first African American
to solo circumnavigate the world. Bill asked if *Amistad*'s tour of the
Great Lakes could be extended in Hammond. Of course. Back when
he had no money and no one would listen to his dream of sending
live video of his voyage to black schoolchildren in Chicago, I let him
use a slip briefly in Belmont without charge, the only time I made an
exception, a pneumatic exception, to the harbor rules for which technically I could have been indicted. Sailing *Amistad* from Navy Pier
to Hammond was a chance to imagine the most profound part of the
black experience.

Amistad is a floating reliquary, as holy as the silver chests of sacred
fragments carried throughout Europe in the Middle Ages. To witness
over three days a thousand black pilgrims tearfully boarding that ship
in Hammond was a religious experience I will never forget. It reignited
my love affair with the black experience.

Several friends passed away. Shortly after retiring from state of Illinois government, Jesse Madison died before I was able to show him
a draft of this book. Gerry Dahl's diabetes dealt its final blow, not
while sailing as he had hoped but alone in his Printer's Row apartment. We were soul brothers and shared that irony of being abruptly
terminated from jobs we so loved. His sense of humor fit mine. Once
in a boring park district meeting on ADA requirements, he stood up
and asked the facilitator, "If con is the opposite of pro, is congress the
opposite of progress?" At a Judd Goldman Adaptive Sailing Foundation charity function, he told a contributor, "I put my pants on like
everyone else—after my legs of course." In his honor we named one
of Hammond's new Freedom 20s *Gerry*. Wulky died while working on
various inventions, one of which was a tire wrench for the disabled
that used the vehicle's motion to undo the wheel lugs in case of a flat
tire. Rich Tinker, after being cancer free for a few years, caught a common cold that his immune system, crippled by chemo, could not fight
off. He died two days later. As he was not religious in the traditional
sense, his family asked me to orchestrate his funeral, which hundreds
of people attended. At the grave site, I quoted Mark Antony's funeral

oration: "My heart is in the coffin there with Caesar, / And I must pause till it come back to me."

In 2009 the Chicago Park District's Recreation Department took back the Rainbow Fleet Sailing Programs from Marine, which was operated by the harbor management company. A position of "manager of sailing" was advertised, at a beginning salary of $20,000 more than my old salary as superintendent of special services. Ironically, in 1990 I had created the identical position, which was eliminated by the harbor management company. Not profitable I assume.

I applied immediately; I don't know exactly why; perhaps it was the same naïveté that suggested recycling me back into the harbors job; perhaps it was more subconscious—that deep love for Chicago.

For over an hour, I was questioned by two interviewers, one of whom took copious notes. The scripted questions concerned the very programs I had established. As in my original harbor job interview with Walter Netsch, I knew far more than they. They seemed interested in my ideas, but it was probably for show, because this time around I was not hired. The rejection form letter, auto-signed "Human Resources Department," made me laugh. The irony would have pleased Zacchaeus.

NOTES

Dawn City

1. The titles of marine director, harbor director, and director of harbors are used interchangeably throughout this book.
2. See Luke 19:1–10. Luke's gospel emphasizes ethical behavior and is the only one that mentions Zacchaeus and famous parables like "The Good Samaritan," "The Prodigal Son," and "The Pharisee and the Tax Collector Who Went to the Temple to Pray."
3. Editorial, *Chicago Tribune*, March 22, 1987.

Harbors as Neighborhoods

1. Lois Wille, *Forever Open, Clear, and Free: The Struggle for Chicago's Lakefront* (Chicago: University of Chicago Press, 1972).
2. "Report of the Citizens' Committee, to Investigate the Operations and Expenditures of the Chicago Park District," *official record, Chicago Park District* (July 1938).
3. "Standards for Operation of Yacht Clubs Located on Park Lands or Waters," *Journal of the Proceedings of the Board of Commissioners, Chicago Park District* (December 26, 1944).
4. Mike Royko, "Those Yacht Clubs Are a Real Menace," *Chicago Tribune*, November 1, 1990, 2.
5. William Shaw, boat seminar, Grebe Shipyard, Chicago, February 1978.

A Boat Slip and Fall

1. Wes Smith, "Lawn Bowlers Strike a Blow for Barrier." *Chicago Tribune*, April 29, 1987.
2. Barry Cronin, "New Park Dist. Harbor Chief a Skilled Boater," *Chicago Sun-Times*, April 12, 1987.

Harold

1. See in-depth discussion on black reform tradition by Gary Rivlin, *Fire on the Prairie: Harold Washington, Chicago Politics, and the Roots of the Obama Presidency* Philadelphia: Temple University Press, 1992; rev. 2013), 183.

2. Dianne Luhmann, church historian, *First Presbyterian Church of Chicago, Its First 175 Years*, a church-produced pamphlet, spring 2008.

Indictments

1. Barry Cronin, "Pfeiffer Is the Latest Harbor Boss in Trouble with Law," *Chicago Sun-Times*, December 8, 1997.
2. *New York Times*, July 10, 1997.
3. Martin and Susan J. Tolchin, *Pinstripe Patronage: Political Favoritism from the Clubhouse to the White House and Beyond* (London: Routledge, 2010).

April Fools

1. William Recktenwald, "Parks Patronage Booming," *Chicago Tribune*, January 24, 1988, 1.
2. Robert J. Nelson, "Black and White of Park District Pay," Voice of the People, *Chicago Tribune*, February 5, 1988, 18.
3. Barry Cronin, "Aide Jabs Parks Chief," *Chicago Sun-Times*, January 15, 1988, 2.

Harbor Fire

1. Peter Kendall, "Historic Coast Guard Station Burns," *Chicago Tribune*, May 18, 1988, A3.

Wulky

1. Stuart Dybek, "The Long Thoughts," in *Childhood and Other Neighborhoods* (Chicago: University of Chicago Press, 1980), 88–102.
2. "It's 100, but It's Far from Perfect; Record-Breaking Heat Stays in Forecast," *Chicago Tribune*, July 15, 1988.

Fog Bowl

1. "McCaskey Faults Park Dist. on Sod," *Chicago Sun-Times*, August 15, 1988.
2. *Chicago Sun-Times*, January 15, 2002, 99–104.

D-Day

1. Steve Neal, "Parks 'Watchdogs' Are Really Madison's Lapdogs," *Chicago Sun-Times*, May 26, 1989, 34.
2. Robert J. Nelson, "At least 'Flunkie' No Criminal," *Chicago Sun-Times*, June 1, 1989, Letters to the Editor.
3. John Kass, "Madison to Quit as Parks Boss," *Chicago Tribune*, December 5, 1989, 2.
4. Basil Talbott Jr., "Jesse Madison's Big Bout," *Chicago Magazine*, November 1987, 145.

Batman

1. O'Malley & Gratteau, Inc., *Chicago Tribune*, April 24, 1990, sec. 1, p. 18.

Paul McCartney

1. Ray Gibson and Mark Caro, "Best Seat in the House? You Can't Touch It," *Chicago Tribune*, July 19, 1992, 1–2.

2. Robert J. Nelson, "McCartney Equality," Voice of the People, *Chicago Tribune*, August 15, 1992.

Golf Dome from Hell

1. The Lakefront Protection Ordinance was a series of policies passed by the city council in the mid-1980s to both limit expansion and new construction and enhance existing lakefront public facilities, part of the overall reform of Chicago's lakefront parks.
2. "Report of Proceedings of the Chicago Plan Commission" (Accurate Reporting Service, Jack Artstein, C.S.R., Chicago, March 14, 1991), 49. See full testimony of Robert J. Nelson, 23–68.
3. Nelson Algren, "Love Is for Barflies," *Chicago: City on the Make* (Chicago: University of Chicago Press, 2011), 49.

MBE/WBE

1. Matt O'Connor, "27-Month Prison Term for Park District Official," *Chicago Tribune*, July 25, 2000, sec. 2, p. 3.

"Lakefront's Small Wonder"

1. M. W. Newman, "New Burnham Boat Station Is Lakefront's Small Wonder," *Chicago Tribune*, June 3, 1991, 11.
2. John Kass, "Parks Board Kills Plan for Harbor Café," *Chicago Tribune*, September 8, 1989, 2–6.

A Reporter Falls Overboard

1. The most egregious example in modern Illinois history was the widespread practice of issuing commercial driver licenses to unqualified applicants in exchange for purchasing fund-raiser tickets for then secretary of state George Ryan. In 1994 Ricardo Guzman, who could not speak English and was incapable of taking the written licensing test, gladly bought fund-raiser tickets in exchange for his license. Later he was driving a truck on the expressway with an illegal loose rear mud flap assembly. Several witnesses would testify they repeatedly warned him about the steel part about to fall off the truck, but because he could not understand English, the warnings were ignored. The piece fell off and a van containing the Reverend Duane "Scott" Willis, his wife, Janet, and family ran over it causing the steel to puncture the van's fuel tank and explode. Six of the Willis children burned to death. After George Ryan was elected governor, a federal investigation uncovered the bribery scandal leading to over seventy-five indictments and convictions, including Governor Ryan. In 2006 he was convicted of corruption and received a federal sentence of six and a half years.

Daley's Underground River

1. John Kass, "Daley Bags 4 Bureaucrats," *Chicago Tribune*, April 23, 1992, 1 and 25; Michael Lev and John Kass, "Some Accept Their Fate but Others Will Fight It," *Chicago Tribune*, April 23, 1992, 26.
2. "The Chicago Park District and Kemper Golf Management Chicago, Inc., Agreement for Operation, Management, and Maintenance of Chicago Park District Golf Facilities," contract, signed April 1, 1993, *official record, Chicago Park District* (April 1993).

A Tale of Two Conventions

1. Norman Mailer, *Miami and the Siege of Chicago* (New York: New American Library, Inc., 1968), 216–17.
2. Bruce Dancis, *Resister: A Story of Protest and Prison during the Vietnam War* (Ithaca: Cornell University Press, 2014). This well-documented memoir relates all the perspectives from the FBI to universities to students both radical and conservative, and the internal disagreements of the antiwar movement. After his release from federal prison, Bruce became a journalist.

From Malcolm X to Muhammad Ali

1. "To Create an Image . . . ," lecture delivered by Malcolm X at the Colgate Rochester Divinity School, February 17, 1965, transcribed by Celia Bucci, December 1992, copyright 1993 by Dr. William Hamilton.
2. See various columns by Steve Neal in the *Chicago Sun-Times*: "Daley Should Take Lead on Parks," January 22, 1993, 31; "Park District Fumbles Sports Programs," March 5, 1993, 37; "Chicago Park Reform Is Overdue," March 8, 1993, 17; "Daley Is Using Parks as Political Base," April 30, 1993, 39.
3. "Chief's Ouster Seen as Imminent," *Chicago Tribune*, December 3, 1992, 5.

So Sad, Too Bad

1. Steve Neal, "Daley Chooses Amateur to Run Parks," *Chicago Sun-Times*, July 7, 1993, 35.

Glatt

1. "Metro Briefings," *Chicago Sun-Times*, September 3, 1993, 4
2. US Court of Appeals for the Seventh Circuit, No. 93 C 3126, decided September 14, 1995. In 1995, John Grant, filed a federal discrimination lawsuit over his being fired for corruption named me as doing the same thing he did, i.e., giving away park district property without authorization—in my case a worthless dry, rotted wooden lifeguard boat. Mr. Grant claimed I should have been fired for corruption, but wasn't because I was white. Grant lost.
3. US Court of Appeals for the Seventh Circuit, No. 95-2932, June 17, 1996.

Filan Report

1. John B. Filan, "Report to the Superintendent Chicago Park District, Preliminary Findings for Certain Departments," Pandolfi, Topolski, Weiss & Co., Ltd., September 23, 1993.
2. John Filan would become Governor Blagojevich's director of management and budget in 2003 and be promoted by the governor to director of the Illinois Finance Authority in 2008. Governor Blagojevich was arrested and indicted in 2009 for corruption, convicted in 2011 on eighteen counts, and sentenced to fourteen years in federal prison.

Afterword

1. Forrest Claypool, "Chicago's Harbors Haven't Had Significant Renovation and Upgrading in 60 Years," *Chicago Tribune*, August 12, 1996, sec. 2, p. 2.
2. See https://www.elections.il.gov/campaigndisclosure/contributionssearchbyall contributions.aspx.
3. Scott Stevenson, "City Harbors Only 76% Full; Economy Took Wind Out of Sails," *Chicago Sun-Times*, September 1, 2013.